HOW IMMIGRANTS IMPACT THEIR HOMELANDS

HOW IMMIGRANTS IMPACT THEIR HOMELANDS

Edited by Susan Eva Eckstein & Adil Najam

DUKE UNIVERSITY PRESS

Durham and London 2013

© 2013 Duke University Press
All rights reserved
Printed in the United States of America on acid-free paper ∞
Designed by Courtney Leigh Baker
Typeset in Warnock Pro by Keystone Typesetting, Inc.
Library of Congress Cataloging-in-Publication Data
How immigrants impact their homelands /
edited by Susan Eva Eckstein and Adil Najam.
pages cm.
Includes bibliographical references and index.
ISBN 978-0-8223-5381-2 (cloth : alk. paper)
ISBN 978-0-8223-5395-9 (pbk.)
1. Emigration and immigration—Economic aspects.
2. Emigration and immigration—Social aspects.
3. Emigration and immigration—Political aspects.
I. Eckstein, Susan. II. Najam, Adil.
JV6217.H69 2013
304.8—dc23
2012048646

CONTENTS

FIGURES AND TABLES

Globalization. It increasingly involves immigration, the movement of people, along with goods, across borders. Since 1960 the number of international migrants has more than doubled.[1] A study in 2010 showed that 215.8 million people, worldwide, lived in a country other than the one they were born in.[2] Many of today's immigrants who live in the so-called Global North, the rich countries, come from the Global South, the poor countries of Africa, Latin America, Asia, the Middle East, and North Africa. Until the mid-1900s, most immigrants to the United States, for example, had come from Europe, while Europe received few immigrants.

To date, concern with contemporary immigrants has focused mainly on how they adapted to where they resettled in the Global North, and, recently, on their transnational ties to the family and communities they left behind. Little attention has been paid to the full range of homeland impacts immigrants have had, unknowingly as well as knowingly, and to conditions accounting for cross-national variability in immigrant impacts in different countries, within individual countries at different times, and among immigrants of different social, cultural, political, and economic backgrounds. How does one account, for example, for the

Chinese who fled a communist revolution in their homeland to provide the bedrock for China's "economic miracle," while wealthy Cubans who similarly fled a communist revolution in their homeland soon after Castro took power, supported an embargo to strangle economic development on the island? And how does one account for men in the Philippines refusing to assume household responsibilities when their wives go abroad to earn money for the family, while nonmigrant wives take over household responsibilities when their husbands go abroad for work? And how does one account for return-migrants to some but not all Central American countries establishing violent gangs? This book, which focuses on the homeland impacts of immigrants to diverse regions of the world and from diverse developing countries, addresses such issues. It addresses a range of impacts far greater and more diverse than studies of immigrant transnationalism note.

The book benefits from the wisdom of scholars who are leading experts of emigration from developing countries. The chapters were commissioned to highlight the range of economic, social, and cultural impacts immigrants from and to diverse regions of the world have had in their home countries. Their impacts will be shown to hinge not merely on immigrant determination and assets, but also on conditions where they went and where they originated, state policies in both the sending and receiving countries, relations between people in the country (and community) of origin and settlement, and nonmigrants' responses to those who go abroad. Combined, these chapters enable the reader to compare how immigrants of different social classes, ethnicities, genders, and cultural backgrounds, from large and small countries, and with different overseas experiences in different regions of the world, have shaped developments in their homelands.

The first chapter provides context. In this chapter, I present an overview of the developing world on the move and then forces shaping immigrant homeland impacts which remaining chapters richly detail.

Chapter 2, by Alejandro Portes, broadly addresses the conditions under which immigrants differently impact their home countries. Often within the context of issues Portes raises, other chapters focus on specific homeland impacts that immigrants from different countries have had. The first of these, chapters 3 and 4, focus mainly on macroeconomic impacts. Min Ye's chapter focuses on China, and Kyle Eischen's on India. Next, my chapter, on Cuba, and David FitzGerald's, on Mexico, address how the interplay between state and societal dynamics, including dynamics across country borders, have led immigrants to unleash social, cultural, and economic changes in their home countries. Chapter 7, by Riva Kastoryano, addresses how experiences in Europe transformed and transnationalized Turkish immigrant identities, values, and practices, and changed Turkey in turn. Chapter 8, by Natasha Iskander, elucidates how the Moroccan government creatively transformed remittances into an instrument of economic development, through its banking system. The final three chapters focus mainly on the homeland sociocultural transformations immigrants have unleashed. Chapter 9, by Rhacel Parreñas, focuses on the transnationalization of mothering that occurs when Filipina women emigrate, and on the effects their uprooting has had on the families they have left behind. Chapter 10, by José Miguel Cruz, focuses on the gang culture and gang life Central American immigrant youth transmitted to their homeland when U.S. officials deported them. And the final chapter, by Victor Agadjanian, Cecilia Menjívar, and Boaventura Cau, focuses on émigrés from Mozambique who, in economic despair, go to South Africa to work and return HIV infected. The authors uncover the tragic social consequences of migration on families and communities in Mozambique.

Boston University's Frederick S. Pardee Center for the Study of the Longer-Range Future helped make this book possible by sponsoring a working-group conference most authors attended, where we discussed drafts of the chapters. The center is committed to improving global understandings, to make the world a better place. I am grateful for the center's financial support and for the wonderful assistance of Theresa White and Meryum Khan, of the center. I am also grateful for the help of Zophia Edwards in the preparation of the manuscript. Most of all, I am grateful to Adil Najam, with whom I organized the conference and the book project. His wisdom, his insight, and his friendship have been invaluable to me. Indeed, he gets credit for the very conception of this book.

Ideally, this book will spark new concern with how developing countries, home to over 80 percent of the world's population, are affected by the exodus of their people. It should also contribute to policy reforms that strengthen the positive effects and minimize the negative effects that the current world on the move has set in motion.

Last but not least, I am grateful to the wonderful staff at Duke University Press. In particular, special thanks to the editor, Valerie Millholland, and to Susan Albury, who shepherded the manuscript through the production process.

Susan Eckstein

Notes

I am grateful for comments by Cecilia Menjívar and Rhacel Parreñas on an earlier version of this preface.

1 Dilip Ratha and William Shah, "South-South Migration and Remittances" (World Bank Working Paper 102, 2007), 3.
2 "2008 World Population Data Sheet," Population Reference Bureau, accessed June 15, 2010, www.prb.org/Publications/Datasheets/2008/2008wpds.aspx.

Immigrants from Developing Countries
An Overview of Their Homeland Impacts

SUSAN ECKSTEIN

Immigration constitutes one of the most important components of to-day's globalization. While not a new phenomenon, it has grown in scale and significance since World War II, especially since the mid-1980s.[1] The number of countries from and to which people have migrated has grown dramatically, with women playing an increasingly important role in the world on the move, not merely as family dependents of men who attain work abroad but as laborers in their own right.[2]

When moving to new countries, today's immigrants do not necessarily sever ties with their homelands. Through transnational engagement even the most humble of immigrants may transform the communities and countries they left behind. Governments and other institutions at times institute reforms to try to influence their impact. Their impact may be unintended and far greater than they realize, owing to conditions in which their home ties become embedded. Their impacts may be political, social, and cultural, even when their main impetus to migrate is economic.

This book addresses the homeland impacts that immigrants from developing countries have had. Most chapters richly detail the experiences of specific immigrant groups. These chapters are written by scholars with deep understandings of the immigrants about which they write. This is the first book of such scope. This introduction provides context for understanding the immigrant experiences detailed in the other chapters. It summarizes characteristics of emigrants, why they uproot, where they mainly resettle and why, and how in moving they changed their homelands.[3]

Emigration from Developing Countries

WHO EMIGRATES?

Seventy-six percent of today's immigrants were born in developing countries. Mexico, India, China, and Turkey, concerns of the chapters in this book, rank among the top ten countries from which people have emigrated.[4] Over 10 million Mexicans and Indians, 7 million Chinese, and 4 million Turks live outside their home countries. India and China, along with Brazil and Russia, constitute the so-called BRIC countries, perceived internationally as up-and-coming. The Indians and Chinese who emigrated in such large numbers felt that their personal lives would improve even more in leaving than were they to remain in their homelands, and they have contributed to the "economic miracles" in their respective countries by moving abroad.

The Philippines and Morocco, the focus of other chapters in this book, rank not among the top ten but among the top fourteen countries in numbers of émigrés. As of 2005, 3.6 and 2.7 million people have emigrated, respectively, from the Philippines and Morocco. These countries rank among the better-off developing-country economies, but their job and earnings opportunities failed to grow apace with their populations, and they do not offer opportunities comparable to those in richer countries.

Yet, none of the twenty countries with the largest out-migrations rank among the (thirty) countries with the highest percent of their populations living abroad, countries with the greatest proportional demographic losses. Jamaica ranks the highest in the world in the portion of its population living abroad. An extraordinary 39 percent of Jamaicans have emigrated. Two other countries addressed in these chapters, El Salvador and Cuba, rank among the thirty countries in the world with the highest percent of their populations having uprooted. El Salvador and Cuba rank seventeenth and thirtieth, respectively. Sixteen percent of Salvadorans and 11 percent of Cubans live abroad. Salvadoran out-migration spiraled as the country experienced a devastating civil war in the 1980s that made living in the country unsafe. However, other Salvadorans followed in the footsteps of those who took refuge abroad, initially for economic reasons but more recently also for security reasons, when gang violence became pervasive. They perceived their life-prospects to be better where their friends and relatives had resettled. The Cuban outmigration also began with a political exodus of opponents to the country's radical transformation after Fidel Castro took power, in 1959. However, out-migration expanded there as well to include economic migrants, especially after the country experienced a deep recession, when Soviet aid and trade abruptly ended, following the break-up of the Soviet Union. The Salvadoran and Cuban cases illustrate that motives for migration may be mixed and that they may change over time, in ways that will be shown to shape immigrant homeland impacts.

In addition, many former Soviet bloc countries, as well as countries in the Middle East, that experienced civil strife and civil wars, such as Serbia, Montenegro, and the West Bank and Gaza, rank among the countries with the highest rates of out-migration. Politically turbulent countries lose their populations to migration, if not to bullets. Refugees, persons who flee their homeland, fearful of religious, ethnic, or political persecution, were they to stay, account for 8 percent of world immigrants.

WHERE DO EMIGRANTS GO?

Where do emigrants resettle? In 2005, reports indicate that 42 percent of emigrants from developing countries, from the so-called Global South, had moved to high-income countries that were members of the Organization for Economic Co-operation and Development (OECD), in the Global North. Another 12 percent had moved to high-income non-OECD countries.[5] Since the late twentieth century, migrants from developing countries have moved in ever-larger numbers to the United States, Australia, and Europe. This book primarily focuses on this migratory flow from the Global South to the Global North.

Most developing-country migration used to be internal, not international—from rural to urban areas. This was especially true in Latin America, until the rates of urbanization in the region reached levels nearly as high as those in industrial, well-to-do countries, even though their cities did not offer comparable economic opportunities. The urban

TABLE 1.1. Origins of International Migrants in 2005–2006

Migrants from	Total (in millions)	South-to-North as % of Total Migration
Latin America and Caribbean	25.9	87
East Asia and Pacific	17.7	84
South Asia	20.2	50
Europe and Central Asia	43.6	36
Middle East and North Africa	11.8	80
Sub-Saharan Africa	14.5	31
High-income Countries	34.0	0
Total	167.7	

option closed down, especially after the neoliberal restructuring of many economies in the mid-1980s, for reasons detailed below. Under these circumstances, both rural and urban residents increasingly turned to emigration as their best hope.[6]

There is a patterning to where immigrants from particular regions, and countries within regions, move. Table 1.1 summarizes this patterning. The percentage of people who have moved from poor to rich countries varies by region. Eighty percent or more of emigrants from Latin America, the Caribbean, East Asia, the Pacific, the Middle East, and North Africa have moved to countries in the Global North, whereas only half of South Asian immigrants and no more than 36 percent of Central Asian and Sub-Saharan African immigrants have. In that immigration to the Global North is greatest from middle-income developing countries, the dynamics of global immigration keep peoples from the poorest regions disadvantaged.[7] In 2005 middle-income countries accounted for 54 percent of immigrants to high-income OECD countries, low-income countries for only 12 percent.

And within regions, immigrants tend to gravitate to specific countries. Migrants on which chapters of the book focus illustrate the selectivity of migration. Mexicans, Philippines, Cubans, and Salvadorans have moved mainly to the United States, while Turks have moved mainly to Germany and Moroccans to France. South Asian Indians, however, have immigrated in large numbers to countries in diverse regions of the world, and shifted their destination countries over the years. They mainly migrated to Great Britain, after it colonized India, and to South Africa, and those who were Muslims fled to Pakistan after it became an autonomous country in 1947. In more recent times, Indians immigrated to Middle Eastern countries and the United States, with different classes of Indians moving to the two regions, laborers to the Middle East and high-skilled workers, on which Kyle Eischen's chapter focuses, to the United States.

The United States has been the magnet for the most immigrants. In 2005, 38.4 million foreign-born lived there, more than three times as many as lived in Russia, the country with the second-largest number of immigrants. Most immigrants to the United States (as well as to Canada, Australia, and New Zealand) used to come from Europe, until opportunities there expanded, first with reconstruction after World War II and then with the formation of the European Union (EU), which allowed labor to move freely among member countries. A dramatic decline in the fertility rate in Europe led to a further drop in transatlantic immigration, and contributed to Europe's shift from a net exporter to a net importer of labor.

Against this backdrop, several European countries, including Germany, France, and Spain, as well as oil-rich Saudi Arabia and Canada, came to rank among the top ten immigrant-receiving countries. The immigration to Saudi Arabia reflects the growing complexity and diversity of destination countries, as select developing countries have become new nodes of economic development. Sparsely populated Saudi Arabia, along with other Gulf oil states, has come to rely on foreign labor for oil-related activity, construction, and service work.[8]

The demographic importance of immigrants in receiving, as well as sending, countries depends not merely on the absolute number of people involved, but also on the size of the native-born populations. Although immigrants have come to constitute about 10 percent of the population in high-income OECD countries (involving European countries, including some former Soviet bloc countries in Central Europe, and countries such as Canada, New Zealand, Turkey, and Japan), and 13 percent in the United States, they account for more than triple that percentage in some of the smaller, high-income non-OECD countries (Hong Kong, Saudi Arabia, Singapore, Israel, and other wealthy Middle Eastern countries) and in several former Soviet bloc countries.[9]

To a certain extent, refugee flows also differ when viewed in absolute numbers and relative to the size of the population of the country where they move. As of 2005, Germany and the United States ranked among the ten countries with the most refugees. But neither Germany nor the United States, nor any other high-income OECD country, ranked among the thirty countries with refugees accounting for most of their immigrants. Refugees accounted for 6 percent of German immigrants and for 1 percent of U.S. immigrants. In contrast, refugees accounted for 14 percent of immigrants to developing countries in general, and for 23 percent of immigrants to the least developed countries. Thus, the countries that can best afford to absorb the humanitarian costs of accommodating displaced persons do not assume their "fair share." Moreover, rich countries tend to acquire refugees in a regularized manner, by criteria they establish, whereas poor countries receive refugees mainly by default, their governments too weak to control who enters their borders. Because most refugees need to flee their homeland quickly when their lives are at risk, they mainly move to neighboring countries. Most such relocations transpire within the Global South. Nine of the ten countries with refugees accounting for the highest percentage of their immigrants are located in the Middle East and Africa. The other country is Armenia, in Eurasia.[10] Also, the partitioning of India and Pakistan, within the Global South, unleashed one of the largest population movements in recorded history, as tens of millions of Hindus and Muslims (and, secondarily, other ethnic and religious groups) relocated across the newly formed borders, to find a safe religious haven, Hindus in India, Muslims in Pakistan.

HOW TO EXPLAIN THE PATTERNING OF IMMIGRATION?

While refugees demonstrate that the motivation for migration may be political, the key driving force is typically economic, rooted in differences in global opportunities. But whatever the reason inducing specific individuals to uproot, immigration must be understood in the context of macrohistorical and institutional processes. State policies, changing demographics, colonial legacies, and transnational social dynamics that immigrants themselves put in place all influence from where and to where people in today's world move.

The economic forces behind migration to the Global North have shifted over the years, as the world economy, and the role of specific countries within it, has changed. In some countries, immigrants have been central to how economies evolved, and in so doing they influenced subsequent migration flows.[11] The massive migration to the United

States in the early twentieth century, for example, was intricately associated with the country becoming the world's most dynamic industrial nation, on a small native-born population base. Then, after World War II, northern European countries rebuilt their industrial economies with so-called guest workers from North Africa and Turkey, the focus of Natasha Iskander's and Riva Kastoryano's chapters in this book, respectively.

By the time global immigration began to reach unprecedented levels in the 1980s, many of the manufacturing jobs in the Global North had disappeared, as companies relocated in poorer countries where labor costs were lower, including in the very developing countries from which many of today's immigrants come. The removal of barriers to trade and investment under global neoliberal restructuring led people with capital to relocate production wherever in the world they believed they could maximize their profits, and then export to global markets.

Under these circumstances, today's immigrants to the Global North move increasingly to high- and low-skilled service-based economies. They gravitate to work that native-born people would rather not do, or lack the skills to do, in sufficient numbers. Particularly noteworthy, women's growing participation in the labor force and the rise in life expectancy in countries in the Global North have contributed to a feminization of immigration. Women from developing countries have responded to a new demand to do work that women in the Global North previously performed, unpaid, as homemakers. Chapters in the book elucidate the range of high- and low-skilled service-sector jobs male and female immigrants from developing countries now do. They work as nurses, nannies, and maids, but also as high-skilled technicians and financiers.

Nonetheless, the increasingly service-based economies have not entirely eliminated demand for foreign labor for other work. Agribusinesses, for example, want immigrants for low-paid farm work, work that the native-born, with better options, resist doing.

People in developing countries respond to demand for their labor, and sometimes even create demand for their labor, in the Global North, largely because economic opportunities in their own countries compare unfavorably. This has been especially true since the neoliberal restructuring that began in the 1980s. Against the backdrop of the severe balance of payments deficits and associated debt crises, governments in developing countries introduced reforms, under pressure from the International Monetary Fund (IMF), that caused living costs to rise, earnings opportunities to decline, income inequality to worsen, and, in many countries, poverty rates to rise. Victims of the reforms came to envision emigration as their best hope. The removal of trade barriers, for example, subjected developing-country economies to foreign competition that often worked to their disadvantage. Mexico is a prime example, as David FitzGerald's chapter shows. Implementation of the North American Free Trade Agreement (NAFTA), in 1994, removed tariffs between the United States, Canada, and Mexico. In Mexico, small-scale agriculturalists who could not compete with imports from U.S. agribusiness lost their means of livelihood. Perceiving few labor-market options in their country, farm laborers looked to the United States for work. Under these circumstances, Mexicans became the main immigrants to the United States.

Yet, no single economic rationality accounts for the economic forces at play. Immigration that serves the interests of certain groups may conflict with the interests of other groups. In particular, immigration that is rational from the vantage point of business, or, more accurately, certain businesses, may not be rational from the vantage point of governments. For example, employers who want a large supply of cheap, foreign-born labor to minimize their production costs, drive up fiscal expenditures for governments that address the social welfare needs of immigrants. Governments may also need to contend with antiforeign, nativistic political backlashes, especially during economic downturns.[12] Native-born workers who believe that immigrants undermine their employment options and weaken their earning power at times channel their resentment politically.

Indeed, behind the "invisible" global market forces propelling migration are governments with their own priorities. Governments in the Global North have adapted their admit policies over the years, primarily due to their changing economic concerns, but also due to their changing political and humanitarian concerns. With their economies offering the best global economic opportunities, they are well positioned to determine whom they let in with legal rights, including how many people, from which countries, with what skills, and on what terms (that is, whether for a defined period of time or indefinitely). Peoples in developing countries are not free to decide for themselves whether to emigrate, where to move, and for how long.[13]

Although governments in the Global North opened their doors to substantially more peoples from developing countries since the 1960s, they nonetheless remain highly selective in who they let in. Washington, for example, gives preference to skilled and moneyed entrants, and to relatives of citizens (after having allotted entry on the basis of national quotas that favored northern Europeans, between the 1920s and 1960s).[14] Over the years, it used immigration as an instrument to maintain and advance its dominant position within the global economy. The Indian information technology (IT) immigrants Kyle Eischen describes in his chapter are beneficiaries of the skill bias of current U.S. immigration policy. So too are the Philippine nurses Rhacel Parreñas describes in her chapter. The demand for medical assistants increased when Washington instituted Medicaid and Medicare in the 1960s.

The situation differs somewhat in Europe. As noted above, while the countries with the strongest economies recruited workers from North Africa and Turkey to assist their reconstruction after World War II, following the formation of the EU, residents could freely move among member countries. The governments in the countries that attracted insufficient labor from member countries introduced strategies to attain non-EU labor. Spain and Italy, for example, extended immigration rights to progeny of their generations-old diasporas, which some Latin Americans, in particular, took advantage of. Also, the Spanish and Italian governments offered short-term work contracts to people from countries in the former Soviet Union, such as Romania, to fill jobs the native-born, with better options, left unfilled. And after Romania joined the EU, Romanians could more easily move to member countries.

Colonial legacies have further influenced migratory flows, even long after colonized countries gained their political independence. Former colonial governments in Europe extended preferential immigration rights to their once colonial subjects. Subsequently, the social networks colonial-era migrants set in motion led their friends and family who initially stayed behind to follow them abroad. The legacy of the Soviet empire, in turn, contributed to migration among countries within the former Soviet bloc, as some of the economies deteriorated and as some of the countries experienced civil strife amid their democratic market transitions. These migrations built on pre–Soviet-era, as well as Soviet-era, intercountry relations. But the Cold War's end also unleashed large-scale migration to Western Europe from Eastern and Central Europe.

Independent of former colonial contexts and macropolitical and economic dynamics that have shaped the world on the move, immigrants on their own have inspired others from their homeland to join them abroad. People move where they have networks to draw on to find work and housing, to ease their adjustment to a foreign land. International networks also influence people's perceptions, correct or not, of where their lives would improve. Indeed, once transnational ties are entrenched, the probability of additional immigration increases.[15] Transnational ties contribute to the formation of a culture of migration, which induces others to move.

Ordinary people who seem powerless, in comparison to states, may take immigration into their own hands covertly and illegally, when they want to move to a country where official policies exclude them. They may be such a force that even the seemingly strong states of the Global North cannot control who settles within their borders and on what terms. "Guest workers" in post–World War II Europe overstayed their temporary migration rights and settled permanently, and they brought family from their homelands who were not initially permitted to accompany them. Also, in the United States (as well as elsewhere in the Global North) foreigners routinely overstay tourist visas when unable to secure legal immigration rights. In so doing, they shift from temporary legal to illegal status. Or they immigrate illegally, at times with the assistance of human traffickers who take advantage of the market for illicit entry. Smugglers charge high fees to navigate border crossings. Around the beginning of the twenty-first century, traffickers charged as much as $10,000 to help Latin Americans enter the United States illegally.

Immigrants without legal rights may be such a force that even governments accommodate them. Washington, for example, extended in 1986 a one-time amnesty to approximately 3 million unauthorized immigrants in the country who met specified requirements. Two decades later, more than 10 million additional immigrants lived in the United States without entry rights. However, political opposition from anti-immigrant groups at the time of writing prevented another amnesty.

Not only determined peoples from developing countries, but businesses in the Global North, are behind covert, illegal immigration. Legitimate businesses, especially in agriculture, food processing, and other labor-intensive, low-skilled activity, fuel demand for illegal immigrants who are unlikely to fight for worker rights and better wages.[16] And middle-class and upper-class families who want inexpensive gardeners and household help also fuel illegal immigration. They often adopt a "don't ask, don't tell" stance about the legality of their employees.

Against this backdrop, the illegal immigrant population in the Global North reflects government resistance to adapting its admit policy to the full range of demand for foreign labor, and employer readiness to hire workers who, if legal, would be more costly. Thus, the problem of illegality is not merely or mainly of the immigrant's making. Illegal immigrants would much prefer to move with legal rights.

While strong states have been unable to control completely who enters their borders and under what terms, it is a great problem for weak states, such as in Africa, that have become a refuge to persons from neighboring countries, persons who flee famines and natural disasters, as well as civil strife, and who seek even modest improvements in their material well-being. In the poorest parts of the world, nearly 80 percent of immigration transpires between countries with contiguous borders, typically involving people who move without official permission.[17]

Some governments in developing countries, however, have managed not to be passive bystanders to the forces behind today's world on the move. Governments in the Philippines, the Republic of Korea, and China, for example, have actively sought contracts for their labor force in Gulf States: contracts for men to work in construction and oil-industry-related jobs, and, more recently, for women to work as domestics and other service jobs.[18] They do so for their own institutional reasons: often to earn hard currency to repay their foreign loans and to finance imports. They view the workers, including such professionals as nurses, medical practitioners, and engineers, as greater economic assets when employed abroad than at home. And prioritizing their economic interests, they tolerate less-than-ideal conditions for their workers abroad.

Homeland Economic Impacts

Immigrants have never had as great and diverse an impact on their home economies as they now do.[19] Migrants may generate social and economic capital abroad that they invest back home. Nonetheless, migration that benefits the individuals involved, and their families, may or may not be good for their home governments, economies, and societies. Analytically, economic impacts can be viewed from the vantage point both of labor and capital.

Poor countries typically suffer most when their skilled people move abroad, because economic development requires human, along with financial, capital. However, the chapters in this book on two BRIC countries, India and China, demonstrate that educated immigrants may play crucial roles in the economic dynamism of their home countries.

The growth in globally organized production since the 1980s has fueled the move of ever more skilled labor from the poorer to the richer countries of the world. A global market for highly skilled labor has evolved, involving Asians especially.[20] Multinational corporations contribute to this migration, in recruiting skilled labor that they circulate among their international subsidiaries.

The exodus of skilled labor from developing countries often involves a so-called brain drain. Caribbean countries have suffered the greatest loss of educated people.[21] The percentage of their university-educated population who lived abroad in 2000 ranged from 59 to 90 percent, depending on the country. A number of African countries lost almost as large a percentage of their highly educated people as Caribbean countries. Some one- to two-thirds of the university-educated populations of Cape Verde, Gambia, Somalia, Mauritius, Eritrea, Ghana, Mozambique, Sierra Leone, and Liberia have left their home countries. And 39 percent of university-educated Vietnamese have resettled elsewhere, many having fled their country's communist turn.

In such instances, developing countries lose not only vital human capital. The governments also experience poor returns from their investment of scarce fiscal funds in the schooling of their people, investment from which wealthier, immigrant-receiving countries benefit. Developing-country governments, in effect, subsidize the skilling of the labor force in the countries where educated immigrants move.

The highly educated who leave poor countries in large numbers include doctors. Countries with the worst global health problems suffer the greatest loss of medical professionals. The rate of emigration of doctors from the least developed countries is three times greater than from high-income (OECD) countries. Over 20,300 Indian, nearly ten thousand Philippine, 5,600 Mexican, and 4,400 South African, Pakistani, and Iranian doctors have left their home countries.[22] These doctors typically put their own economic interests above their nation's health-welfare needs. They can earn substantially more money in the

Global North, where most of them move. Rarely do they return to their home countries, other than to visit.

Nonetheless, the migration of skilled labor is not necessarily a zero-sum phenomenon for the countries involved. As Alejandro Portes delineates in his chapter in this book, developing countries are most likely to benefit if their skilled laborers do not permanently uproot but return-migrate and invest income and skills they acquired abroad. But he also notes that the development impact is not explicable solely at the individual level. Home governments need to provide adequate infrastructure to encourage productive investment.

Min Ye, in her chapter, specifically details how China benefited from its diaspora acquiring, abroad, banking and manufacturing expertise, plus capital that they subsequently invested in homeland businesses.[23] In an ironic turn of history, many of the overseas Chinese who masterminded China's cutting-edge "manufacturing revolution" had emigrated for political reasons, opposed to China's communist turn. But they returned, to invest if not live, when they considered it in their economic interests to do so. They even convinced local and national-level officials on the mainland to create attractive investment conditions for them.

Similarly, Eischen, in his chapter, details how South Asian Indian IT workers applied skills, experience, and capital, as well as contacts, that they acquired in California's Silicon Valley to develop a globally competitive IT sector in India. Eischen also demonstrates that immigrant contributions may be symbiotic across borders, with both the country of origin and settlement benefiting, and synergistically so. The Indians involved have contributed to the formation of a transnationally embedded high-tech economic niche. Skilled Indian IT workers enmesh themselves in economic relations across borders, relations that contribute to cutting-edge, complementary developments both in California and India. The large number of Indian doctors who have emigrated have had no comparable positive professional impact in India. Consequently, from the homeland vantage point, they, in contrast, constitute a "brain drain."

As in China, in India the government was instrumental in creating the bedrock for the economic transformation in which immigrants have come to play a central role. The government aggressively invested in the technical and professional training of its "best and brightest," in institutions more difficult to enter than Harvard. Once trained, graduates qualify for jobs in the United States, where they have been instrumental in the U.S. technology boom, especially in California.

Returns to the Indian government's human-capital investment rested partially on U.S. immigration policy, although not intentionally so. Washington extended about one-third of its skilled-worker visas to Indians.[24] It thereby enabled Indians to acquire economically lucrative IT experience in the United States. But in only permitting temporary migration, for up to six years, it compelled IT workers to return home (unless they found ways to evade and bypass the six-year cap). Return-migrants, some of whom accumulated large fortunes in the United States, helped develop India's IT sector, with close links to Silicon Valley where they had worked. Their success in the United States, and the networks they formed there, generated economic and social capital for software service markets for companies founded in India by returnees, where they capitalized on the country's low-wage, high-skilled labor force.

Indians in the IT sector who moved back and forth across country borders contributed to "brain circulation," as distinct from a "brain drain."[25] Brain circulation involves immigrants' applying skills, capital, contacts, and experience in their homeland that they had acquired abroad, while often building on and maintaining economically useful ties they established when living abroad. Immigrants may return permanently or temporarily to their country of origin.

Sometimes developing countries also benefit from entrepreneurial émigrés who establish businesses abroad that involve their home countries. Such "transnational entrepreneurs," as Portes notes in his chapter, may generate jobs and income in their country of origin, as well as where they resettle.[26] Travel agencies specializing in trips, and companies specializing in exports, imports, and remittance transfers, between the new and home countries, are cases in point.

Developing countries may also benefit from the emigration of their less-skilled people, as many country studies in this book demonstrate. Low-skilled workers often cannot find adequate work in their home countries, because there are too many of them relative to demand for their labor. Although developing countries have long lacked adequate employment options for low-skilled laborers, the problem, following neoliberal restructuring, exploded. Not only did the removal of trade barriers leave small-scale agriculturalists in countries such as Mexico unable to compete with imports from large-scale farmers in the rich countries, but privatizations of state-owned enterprises led the more efficient and profit-oriented new owners to downsize their workforce, and fiscal belt-tightening led governments to cut back services, and employment in turn. The new export-processing zones that, in contrast, generated jobs, typically did not expand sufficiently to absorb the labor displaced in other sectors. Under these circumstances, the economies of developing countries suffer little when their low-skilled laborers emigrate, and they may benefit from the money such émigrés remit from abroad. Developing country governments may also benefit politically from the diminution of domestic labor-market pressures.

Worker migration may be permanent or temporary. Temporary migration includes agriculturalists who go abroad seasonally, during the "dead season" in farming in their home country, to supplement their inadequate earnings at home. The Mozambicans who go to South Africa, and some of the Mexican migrants who go to the United States, described in chapters in this book, are seasonal migrants. Gulf States also contract temporary migrants.

Yet others return-migrate, either because they experienced job or other difficulties abroad, or, if they are fortunate, because economic opportunities improved in their country of origin while they lived abroad. Return-migration to Mexico and Brazil, for example, picked up after work prospects contracted in 2008 in the United States, when it experienced its worst economic downturn since the Great Depression. At the same time, economic conditions in the two Latin American economies improved.

Nonetheless, return-migrants do not necessarily have positive experiences when they reinsert themselves into their country-of-origin economies. For example, 70 percent of businesses launched by Brazilian returnees very quickly failed, according to one study, because they applied entrepreneurial ideas and experiences they acquired in the United States that proved ill-suited to their home communities.[27] And, in Mexico, FitzGerald found that return-migrants resisted exploitative work conditions that they had tolerated before emigrating. Rather than accommodate migrant demands, employers preferred not to hire them. Return-migration thereby fueled new social and economic tensions.

Returnees do not necessarily go back to their communities of origin, especially if opportunities there either did not improve or deteriorated during their years abroad, while improving elsewhere. In Mexico, return-migrants have shied away from resettling where drug-related violence surged, and Iskander shows that the Moroccan government's channeling of remittance deposits to promote regional over local development induced return-migrants to resettle where they perceived their economic opportunities to be best. Similarly, Eischen shows that when Indians who worked in Silicon Valley return to their home country they often settle in new high-tech hubs, not necessarily where they grew up. These instances point to the manner in which changing homeland conditions shape how migrants impact their home communities and countries.

In sum, individuals, families, and developing-country economies and governments may all benefit from migration. While migrant experiences have hinged on where they moved and when, at times migrants have created opportunities where they resettled, including in ways that have stimulated developments in their homelands. Yet, developing-country economies often suffer from migration, from the loss of human capital, and families left behind often suffer, as detailed below, when some members migrate.

CAPITAL: IMMIGRANT INVESTMENT AND REMITTANCES

Labor migrants, even when unskilled, often remit some of their foreign earnings. Indeed, remittances to developing countries surged with immigration in recent decades. Migrants mainly remit earnings to family they leave behind, but they sometimes also invest in community projects, and in property and businesses. Their home governments may implement measures that not only encourage the sending of remittances, but channel the transnational transfers so as to access the money for their own institutional use. However, migrants, their families, their home communities, and their home governments do not necessarily benefit equally from remittances, and remittances may generate unintended and undesirable consequences from both a state and societal vantage point.

Indicative of how important remittances have become, in 2008 immigrants from developing countries sent $338 billion to their homelands (see table 1.2), up from $57.5 billion just twelve years earlier.[28] Many developing countries have come to receive more money from their diasporas through remittances than wealthy governments provide via multilateral and bilateral aid. Diasporas, in the aggregate, sometimes even remit more money than multinational companies invest in their home countries. Accordingly, immigrants have become a vital source of funds for capital-poor countries of origin.

TABLE 1.2. Remittances to Developing Countries (billions of dollars)

	2006	2008
Developing Countries	235	338
East Asia and Pacific	58	86
Europe and Central Asia	37	58
Latin America and Caribbean	59	65
Middle-East and North Africa	26	35
South Asia	43	73
Sub-Saharan Africa	13	21
Low-income Countries	20	32
Middle-income Countries	215	306
World	317	444

India, China, and Mexico receive, by far, the most remittances. In 2010 they are estimated to have received, respectively, $55 billion, $51 billion, and $23 billion.[29] The Philippines was the fourth largest recipient of remittances. It received $21 billion. Many other Latin American and South Asian countries, as well as North Africa, the former Soviet bloc, and some Western European countries, also rank among the top remittance-receiving countries. The countries receiving the most remittances mainly benefited from migrations of their people to the Global North. In contrast, migrants who move within the Global South, such as within sub-Saharan Africa, remit far less, even though their home countries, and people there, are the most in need.[30]

From the vantage point of developing countries, the financial importance of remittances rests not merely on the total amount immigrants send home but also on the size of the economies to which they remit. India, China, and Mexico do not rank among the thirty countries where remittances account for 9 percent or more of GDP (including for as much as 36 percent, in the case of Tajikistan). Remittances play greatest importance in the economies of several former Soviet bloc countries, and economies in Central America, the Caribbean, the Middle East, and Africa, in some of the smallest economies in the world. In these countries the infusion of remittances may, in part, offset the heavy loss of labor to migration.

Detailed in a number of chapters, recipients typically use remittances to finance, in declining order, basic necessities, consumer-goods purchases, the schooling of their children, and home improvements. Occasionally, remittances finance businesses, typically small in scale. Migrants from some countries also collectively invest, through home-town associations, in community projects, such as roads, schools, and church renovations, as FitzGerald and Portes note in their chapters. Although rare, successful immigrants sometimes invest in capital-accumulating businesses of such scale that they fuel economic transfor-mations in their countries of origin, as illustrated in the chapters on Indians and Chinese. Migrants from India and China invest in family ventures in their homelands, but also in publicly traded companies that combine their own with nonimmigrant (including government) capital.

Min Ye documents how overseas Chinese cultivated economically instrumental ties with mainland officials, through which they influ-enced state investment policy to their personal advantage, as well as to the advantage of the economy at large. Overseas Chinese in Hong Kong paved the way, benefiting from special relations their "host society" had with the mainland. However, Chinese throughout Asia, and in the United States, also contributed to the "economic miracle."[31] They had the cultural, social, and economic capital to take advantage of China's cheap, dependable, and abundant labor, to enrich themselves on a scale not possible where they had moved, where labor costs were substantially higher. But their economic impact was contingent on state interven-tions that created a favorable investment climate.

From a global vantage point, both the Indian and Chinese govern-ments have been exceptional in their ability to transform their diasporas into major agents of development. While unable to achieve the same impressive and internationally competitive results, the Moroccan gov-ernment very creatively convinced its overseas workers not only to send remittances but also to channel the money that they initially remitted informally to family they left behind, via couriers and on home visits, through the formal state-banking system, in a manner that financed important development initiatives from which the country benefited. As Iskander insightfully details in her chapter, the Moroccan govern-ment needed to reinvent itself for this to transpire, and it did so by collaborating with migrants. It reformed a state bank to be responsive to migrant needs and wants. In a remarkable example of how effective "street level bureaucrats" may be, the government commissioned over-seas staff of the bank to meet and socialize with migrants where they lived and worked, to learn how the bank might best serve them.[32] In response, the bank introduced homeland mortgage opportunities, unemployment insurance, burial and other community social and economic services, and secure, rapid, and inexpensive financial transfer services. And once the bank addressed their needs and wants, migrants directed their remittances through branch offices where they had moved, all while the bank invested in government bonds that financed development projects.[33]

Deploying a different strategy than the Moroccan state, Turkish governments also cultivated their diaspora in Europe, encouraging them to invest back home, at the same time that Turks abroad influenced home-government policies from which they benefited. Riva Kastoryano highlights how, in the context of the EU, the Turkish diaspora reimagined itself in ways that impacted Turkey. Turks who moved to EU member-countries, especially to Germany and France, created new pan-European Turkish identities and organizations, which contributed to what Kastoryano calls transnational of transnationalism. Transnational transnationalists became important investors in Turkey, while also contributing to the Islamization of Turkish politics. Meanwhile, political changes in Turkey led to complex and changing relations with Turks in Europe.

The efforts of most developing-country governments to leverage remittances for economic development, however, have been less effective.[34] David FitzGerald and I, in our chapters on Mexico and Cuba, show this to be true. Governments in both countries initiated measures to encourage the sending of remittances to finance public-sector investment. In Mexico the national government introduced an imaginative program whereby it, as well as local and state governments, matched funds Mexicans abroad channeled to their home communities. But because the program only involved funds immigrants channeled through their hometown associations for collective projects, not the much larger amount of money they privately transmitted to their families, it fueled little economic development.

In Cuba, the government introduced several measures to encourage the sending of remittances when faced with an economic crisis caused by the ending of Soviet aid and trade. But it proved far more effective in attracting remittances for personal consumption than for investment. Although it tried to direct remittances to the state banking system, in the form of savings, Cubans resisted. The Cuban case illustrates that even when a state owns most of an economy it cannot direct remittances as it chooses, when remittance recipients consider their interests best served otherwise.

Even if ineffective in enticing their diasporas to remit in ways that foster significant economic development, many governments in developing countries have restructured institutions and shifted their public discourse to encourage their diasporas to maintain economically consequential homeland ties. They increasingly portray their diasporas as long-distance nationalists and heroes.[35] Some governments have even introduced annual holidays to honor "the absent ones," and restructured institutions in diaspora-friendly ways, for example, in establishing ministries (or departments within ministries) dedicated to diaspora relations, and in extending political representation and voting privileges to their immigrants.[36]

Nonetheless, several chapters demonstrate that remittances are not necessarily problem-free for receiving countries. Remittances may generate unintended and unwanted consequences from the vantage point of the population at large, the economy, and governments. Remittances obtained through no work effort on recipients' part may undermine motivation to work. Remittances may also fuel consumption at the expense of savings and investment, including the consumption of imported luxury goods that divert hard currency from more productive use. Only when consumption fuels demand for domestically produced goods does it stimulate economic growth.[37] In addition, remittances may informally dollarize economies and infuse foreign money that both devalues the worth of local currencies and drives up prices, including prices for basic necessities. In turn, my chapter on Cuba shows that in state socialist economies remittances that help a government address its hard currency needs may erode, simultaneously, state control over the economy and society. The chapter also shows how a government may manipulate exchange rates and impose service charges on remittances to its own advantage, at remittance recipients' expense.

In sum, the impact of transnational financial transfers depends on the amount immigrants remit, but also on the uses made of the money and the economies in which the money becomes embedded. Governments in developing countries interested in accessing hard currency have instituted a range of policies to induce investment and the sending of remittances by their diasporas, and to channel the money through state institutions. However, India, Morocco, and China aside, rarely have governments successfully induced their diasporas to remit foreign earnings on a scale and in a manner that has fueled macroeconomic development. In many capital-poor countries, the main beneficiaries of remittances are the direct recipients.

IMMIGRANTS' SOCIAL AND CULTURAL IMPACTS IN THEIR HOMELANDS

Immigrants also set in motion social and cultural changes in their homelands, including changes they do not realize and changes generating adverse consequences. They have become agents of globalization, transmitters of foreign ideas and practices learned abroad, including in conjunction with their transnational economic involvements. Remittances, in particular, sometimes transform the social relations in which they become enmeshed. Nonetheless, independent of remittances, émigrés may transmit—on homeland visits, via long-distance telephone, e-mail, and video communications, and upon return-migration, should their stay abroad be temporary—values and ideas acquired where they resettle. The very uprooting of people may even spur social and cultural changes in émigrés' home communities, when, for example, the working age population leaves and mainly elderly and children are left behind.

TRANSFORMATION OF HOMELAND CULTURAL PRACTICES

Immigrants transmit back home values and norms that they learn where they resettle, dubbed cultural remittances, such that cultural differences between migrants and nonmigrants may dissipate.[38] These cultural transfers, in turn, may stimulate subsequent immigration and transform the cultural practices immigrants bring with them. Immigrants may also establish transnational ties that come to have their own distinctive social and normative dynamics, referred to as "new transnational spaces" and "transnational social fields."[39]

Invariably, immigrants stir new yearnings for Western materialism. Many chapters in this book show how transnational income transfers fuel consumption of nonessentials, as well as of basic necessities. This is true in communist as well as market-based homeland economies.[40]

The new materialism that remittance recipients enjoy may also stir resentments among nonrecipients. People who can barely eke out a living resent those who enjoy a lifestyle through no work effort on their part, thanks to remittances they receive from friends and family abroad.

And remittances may exacerbate inequality in the distribution of societal wealth, since the poorest people tend not to migrate and therefore not to have access to remittances.[41]

Moreover, the new immigrant-based materialism, and desire for it, may transform and transnationalize homeland bases of status and prestige. Émigrés who make materialism possible acquire respect and prestige in their homeland, irrespective of how they earn a living. In the process, previous domestic bases of stratification, associated with education, skills, and work, may lose meaning. I show this to be true in Cuba.

Meanwhile, the transnationalization of prestige, plus the transnationalization of social networks and new materialistic yearnings, make additional emigration all the more likely. This is especially true among youth with the greatest earning potential abroad. Communities are losing their most able-bodied people, as FitzGerald illustrates in rural Mexico, and Portes describes more generally.

Immigrants also transmit normative and cultural practices that they learn from the specific people with whom they associate abroad, a phenomenon known as segmented assimilation.[42] They may socialize with upper- and middle-class people, as do the Asian Indians Eischen describes. Through their social and economic ties, Indian IT immigrants absorb the distinctive entrepreneurial subculture entrenched in Silicon Valley. At the other extreme, immigrants may become enmeshed in lower-class, racialized, and ghettoized social networks. The Central American youth who entered the United States without documentation, described by José Miguel Cruz in his chapter, are illustrative. Poor, young Central Americans have affiliated with gangs in the inner cities where they settled. When immigration authorities deported them back to their home countries, some of them brought the violent, criminal lifestyle that they learned in the United States with them—illustrating the negative nature of certain so-called social remittances. This was especially true of Salvadoran youth who had lived in Los Angeles. Upon their forced return to their homeland, they transnationalized U.S. gangs, to the point of making their home country unsafe, as well as neighboring countries to which they took their gangs. U.S. authorities concerned about law and order in America thus had the unintended effect of eroding law and order in countries where the undocumented immigrants originated, and in other countries as well.

While immigrants may serve as host-to-home-country cultural transmitters, Cruz, as well as Parreñas in her chapter on the Philippines, show that the flow of social and cultural influences is not necessarily unidirectional. The flow may be circular, back to the host country, and transmitted to "third" countries, with ideas and practices possibly reinterpreted and modified in the process, partly depending on the context in which they become embedded.

Immigrants may also bring their own home-country beliefs, values, and cultural practices with them when they move abroad, which they transmit to people where they resettle—what might be referred to as "social and cultural remittances in reverse." Although these immigrant impacts are beyond the scope of the book, noteworthy social and cultural remittances may undergo change when embedded across borders.

Meanwhile, nonmigrants do not necessarily welcome foreign ideas and practices migrants bring back with them, to the point that they may actively resist the influences. Return-migrants may experience what FitzGerald, in his chapter on Mexico, describes as dissimilation.

WHEN WOMEN VERSUS MEN EMIGRATE

Immigrants' sociocultural impact in their homeland hinges also on their gender. Women are increasingly moving abroad on their own, independent of spouses and children. Women migrants include professionals, especially nurses, as well as nonprofessionals who work, for example, as domestics.[43]

As the earning power of men has deteriorated in many developing countries in the neoliberal era, women have responded to new demand for their labor in wealthier countries. Meanwhile, recognizing demand for the women's labor, but seeking to avoid absorbing costs of providing schooling, health care, and other social services for children, governments in the Global North have increasingly been granting individual, not family, entry visas. Women, as a result, are pressed to leave their families behind, however saddened they are by the separation.

There is a patterning to the emigration of women, just as there is to emigration in general. While female migration has grown globally since 1980, it has increased to certain regions more than to others. Overall, now accounting for nearly half of all immigrants, women's share of migration ranges from a low of 40 percent in the Middle East and North Africa to a high of 57 percent in Europe and Central Asia.[44] The Filipina women Parreñas describes are illustrative of the women from developing countries who comprise 51 percent of immigrants to high-income OECD countries.

The emigration of women, independent of their families, has contributed to the formation of new, transnational households, and a new structuring of relations among kin. When emigrating, women do not typically abandon their commitment to mothering but do it differently, across borders, often with different and more tension-ridden consequences.

Whatever the economic gains, migration may transpire at great social and psychological costs to families. Often, marriages are strained, at times beyond repair, and children suffer psychologically. No material lifestyle gains that remittances make possible compensate for the loss of everyday companionship. Meanwhile, children suffer when parents abroad are unavailable to tend to their everyday needs, to discipline them, and to provide them with emotional support. Adolescents, in particular, suffer. Many drop out of school, experiment with drugs, and get pregnant. Yet, as Parreñas documents in the Philippines, the costs to families, the most fundamental building block of society, differ when men, instead of women, fathers, instead of mothers, emigrate, because men respond differently than women to the migration of their spouses and because children interpret the physical absence differently when their fathers and mothers migrate. Most Philippine migrants now are women, many of whom are mothers who left their children in their homeland. While focusing on the Philippines, but pointing to similar experiences in Sri Lanka and some former Soviet bloc countries, Parreñas describes how when men go abroad wives typically take over their husband's household responsibilities.[45] However, when women emigrate to earn money for the family their spouses typically resist assuming responsibility for the household chores their wives addressed when home. Instead, other women—sisters, aunts, and grandmothers—are called upon to serve as surrogate mothers, while the biological mothers do what they can long-distance, transnationally. In turn, children resent the family's restructuring. They continue to assess mothering through conventional lenses, as their government, their clergy, and their fathers convince them to do.

Victor Agadjanian, Cecilia Menjívar, and Boaventura Cau demonstrate that when men emigrate and leave their families behind, the homeland social consequences may even be deadly, if they move to disease-ridden places. The authors trace how Mozambican men who go to South Africa for work, to earn money their families desperately need to subsist, may, upon their return, infect their wives with the HIV virus they contracted abroad, when having extramarital affairs. In other instances, migrant men take up permanently with new women in South Africa, abandoning their Mozambican wives. Insecure, some wives themselves take up with other men. If HIV-infected by their migrant spouses, they spread the disease to their new partners. Individuals suffer, relations are ruined, and communities are devastated, all because homeland economic opportunities were too meager to meet basic family needs.

THE CHAPTERS THAT follow bring to life some of the range of homeland effects immigrants have had, for better and for worse. Immigrants have transformed the lives of the families, communities, and even countries they left behind, in ways heretofore inadequately documented and understood, and in ways they do not necessarily realize. This book represents an effort to address these lacunae in our knowledge, in selective countries. The first chapter to follow, by Alejandro Portes, addresses conditions under which migrants become agents of homeland development. The remaining chapters focus on country studies, the first five primarily on economic impacts immigrants have had, in both free-market countries and remaining communist countries—in China, India, Cuba, Mexico, and Turkey. The final three chapters highlight homeland social consequences immigrants have unleashed: in the Philippines, Central America, and Mozambique.

Notes

My thanks to Cecilia Menjívar and Rhacel Parreñas for comments on an earlier version of this chapter.

1 Unless otherwise indicated, for data I cite see *Migration and Remittances Factbook 2009* (Washington, DC: The International Bank for Reconstruction and Development/The World Bank, 2009).
2 See Stephen Castles and Mark Miller, *The Age of Migration in the Modern World* (London: Macmillan, 1998).
3 This book does not focus in depth on the homeland political impacts immigrants sometimes have. However, some political impacts are discussed in conjunction with other homeland impacts.
4 For an even higher estimate, 82 percent, see Dilip Ratha and William Shaw, "South-South Migration and Remittances" (World Bank Working Paper 102, 2007), 5.

5 I use the terms *Global North, wealthy countries,* and OECD *countries* inter-changeably, but adopt the term used in specific sources. Members of the OECD include the United States, Canada, New Zealand, and countries in Western and Central Europe, as well as Israel, Korea, Mexico, Chile, and Turkey. I use the term *Global South* to refer to the less well-off developing countries where immigrants addressed in the book originate.

6 On the declining ability of cities to absorb rural migrants, and conditions contributing both to rural and urban immigration, see Norman Long and Bryan Roberts, "Changing Rural Scenarios and Research Agendas in Latin America in the New Century," *New Direction in the Sociology of Global Development: Research in Rural Sociology and Development* 11 (2005): 55–89. As rural people in Latin America have come to rely on nonagricultural work for income, remittances, along with skills learned abroad, influence what return-migrants do and where they resettle. Iskander describes similar trends among Moroccan migrants in her chapter in this book.

7 Some developing countries with high emigration rates themselves have become homes to immigrants from other countries. This is true, for example, of Mexico and India.

8 See Castles and Miller, *The Age of Migration in the Modern World*, especially chapter 6.

9 Movement within the Soviet Union, prior to its dissolution, was considered internal migration, not immigration.

10 Iran is the world's principal haven for refugees. Castles and Miller, *The Age of Migration in the Modern World* , 6.

11 For analyses of the relationship between global capitalist developments and immigration, see Castles and Miller, *The Age of Migration in the Modern World*, as well as Ewa Morawska, *A Sociology of Immigration: (Re)Making Multifaceted America* (Basingstoke, UK: Palgrave Macmillan, 2009).

12 On antiforeign movements during bad economic times, see John Higham, *Strangers in the Land: Patterns of American Nativism, 1860–1925* (New York: Atheneum, 1972).

13 Aristide Zolberg, "From Invitation to Interdiction: U.S. Foreign Policy and Immigration since 1946," in *Threatened Peoples, Threatened Borders: World Migration and U.S. Policy*, ed. Michael Teitelbaum and Myron Weiner (New York: W. W. Norton, 1989), 117–59.

14 Aside from increasingly privileging workers with specific skills, by granting entry on the basis of H1-B visas, since 1992 the U.S. government annually grants entry to ten thousand foreigners who agree to invest $1 million or more in businesses that create at least ten jobs in the country.

15 Douglas Massey et al., *Worlds in Motion: Understanding International Immigration at the End of the Millennium* (New York: Oxford University Press, 1998).

16 Illegal immigration also involves trafficking in the global sex trade. Women and girls account for most of this multi-billion dollar exploitative trade.

17 Ratha and Shaw, "South-South Migration and Remittances," v.

18 Castles and Miller, *The Age of Migration in the Modern World*, chapter 6.

19 Morawska, *A Sociology of Immigration*, 39.

20 Castles and Miller, *The Age of Migration in the Modern World*, 146.

21 Frédéric Docquier and Abdeslam Marfouk, "Measuring the International Mobility of Skilled Workers (1990–2000)" (World Bank Policy Research Working Paper, 2004).

22 England, Germany, Italy, and Spain also rank, along with India, the Philippines, Mexico, South Africa, Pakistan, and Iran, among the top ten countries from which doctors emigrate.

23 Yet, China has experienced a net loss of skilled labor. Only one in four Chinese who studied abroad in the past decade returned to China to work. Students who obtained science and engineering doctorates from American universities were the least likely to return (Sharon LaFraniere, "Fighting Trend, China Is Luring Scientists Home," *New York Times*, January 7, 2010). These statistics suggest that countries of origin and settlement may both benefit from the migration of skilled labor, including from the foreign training of such labor. However, they do not necessarily benefit equally.

24 *New York Times*, February 29, 2000.

25 AnnaLee Saxenian, "From Brain Drain to Brain Circulation: Transnational Communities and Regional Upgrading in India and China," *Studies in Comparative International Development* 40, no. 2 (summer 2005): 35–61.

26 Alejandro Portes, William Haller, and Luis Guarnizo, "Transnational Entrepreneurs: An Alternative Form of Immigrant Economic Adaptation," *American Sociological Review* 67 (April 2002): 278–98.

27 Maria Sacchetti, "From N. E. Back to Brazil, with Regret," *Boston Globe*, July 8, 2009.

28 This data reflects only officially recorded remittances and thus underestimates total remittances.

29 *Migration and Remittances Factbook 2011* (Washington, DC: International Bank for Reconstruction and Development/World Bank, 2011).

30 Ratha and Shaw, "South-South Migration and Remittances," v, 11.

31 The Chinese government, at the local and national levels, framed Hong Kong and Taiwanese investment as foreign, in the context of the Chinese economic reforms of the 1970s. The overseas Chinese accordingly qualified for investment prerogatives denied to domestic Chinese at the time. And when Hong Kong was formally reincorporated into China, in 1997, the Chinese who had settled there maintained investment privileges.

32 Michael Lipsky coined this term. See his *Street-Level Bureaucracy: Dilemmas of the Individual in Public Services* (New York: Russell Sage Foundation, 1980).

33 Iskander, however, notes that the conditions that induced Moroccan migrants, from the 1960s through the 1980s, to remit through a state bank, did not appeal to later migrants, who, more educated, uprooted with less intent to maintain homeland ties.

34 For an overview of studies addressing how and to what extent remittances have fostered economic development, see Susan Pozo, ed., *Immigrants and Their International Money Flows* (Kalamazoo, MI: W. E. Upjohn Institute for Employment Research, 2007).

35 Nina Glick Schiller and Georges Fouron, *Georges Woke Up Laughing: Long-Distance Nationalism and the Search for Home* (Durham, NC: Duke University Press, 2001).

36 See Robert Smith, *Mexican New York* (Berkeley: University of California Press, 2006) and "Contradictions of Diasporic Institutionalization in Mexican Politics: The 2006 Migrant Vote and Other Forms of Inclusion and Control," *Ethnic and Racial Studies* 31, no. 4 (May): 708–41; Roger Waldinger and David FitzGerald, "Transnationalism in Question," *American Journal of Sociology* 109, no. 5 (March 2004): 1177–95.

37 J. Durand and D. Massey, "Migradollars and Development: A Reconsideration of the Mexican Case," *International Migration Review* 30, no. 2 (1996): 423–44.

38 On social and cultural remittances, see Peggy Levitt, *Transnational Villagers* (Berkeley: University of California Press, 2001).

39 For an early discussion of such "transnational spaces," see Nina Glick Schiller and Georges Fouron, "Transnational Lives and National Identities: The Identity Politics of Haitian Immigrants," in *Transnationalism from Below*, ed. Michael Smith and Luis Guarnizo (New Brunswick, NJ: Transaction, 1998), 130–64.

40 This is also true in communist China. See Anita Chan, Richard Madsen, and Jonathan Unger, *Chen Village: Revolution to Globalization* (Berkeley: University of California Press, 2009).

41 Castles and Miller, *The Age of Migration in the Modern World*.

42 Alejandro Portes and Min Zhou, "The New Second Generation: Segmented Assimilation and Its Variants Among Post-1965 Immigrant Youth," *Annals of the American Academy of Political and Social Sciences* 530 (1993): 74–98.

43 See Sherba George, *When Women Come First* (Berkeley: University of California Press, 2005), as well as Parreñas's chapter in this book. Also see Pierrette Hondagneu-Sotelo, *Domestica: Immigrant Workers Cleaning and Caring in the Shadows of Affluence* (Berkeley: University of California Press, 2001) and Pierrette Hondagneu-Sotelo, ed., *Gender and U.S. Immigration* (Berkeley: University of California Press, 1999).

44 *Migration and Remittances Factbook 2009.*

45 Romania is a case in point. One-third of the country's labor force now works abroad. While remittances that migrants send home have helped eradicate extreme poverty in Romania, when women in particular leave, children suffer. Child drug addiction and depression have increased, and performance in school has deteriorated. Dan Bilefsky, "In Romania, Children Left Behind Suffer the Strains of Migration," *New York Times*, February 15, 2009.

2

Migration and Development
Reconciling Opposite Views

ALEJANDRO PORTES

Debates and research on the consequences of contemporary south-north migration have overwhelmingly focused on the impact they have had on the nations and localities at the receiving end.[1] Much less attention has been paid to the effects of such movements on the countries left behind. The general view among analysts and the public is that out-migration should be good for sending countries because of the safety valve to poverty and unemployment that it provides and, above all, because of the river of remittances sent by expatriates that contributes significantly to the survival of families and the financial stability of sending nations.[2]

Arrayed against these optimistic views are a number of scholars from the Global South who have become fierce critics of out-migration and its consequences for their nations. From their point of view, migration is not only a symptom of underdevelopment, but a cause of it, as it depopulates entire regions, turns sending families from producers into rentiers, and allows governments to escape their responsibilities by relying on migrant remittances. Such views have been summarized in a number of public documents, of which perhaps the best known is the *Declaration of Cuernavaca*, written in 2005:

> The development model adopted in the immense majority of labor-exporting American countries has not generated opportunities for growth nor economic or social development. On the contrary, it has meant the emergence of regressive dynamics; unemployment and job precarization; loss of qualified workers; productive disarticulation and stagnation; inflation and greater economic dependency. As a consequence, we experience a convergence between depopulation and the abandonment of productive activities in areas of high emigration.[3]

How can we reconcile these opposing views? On the one hand, we have the governments of sending nations pleading with the United States and Western European countries to let their nationals in and not to deport them, so that they can continue to send remittances. On the other hand, development experts from the same countries denounce the very same outflows as inimical to the national interest. Adjudicating between these opposite views requires us to make several practical and conceptual distinctions in order to separate disparate phenomena obscured under blanket statements:

1　Between the *structural importance* of migration flows and their *change potential*; the latter being a subset of the former.
2　Between high human-capital and those primarily composed of manual workers labor outflows.
3　Between cyclical or temporary and permanent or quasipermanent migrations.

The first distinction calls attention to the possibility that out-migration acquires structural importance for sending nations not by developing those nations, but precisely by consolidating entrenched elites inimical to their development. The "safety valve" function of large outflows and the role of remittances in buttressing public finances play a role in this process: they do not change the institutional underpinnings of economic stagnation and social inequality, but can actually perpetuate them. This is, in part, the reason why, as critics of migration argue, there are no documented instances in which such movements have actually lifted sending countries out of poverty and a subordinate position in the global system. It should be noted, however, that remittances might, contrary to this thesis, undermine elite hegemony by providing recipients with alternative sources of earnings and information.[4]

In turn, the change potential of migration does not always yield effects conducive to or congruent with developmental goals. Migration-induced social change is not always for the better. To see these differences more clearly, it is best to organize the discussion on the basis of the second distinction, namely that between manual and high-human capital flows, although a full discussion would also take gender into account, as the chapters in this book by Rhacel Salazar Parreñas and by Victor Agadjanian, Cecilia Menjívar, and Boaventura Cau suggest. The two skill-based movements possess different dynamics, but as we shall see, their potential contribution to sending countries' economic and social development hinges largely on the same set of factors.

The International Migration of Manual Labor

PERSPECTIVES ON LABOR MIGRATION

The mass migration of peasants and workers out of the Global South and into wealthy nations is what critics of these flows commonly have in mind. Despite sustained criticism by nativists in host nations, these movements can play a significant positive role in their economies by, among other effects, compensating for declining and aging populations and meeting demand in labor-intensive sectors of economies, such as in agriculture, construction, and low-tech industries.[5] Two economic schools have generally favored the onset and continuation of these flows. The first is the orthodox economic position, associated with the classic studies of Brinley Thomas and Arthur D. Lewis.[6] It sees these movements as natural equilibrating mechanisms between labor-surplus regions, where the marginal productivity of labor is near zero, and those where it can be put to productive use. Migration helps both regions by allowing productive investments in receiving areas, while helping raise wages in sending regions.[7]

The second school is the "New Economics of Migration," which also takes a positive stance toward such flows, but for different reasons. They are seen as a functional alternative to imperfect credit and futures markets in sending rural areas and as insurance against unforeseen economic downturns. The migrant worker functions, in a sense, as his family's social security and credit card all rolled into one.[8] For this school, migrant remittances always have positive effects in sending economies because they stimulate demand that is met by domestic production. Douglas Massey and his coauthors argue, for example, that every "migradollar" sent by Mexicans in the United States generates a $2.90 contribution to Mexico's GNP.[9] Supporters of these theories also tend to stress the role of social networks in maintaining the continuity of cross-border labor flows: the knowledge of others who have previously undertaken the journey represents the prospective migrant's "social capital," as it lowers the costs and the uncertainty of the move.

Yet, authors of this school tend to neglect another, less positive consequence of social networks, namely that the cumulative processes of out-migration that they facilitate may end up emptying sending areas of their able-bodied population and weakening their productive structures. In the end, there would be few people to send remittances to and nowhere to make productive investments. Places of out-migration can thus become "ghost towns" or "tinsel towns," decorated once a year for the patron saints' festivities, but otherwise populated only by the old and the infirm. Already, close to 50 percent of Mexico's municipalities report having lost population during the last intercensal period.[10]

Whether social networks structure migrant flows in ways conducive or contrary to local and national development depends ultimately on the timing of these movements. Cyclical flows, where migrant workers spend a certain time abroad but eventually return to their towns and families, tend to produce positive developmental outcomes, as described by the New Economics school: families stay put, their consumption generates positive spinoff effects, and migrants' accumulated savings can be put to use productively in local economies. Permanent out-migrations tend to have the opposite effects. These are the movements that can depopulate townships and entire regions. Migrant workers who settle abroad take their families with them, thus weakening the incentive to continue sending remittances or making investments at home. The migrant's economic focus shifts in the direction of surviving and moving ahead in the host society.[11]

Not incidentally, children raised abroad by poor migrant families experience all the disadvantages of a strange culture and language, plus poor schooling, without many countervailing resources. The result is a process of "segmented assimilation," in which many second-generation youths end up assimilating into the lower rungs of the host society, stagnating in manual jobs not too different from those of their parents or moving ever downward into the world of gangs, violence, and the drug trade, as José Miguel Cruz describes among Salvadoran migrants to Los Angeles, in his chapter in this book. Such youths are lost not only to their country of origin, but to their families and to themselves.[12] Yet, the meaning of circular migration, as opposed to permanent migration, requires additional elaboration in order to avoid tautological statements.

TRANSNATIONAL COMMUNITIES

A silver lining in the consolidation of permanent expatriate settlements is the rise and growth of transnational organizations linking these settlements with areas of out-migration. It is a fact supported by hundreds of studies that migrants do not simply "leave"; instead, they maintain intense ties both with their families and communities left behind. The concept of *transnationalism* has been coined to refer to this intense traffic of communication, information, and resources across places of origin and destination.[13] The research literature has also established that the immigrants most likely to take part in these organizations and activities are not the most recent arrivals, but those better established and with a more solid economic position in the host countries.[14]

Better-established first-generation immigrants create organizations of the most varied kind—from hometown committees to civic associations and branches of home-country political parties. Tables 2.1 and 2.2 reproduce findings from a recent national survey of organizations created by Colombian, Dominican, and Mexican expatriates in the United States. Table 2.1 is an inventory of all such organizations by type that documents their notable diversity. Table 2.2 presents data on the membership of these organizations that again demonstrate their being composed primarily by older, firmly settled, and more educated migrants. Migrants who perform manual labor and who have become more secure financially are also likely to take part in these activities, reversing, at least in part, the negative consequences of their departure.

Transnational organizations engage in a variety of philanthropic and civic activities in their home localities and regions. Their work has been referred to as a form of "globalization from below," through which poor people seek to mitigate the growing inequalities and lack of opportunity foisted on them by capitalist-driven "globalization from above."[15] Remittances to families, philanthropic contributions to towns, and public works planned and funded by transnational organizations are illustrative of the forms in which globalization from below takes place.[16]

TABLE 2.1. Latin Immigrant Organizations in the United States by Type

Type	National Origin Colombian %	Dominican %	Mexican %	Total %
Civic/cultural organizations	47.30	30.00	6.82	16.23
Other cultural organizations	10.16	15.29	0.54	3.66
Economic organizations	4.44	2.35	0.70	1.52
Hometown associations	1.90	3.53	63.80	47.04
Federations of hometown associations	0.00	0.00	4.26	3.10
State-of-origin associations	0.32	1.18	8.68	6.48
International philanthropic organizations (Lions, Rotaries, Kiwanis)	6.98	3.53	0.00	1.58
Home country philanthropies	3.17	0.00	0.00	0.56
Political committees	7.93	10.00	0.46	2.70
Professional associations	8.89	14.12	0.70	3.44
Religious groups	1.59	1.18	0.23	0.56
Social service agencies	2.86	17.06	3.26	4.51
Sports groups	0.63	1.76	10.00	7.55
Student organizations	3.81	0.00	0.54	1.07
Total	100.00	100.00	100.00	100.00
N	315	170	1,290	1,775

Transnationalism, however, is not a panacea and does not completely neutralize the negative effects of permanent out-migration. This is so for three reasons: First, as depopulation of sending regions advances, there are fewer kin to send remittances to and less economic infrastructure to build on. For migrant resources to be invested productively, there must be "something" that they can return to. Otherwise, no investments can be made, or they would be of the purely symbolic kind, building the "tinsel towns" for the annual festivities, but without any effective developmental potential.[17]

Second, regardless of migrants' good intentions, the resources that they can commit to developmental projects are modest. Recall that labor migrants are former peasants and workers and that their wages in the host labor market are low. While some may become successful entrepreneurs, the mass of their pooled contributions can have signifi-

TABLE 2.2. Characteristics of Members of
Latin American Immigrant Organizations in the United States

	Colombian	Dominican	Mexican	Total
AGE				
30 years or less, %	12.1	11.1	24.8	15.2
40 years or more, %	53.2	53.8	33.6	48.3
EDUCATION				
Less than high school, %	7.4	29.7	28.7	20.9
College degree or more, %	52.3	50.5	27.0	45.7
OCCUPATION				
Manual laborer, %	18.0	26.4	40.1	26.6
Professional/Business owner, %	49.8	61.5	36.0	50.3
KNOWLEDGE OF ENGLISH				
Very little, %	11.9	18.7	5.0	12.4
Well or very well, %	64.2	49.7	60.9	58.5
LEGAL STATUS				
Does not have entry visa, %	6.3	3.5	27.9	10.7
U.S. citizen, %	56.3	48.5	38.4	49.1
LENGTH OF U.S. RESIDENCE				
Less than 5 years, %	10.1	5.8	10.4	8.7
Ten years or more, %	68.9	66.8	69.5	69.3
AVERAGE TRIPS TO HOME COUNTRY FOR ORGANIZATIONAL MATTERS				
Never or rarely, %	6.7	3.6	30.0	11.5
At least three trips a year, %	40.0	35.7	20.0	33.3

cant positive effects in their hometowns, but very limited ones at the regional and, especially, national levels.[18] This is another form of saying that expatriate communities cannot be counted on to develop sending nations by themselves, either through their remittances or through their philanthropic activities.

Third, active transnational activism is, by and large, a one-generation

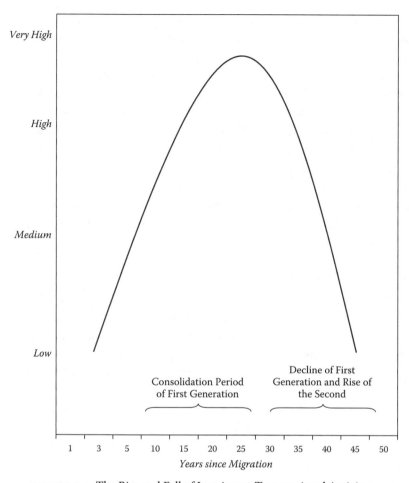

Very High

High

Medium

Low

Consolidation Period
of First Generation

Decline of First
Generation and Rise of
the Second

1   3   5   10   15   20   25   30   35   40   45   50

Years since Migration

FIGURE 2.1. The Rise and Fall of Immigrant Transnational Activism

phenomenon. While, as shown by the research literature, it strengthens with the consolidation of migrants' economic and legal position in the host society, their offspring cannot be counted on to continue these activities or, at least, carry them on with the same level of fervor.[19] The power of assimilative forces generally leads to a reorientation of the second generation toward their lives and prospects in what is now their country, to the detriment of the transnational concerns and goals of their parents.[20] The level of commitment to transnational activism may thus be portrayed as a bell curve moving along with the passage of time: low at arrival; increasing with the consolidation of the first generation, and declining with the passage of that generation from the scene and the arrival of the second. Figure 2.1 graphically portrays the process.

For these reasons, transnationalism can be regarded as, at best, a palliative for the deleterious effects of permanent population loss in sending nations. While cyclical flows, as defined next, might be counted upon to make a significant contribution to development, the demographic and economic consequences of permanent departures lead, on balance, in the opposite direction. Although it is true that mass out-migration can have structural significance in helping consolidate the power of dominant classes in sending nations, this result is not conducive, for reasons already given, to their developmental transformation. Despite the rise of transnational organizations and activism, the overall change potential of permanent settlement abroad is not positive, since the contributions cannot match, in the long term, the hollowing-out effect of such movements.

CYCLICAL LABOR MIGRATION

The concept of cyclicality is not straightforward. Numerous forms and periodicities of migration may or may not fall under its rubric. At one extreme, we must consider the phenomenon of forced repatriation of unauthorized migrants that may be classified as a kind of "temporary" migration, albeit of an involuntary sort. On the other hand, migrants permanently settled abroad may return frequently for visits or vacations or even own a second home in their native country. The same type of migrant may also participate regularly and invest in transnational organizations, thereby investing their everyday lives with a sort of "virtual" cyclicality.

All of these and other experiences exist in reality, but they do not qualify as truly cyclical. The cyclical pattern may be defined, in its pure type, as labor displacements abroad, wherein migrants orient their life and work toward the goal of return, do not bring their immediate families for resettlement, send regular remittances to family and kin and invest or save for investments at home, and actually return after limited periods abroad.

Based on this definition, a continuum of migratory types may be defined. Excluding coerced returns, with problematic developmental implications, there is a theoretical progression where the "pure" type of cyclical migrant is hypothesized to have the greatest developmental impact, while those settled with their families abroad have the least. *Developmental impact* is defined as including economic investments, but also transfers of information and skills from abroad, plus the avoidance of depopulation. The available data indicate that long-term and economically secure immigrants are the most likely to take part in transnational organizations, but they represent a minority of the expatriate population. The rest have effectively cut their ties with the home country, except for occasional visits or vacations whose developmental impact is nil.[21]

Such a framework helps bring together a series of disparate findings in the empirical literature: from the regular transfers of money and know-how that buttress the optimistic perspective of the "New Economics of Migration" to the grim data on depopulation and impoverishment that underlie the *Declaration of Cuernavaca* and similar statements.[22]

No extensive data exist at present on the effects of forced repatriation. While, in principle, involuntary returnees could also make economic and skill transfers to their places of origin, the traumatic circumstances of apprehension and forced departure lead me to be skeptical of such effects. This form of return migration contrasts, in every respect, with the deliberate, planned manner in which true cyclical migrants organize their lives abroad, with an eye toward their families and their future lives at home.

The Migration of Professionals

The migrations of manual laborers are not the only type of economically driven population movements in the global economy. The same wealthy societies that generate demand at the bottom of their labor markets also do so at the top. These increasingly information-driven societies require foreign-trained talent to supplement their domestic professional and technical labor pools. The information-technology revolution in the United States, centered in Silicon Valley, generated a vast demand for engineers, computer scientists, and programmers that American universities by themselves could not supply.[23] The deficit has been covered by importing talent, as Kyle Eischen describes in his chapter on high-skilled Indian immigrants to the United States.

Recognizing this need, Congress created in 1990 the H1-B visa program, under which highly skilled professionals can be hired for temporary work in the United States. The visas and work permits are issued for a maximum of three years and are renewable for another three. In practice, many "H1-B workers" eventually manage to shift their status to permanent residents. In 1990, the authorized ceiling for this program was 65,000. Successive congressional acts increased the ceiling. In 2002 and 2003, H1-B permits were issued to 195,000 and 360,498 professional foreign workers and their families, respectively, and by 2006, the figure had increased to 431,853. Principal specialty areas represented among these temporary immigrants include computer science, engineering, and information technologies. Emerging Third World countries such as India and China, discussed in other chapters of this book, are the principal sources of this inflow, followed by large Latin American countries such as Colombia and Mexico, and by countries of the British Commonwealth, mainly Canada.[24]

Called "brain drain" in sending countries, professional outflows can be examined through the same theoretical lenses used for the analysis of labor migrations. Neoclassical economists view these movements as natural, equilibrium-restoring mechanisms between low-wage and high-wage countries, the latter being able to better reward workers according to their productivity.[25] This neoclassical approach is contradicted by the fact that professional out-migrations do not generally originate in the poorest countries, where salary differentials are at a maximum, but in emerging, mid-income, and even developed countries, where such differentials are much lower. In addition, the theory is unable to explain why most professionals in sending countries do not migrate, despite being exposed to the same wage differentials.[26]

While the New Economics school has not explicitly addressed the topic of professional outflows, its key concept of "relative deprivation" can be readily applied to correct the shortcomings of the neoclassical analysis: professionals at risk of moving abroad are those subject to high levels of relative deprivation. This situation can come about in two ways: first, if their incomes are not high enough to allow them a middle-class life, according to local standards. In these cases, it is not the invidious comparison with higher incomes abroad, but with those earned by other professionals at home, that can create a powerful incentive to move abroad.[27] Second, the situation arises if their training is so superior to local employment opportunities that they see their chances for professional development as seriously compromised. In these cases, the point of reference is professionals in First World countries, not because of their incomes, but because of their much better working conditions.[28]

A third theoretical perspective—world-system analysis—can be invoked to provide broader context to the relative-deprivation hypothesis. The operative concept in this case is "structural imbalancing," which denotes how the cultural and technological penetration by advanced nations into less-developed nations ends up compromising the chances of the latter to create and retain pools of domestic talent.[29] Schematically, the process runs as follows: professional standards and training practices are disseminated from core nations to the rest of the world and are readily copied by emerging countries aiming to "catch up" with the West. Young professionals trained according to these First World standards look for occupational opportunities that allow them to put their advanced skills to use and to develop them further. Unfortunately, such opportunities are scarce in the local economy, with the result that many experience rising relative deprivation. In the interim, high-tech firms and universities in the advanced world experience scarcities of domestic talent and seek to supplement it by recruiting abroad. Naturally, the first place to look is among well-trained labor pools created by imported professional standards in less-developed nations.

The fit between the goals of young professionals experiencing relative deprivation at home and the demand for high human capital abroad sets the stage for the brain drain. In this manner, poorer countries end up subsidizing the high-tech labor needs of rich countries. Structural imbalancing ensures that the effort of emerging Third World nations to imitate advanced nations is compromised, at every step, by the better fit between talent trained according to the most modern standards and the labor needs of the countries from which these standards emanated in the first place. Figure 2.2 graphically summarizes the process.

Until recently, theorizing about determinants and consequences of the brain drain pretty much ended here. However, two developments have added complexity to the picture and, in the process, significantly altered its somber conclusions. First, temporary professional migration promoted by such legislation as the H1-B program creates strong incentives to return home in a relatively short period. While, as noted above, many H1-B workers manage to extend their stays, the expectation and reality of the program is that the majority return, thus creating a cyclical flow. Cyclical professional migration contributes to development in sending nations for the same reasons that cyclical manual labor movements do: returnees bring their new skills, innovations, and savings that can be invested productively at home. The extent to which the return flow of professionals pays off depends largely on the existing infrastructure: sending countries that possess a modicum of universities, research centers, and firms able to absorb scientific and technological innova-

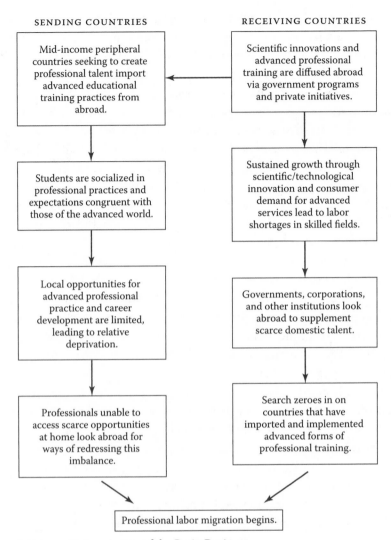

SENDING COUNTRIES   RECEIVING COUNTRIES

Mid-income peripheral countries seeking to create professional talent import advanced educational training practices from abroad.

Scientific innovations and advanced professional training are diffused abroad via government programs and private initiatives.

Students are socialized in professional practices and expectations congruent with those of the advanced world.

Sustained growth through scientific/technological innovation and consumer demand for advanced services lead to labor shortages in skilled fields.

Local opportunities for advanced professional practice and career development are limited, leading to relative deprivation.

Governments, corporations, and other institutions look abroad to supplement scarce domestic talent.

Professionals unable to access scarce opportunities at home look abroad for ways of redressing this imbalance.

Search zeroes in on countries that have imported and implemented advanced forms of professional training.

Professional labor migration begins.

FIGURE 2.2. Determinants of the Brain Drain

Source: Alejandro Portes, Cristina Escobar, and Alexandria Walton Radford. "Immigrant Transnational Organizations and Development: A Comparative Study." *International Migration Review* 41 (spring 2007), 242–81.

tions will obviously be better placed to make use of their professional returnees than those that lack such institutions.

Second, the advent of the transnational perspective in migration studies has modified the lens through which permanent, professional out-migration was previously seen. From a brain-drain outlook, such flows amounted to a permanent loss for sending countries whose sole recourse was to try to attract their migrants back.[30] However, the discovery that immigrant transnationalism increases with length of residence in host countries and with levels of education leads to the expectation that professional expatriates will be at the forefront of these activities.[31] Data from recent studies of transnational organizations, including those presented in table 2.2, lead to the same conclusion.

Unlike manual labor migrants whose transnational philanthropy leads, at best, to public works and services in their hometowns, a community of professional expatriates can make a significant contribution to the scientific and technological development of their home countries. The reasons for doing so are straightforward. In addition to national loyalties and the weight of nostalgia, migrant professionals often have a sense of obligation to the institutions that educated them. When, on the basis of that education, they achieve wealth, security, and status abroad, it is only natural that at least some will seek to repay the debt. Some do so through philanthropic activities, others through transferring information and technology, still others through sponsoring the training of younger colleagues. Professionals who have become successful entrepreneurs abroad may go further and endow their alma maters or even found institutions of higher learning and research at home.[32]

Professional transnationalism has another important facet: unlike immigrants who perform manual labor, and whose return home is often made difficult by their legal status or by their modest resources, professionals with a well-established position abroad have the option of making their journey cyclical. They can do so because they face no legal difficulties in traveling and because they command the necessary resources. Hence, they are able to continue living and working abroad while making investments at home or involving themselves actively in philanthropic and educational pursuits there.

While not all expatriate professionals and scientists take part in these activities, those who do can make a more significant contribution to national development than short-term professional migrants. This is so because, unlike H1-B and similar contract workers, long-term professional migrants are more likely to have acquired the skills, experience, and resources to have a major impact at home, should they wish to do so.

The recent research literature on economic transnationalism supports this line of argument. First, surveys show that transnational entrepreneurs are recruited among the better-educated and better-established members of their respective immigrant communities, making up the bulk of the business class in these communities.[33] Second, as the cases of China, India, and Israel show, the growth of sizable expatriate populations of scientists and engineers does not necessarily mean the hollowing out of these countries' scientific and research institutions, but may energize them through a dense traffic of personnel, resources, and ideas. AnnaLee Saxenian, as well as Kyle Eishen, in this book, attributes the growth of dynamic information technology (IT) poles in cities like Bangalore, Shanghai, and Tel Aviv to the entrepreneurial initiatives of their professionals abroad.[34] Similar conclusions are reached by Min Ye, in her chapter in this book, and by Maggi Leung, in her study of transnational investments and the activities of overseas Chinese.[35]

A word of caution is necessary at this point. The positive developmental potential of settled professional communities abroad depends, as in the case of H1-B temporary workers, on the existence of an infrastructure capable of absorbing technological innovations and investments. For this potential to materialize, governments of sending countries must be proactive in creating suitable conditions for returnees. These conditions range from stable property regimes to support scientific and technological research facilities that can dialogue with expatriates and understand the import of what they have to offer. Natasha Iskander describes in her chapter on Morocco how governments can even channel, through dialogue with migrants, remittances to foster development. A laissez faire approach that merely waits for the market to work out its "magic" through spontaneous remittances and knowledge transfers will not work. Governments must meet their half of the bargain, since, in the absence of suitable conditions that only they can create, the best-intentioned transnational projects cannot succeed. Again, for professional migrants to help transform the technical and industrial structures of their home nations, there must be "something" that they can return to.

Figure 2.3 summarizes the analysis presented so far, with a typology of international migration. Its aim is to reconcile opposite positions concerning the role of migration in development, by showing when and under what conditions such flows can make a positive contribution to sending communities and countries and showing when they will have the opposite effects. The very complexity of these movements ensures

TYPES / DURATION	Cyclical	Permanent
Manual Labor Flows	Developmental • Overcomes inefficiencies in sending countries' credit and product markets • Transfers skills and resources, strengthening local productive structures • Preserves demographic growth of sending regions	Nondevelopmental • Leads to depopulation of sending areas and weakening of productive infrastructures • Long-term decline of migrant remittances • Migrant children placed at risk of downward assimilation in host societies • Rise of transnational organizations and activities as a partially countervailing force
Professional-Technical Labor Flows	Developmental • Transfers scientific-technological knowledge to sending countries • Encourages new productive investments of migrant savings when suitable infrastructures are present • Preserves quality and growth of national scientific/technological establishment	Mixed • Loss of talent trained with scarce national resources • Transnational entrepreneurship and activities by expatriates can neutralize initially negative effects through significant transfers of capital and technology • Outcomes contingent on institutional context and government proactivity in sending nations

FIGURE 2.3. International Migration: Its Types and Developmental Effects

that the overall picture will be mixed: some countries have and will continue to benefit from their expatriates, making use of their transfers to transform their productive structures and increase their export capacity; others have used their departure and their remittances merely to perpetuate the existing sociopolitical order and the rule of entrenched elites; in still others, the overall balance is still uncertain. Not surprisingly, this opaque picture has given rise to militantly opposite pronouncements about the effects of migration. The purpose of the preceding diagrams is to help clarify this complexity so that conditions can be identified that make migration flows positive, on average, for sending regions and countries.

IN CONCLUSION, I would like to return to the first point of the introduction, namely that international migration flows receive more attention for their real or imaginary effects in the receiving societies than for their effects in places of origin. Governments of host nations generally follow suit, enacting policies designed to stem or channel the flow according to purely domestic interests, with nary a thought about the implications of these policies for migrant-sending nations. Governments of sending nations have not proven much more enlightened, as their interests in migration seldom extend beyond the size and growth of remittances sent by their expatriates.[36] In this context, it has fallen to immigrants themselves to correct the situation by implementing a myriad of transnational activities that seek to connect and reconcile the needs and interests of people living both in the sending and receiving countries.

This form of globalization from below is by itself insufficient to neutralize the negative developmental consequences of permanent out-migration. Instead of a zero-sum game, international migration could be transformed into a win-win process, if sending and receiving governments would take active steps in organizing it as a managed labor-transfer program. Such a program could be constructed on the basis of five general principles:

1 Cyclical labor flows, especially of manual workers, are preferable to permanent out-migration.
2 The cyclical character of migration should be grounded on a schedule of real incentives in both receiving and sending nations, so that return is voluntary and planned.
3 Governments of advanced nations should cooperate with their sending-country counterparts in creating the necessary infrastructure of health, education, and investment opportunities for families of labor migrants to remain at home and for migrants to be motivated to return.
4 Similar support should be provided in the construction of scientific and technological centers that can establish a dialogue with expatriate professionals and benefit from their knowledge and investments.

5 For migrants who settle permanently abroad, additional facilities should be created so that they are encouraged to transform their journey through investments and philanthropic activities at home.

The best research shows that there is no contradiction between active transnationalism and the successful social and political incorporation of permanent immigrants in host nations. Rather than pay attention to the misguided chorus of nativists denouncing whatever migrants do, the governments of host nations should follow scientific knowledge by working along the paths already charted by the self-initiated productive transnationalism of many expatriates. Similarly, instead of worrying exclusively about their balance of payments and the flow of remittances, the governments of sending countries should pursue a line of action guided by the long-term developmental potential of migration, rather than its short-term economic consequences. In such a fashion, the sorry outcomes seen and denounced by Third World scholars in documents like the *Cuernavaca Declaration* can give way to a world in which international migration and development become mutually supportive.

Notes

1 This is a revised version of the annual lecture sponsored by *Ethnic and Racial Studies*, City College of London, May 8, 2008. I thank Martin Bulmer, Stephen Castles, and Susan Eckstein for their comments. Responsibility for the contents is exclusively mine. The data on which this chapter is partially based were collected by the Comparative Immigrant Organizations Project, supported by grants from the MacArthur and Russell Sage Foundations.
2 Luis E. Guarnizo, "The Economics of Transnational Living," *International Migration Review* 37 (fall 2003): 666–99; Douglas S. Massey, Joaquin Arango, Graeme Hugo, Ali Kouaouci, Adela Pellegrino, and J. Edward Taylor, *Worlds in Motion: Understanding International Migration at the End of the Millennium* (Oxford: Clarendon, 1998); Sergio Diaz-Briquets and Sidney Weintraub, *Migration, Remittances, and Small Business Development, Mexico and Caribbean Basin Countries* (Boulder, CO: Westview, 1991).
3 Raúl Delgado-Wise and Humberto Márquez Covarrubias, *The Reshaping of Mexican Labor Exports under NAFTA: Paradoxes and Challenges* (Zacatecas, Mexico: University of Zacatecas, International Network of Migration and Development, 2006).
4 Stephen Castles, "The Factors That Make and Unmake Migration Policies," *International Migration Review* 38 (fall 2004): 852–84; Raúl Delgado-Wise,

"Globalización y migración laboral internacional: Reflexiones en torno al caso de Mexico," in *Nuevas tendencias y desafíos de la migración internacional*, ed. R. D. Wise and M. Favela (Mexico City: Miguel Angel Porrua, 2004); Joshua S. Reichert, "The Migrant Syndrome: Seasonal U.S. Wage Labor and Rural Development in Central Mexico," *Human Organization* 40 (1981): 59–66.

5 Frank D. Bean and Gillian Stevens, *America's Newcomers and the Dynamics of Diversity* (New York: Russell Sage Foundation, 2003); Alejandro Portes and Rubén G. Rumbaut, *Immigrant America: A Portrait*, 3rd ed. (Berkeley: University of California Press, 2006), chapter 3.

6 W. Arthur Lewis, *The Theory of Economic Growth* (London: Allen and Unwin, 1959); Brinley Thomas, *Migration and Economic Growth: A Study of Great Britain and the Atlantic Economy* (Cambridge: Cambridge University Press, 1973).

7 Michael Todaro, *Internal Migration in Developing Countries* (Geneva: International Labor Office, 1976).

8 Oded Stark, "Migration Decision Making," *Journal of Development Economics* 14 (1984): 251–59; Oded Stark, *The Migration of Labour* (Cambridge: Basil Blackwell, 1991).

9 Douglas S. Massey, Rafael Alarcon, Jorge Durand, and Humberto Gonzalez, *Return to Atzlan: The Social Process of International Migration from Western Mexico* (Berkeley: University of California Press, 1987); Massey, Arango, Hugo, Kouaouci, Pellegrino, and Taylor, *Worlds in Motion.*

10 Delgado-Wise and Covarrubias, *The Reshaping of Mexican Labor Exports under NAFTA.*

11 Wayne A. Cornelius, "The Structural Embeddedness of Demand for Mexican Immigrant Labor: New Evidence from California," in *Crossings, Mexican Immigration in Interdisciplinary Perspective*, ed. M. Suarez-Orozco (Cambridge, MA: Center for Latin American Studies, Harvard University, 1998), 115–55; David E. Lopez and Ricardo D. Stanton-Salazar, "Mexican-Americans: A Second Generation at Risk," in *Ethnicities: Children of Immigrants in America*, ed. R. G. Rumbaut and A. Portes (Berkeley: University of California Press and Russell Sage Foundation, 2001), 57–90.

12 Alejandro Portes, Patricia Fernandez-Kelly, and William Haller, "Segmented Assimilation on the Ground: The New Second Generation in Early Adulthood," *Ethnic and Racial Studies* 28 (November 2005): 1000–1040; Edward E. Telles and Vilma Ortiz, *Generations of Exclusion: Mexican-Americans, Assimilation and Race* (New York: Russell Sage Foundation, 2008); Jaime D. Vigil, *A Rainbow of Gangs: Street Cultures in the Mega-City* (Austin: University of Texas Press, 2002).

13 Patricia Landolt, "Salvadoran Economic Transnationalism: Embedded Strategies for Household Maintenance, Immigrant Incorporation, and Entrepreneurial Expansion," *Global Networks* 1 (2001): 217–42; Peggy Levitt and Nina

Glick-Schiller, "Conceptualizing Simultaneity: A Transnational Social Field Perspective on Society," *International Migration Review* 38 (fall 2004): 1002–39; Steven Vertovec, "Migrant Transnationalism and Modes of Transformation," *International Migration Review* 38 (fall 2004): 970–1001.

14 Luis E. Guarnizo, Alejandro Portes, and William J. Haller, "Assimilation and Transnationalism: Determinants of Transnational Political Action among Contemporary Immigrants," *American Journal of Sociology* 108 (May 2003): 1211–48; Alejandro Portes, William Haller, and Luis E. Guarnizo, "Transnational Entrepreneurs: An Alternative Form of Immigrant Adaptation," *American Sociological Review* 67 (April 2002): 278–98; Alejandro Portes, Cristina Escobar, and Alexandria Walton Radford, "Immigrant Transnational Organizations and Development: A Comparative Study," *International Migration Review* 41 (spring 2007): 242–81.

15 Alejandro Portes and Josh DeWind, "A Cross-Atlantic Dialogue: The Progress of Research and Theory in the Study of International Migration," *International Migration Review* 38 (fall 2004): 828–51.

16 Jose Itzigsohn, Carlos Dore, Esther Fernandez, and Obed Vazquez, "Mapping Dominican Transnationalism: Narrow and Broad Transnational Practices," *Ethnic and Racial Studies* 22 (March 1999): 316–39; Landolt, "Salvadoran Economic Transnationalism"; Robert C. Smith, *Mexican New York: Transnational Worlds of New Immigrants* (Berkeley: University of California Press, 2005).

17 David FitzGerald, *Negotiating Extra-Territorial Citizenship: Mexican Migration and the Transnational Politics of Community* (San Diego: Center for Comparative Immigration Studies, University of California, 2000); Alejandro Portes, Cristina Escobar, and Alexandria Walton Radford, "Immigrant Transnational Organizations and Development: A Comparative Study," *International Migration Review* 41 (spring 2007), 242–81.

18 Patricia Landolt, Lilian Autler, and Sonia Baires, "From 'Hermano Lejano' to 'Hermano Mayor': The Dialectics of Salvadoran Transnationalism," *Ethnic and Racial Studies* 22 (1999): 290–315; Portes, Haller, and Guarnizo, "Transnational Entrepreneurs."

19 William Haller and Patricia Landolt, "The Transnational Dimensions of Identity Formation: Adult Children of Immigrants in Miami," *Ethnic and Racial Studies* 28 (November 2005): 1182–1214.

20 Patricia Fernández-Kelly and Lisa Konczal, "'Murdering the Alphabet': Identity and Entrepreneurship among Second Generation Cubans, West Indians, and Central Americans," *Ethnic and Racial Studies* 28 (November 2005): 1153–81.

21 Portes, Haller, and Guarnizo, "Transnational Entrepreneurs"; Itzigsohn, Dore, Fernandez, and Vazquez, "Mapping Dominican Transnationalism"; Landolt, "Salvadoran Economic Transnationalism."

22 Stark, "Migration Decision Making,"; Stark, *The Migration of Labour*; Douglas
     S. Massey, Luin Goldring, and Jorge Durand, "Continuities in Transnational
     Migration: An Analysis of Nineteen Mexican Communities," *American Jour-
     nal of Sociology* 99 (1994): 1492–1533; Douglas S. Massey, Jorge Durand, and
     Nolan J. Malone, *Beyond Smoke and Mirrors: Mexican Immigration in an Era
     of Economic Integration* (New York: Russell Sage Foundation, 2002); Delgado-
     Wise and Covarrubias, *The Reshaping of Mexican Labor Exports under*
     NAFTA; Stephen Castles, "Comparing the Experience of Five Major Emigra-
     tion Countries," in *Migration and Development: Perspectives from the South*,
     ed. S. Castles and R. Delgado-Wise (Geneva: International Organization for
     Migration, 2008), 255–84.
23 AnnaLee Saxenian, *The New Argonauts: Regional Advantage in a Global
     Economy* (Cambridge, MA: Harvard University Press, 2006).
24 Office of Immigration Statistics, *2003 Yearbook of Immigration Statistics*
     (Washington, DC: Department of Homeland Security, 2004); Office of Immi-
     gration Statistics, *2007 Yearbook of Immigration Statistics* (Washington, DC:
     Department of Homeland Security, 2008).
25 George Borjas, "Economic Theory and International Migration," *International
     Migration Review* 23 (1989): 457–85; George Borjas, *Friends or Strangers: The
     Impact of Immigrants on the U.S. Economy* (New York: Basic Books, 1990).
26 Enrique Oteiza, "La migracion de profesionales, técnicos y obreros calificados
     argentinos a los Estados Unidos," *Desarrollo economico* 10 (1971): 429–54;
     Portes and Rumbaut, *Immigrant America*, chapter 2.
27 Oteiza, "La migracion de profesionales, técnicos y obreros calificados argen-
     tinos a los Estados Unidos"; Alejandro Portes and Adreain R. Ross, "Modern-
     ization for Emigration: The Medical Brain Drain from Argentina," *Journal of
     Interamerican Studies and World Affairs* 13 (1976): 395–422.
28 Rafael Alarcon, "Recruitment Processes among Foreign-Born Engineers and
     Scientists in Silicon Valley," *American Behavioral Scientist* 42 (June/July 1999),
     1381–97.
29 Saskia Sassen, *The Mobility of Labor and Capital: A Study in International
     Investment and Labor Flow* (New York: Cambridge University Press, 1988);
     Alejandro Portes and John Walton, *Labor, Class, and the International System*
     (New York: Academic Press, 1981), chapter 2.
30 Oteiza, "La migracion de profesionales, técnicos y obreros calificados argen-
     tinos a los Estados Unidos."
31 Guarnizo, Portes, and Haller, "Assimilation and Transnationalism"; Portes,
     Escobar, and Radford, "Immigrant Transnational Organizations and Devel-
     opment."
32 Maggi W. H. Leung, "Homeward-Bound Investors: The Role of Overseas Chi-
     nese in China's Economic Development," in *Global Migration and Develop-
     ment*, ed. T. van Naerssen, E. Spaan, and A. Zoomers (New York: Routledge,

2008), 288–308; AnnaLee Saxenian, *Silicon Valley's New Immigrant Entrepreneurs* (San Francisco: Public Policy Institute of California, 1999); AnnaLee Saxenian, *Local and Global Networks of Immigrant Professionals in Silicon Valley* (San Francisco: Public Policy Institute of California, 2002); Vertovec, "Migrant Transnationalism and Modes of Transformation."

33 Portes, Haller, and Guarnizo, "Transnational Entrepreneurs"; Guarnizo, "The Economics of Transnational Living."

34 Saxenian, *Local and Global Networks of Immigrant Professionals in Silicon Valley*; Saxenian, *The New Argonauts*.

35 Leung, "Homeward-Bound Investors."

36 Castles, "The Factors That Make and Unmake Migration Policies."

3

How Overseas Chinese Spurred the
Economic "Miracle" in Their Homeland

MIN YE

China ranks among the top countries in the world in the number of its people who have emigrated. Known as *overseas Chinese*, they left their homeland under various historical circumstances and went to a variety of countries. They have differed in how they adapted, where they resettled, and how they impacted their homeland from their new land.[1] Chinese emigrants became instrumental in the industrial transformation of their home country since the late 1970s. They became the largest investors in their homeland, and influenced the government's reform policies.

These economically influential overseas Chinese emigrated in a historically tumultuous period, after nationalist government rule collapsed and the communists took over. They mostly fled to Hong Kong, Macao, Taiwan, and Southeast Asian countries, because they opposed the communist revolution of 1949. They helped the places where they settled industrialize and experience some of the highest economic growth rates in the world. But they returned to their homeland thirty years later, where they oversaw the revival of capitalism and an industrial revolution.[2] In John Kao's words, they contributed to the formation of "a de facto Chinese commonwealth," a fourth global economic power, alongside the United States, Japan, and Western Europe.[3] The overseas Chinese who came to play such extraordinary roles both where they settled and from there in their homeland had human, economic, and social-capital assets that they creatively put to work to develop globally competitive industries.

Since the late 1970s, overseas Chinese have heavily invested in China. In 2007, they infused more than $40 billion in foreign direct investment (FDI), plus nearly $20 billion in remittances. They benefited from the rapid industrialization of Asia after World War II, industrialization that they helped spur.[4] Abroad, they accumulated considerable financial resources, along with technological expertise and market connections, that they channeled to China once they perceived economic conditions there propitious. The communist Chinese government helped create those conditions, beginning in 1978. At both the national and local levels, officials became remarkably receptive to overseas Chinese, who even influenced government economic policy.

The early overseas Chinese investors in the Communist Peoples Republic of China (PRC) were predominantly first-generation immigrants.[5] They were born in mainland China and uprooted around the time of the revolution in 1949. They maintained strong roots to their birthplaces and to extended family who remained there, such that they continued to be emotionally attached to China, despite their political opposition to the communist regime. Consequently, when the PRC introduced economic reforms and began to allow the investment of overseas Chinese in the late 1970s, they responded quickly. According to surveys, the immigrants invested in the PRC primarily for economic, but also for sentimental, reasons.[6]

Overseas Chinese is an evolving and even contested concept, depending on the definition of homeland. As this chapter examines industrialization in the PRC, or mainland China, I include residents of Hong Kong, Macao, and Taiwan as overseas Chinese. This practice is consistent with the PRC's official account of transnational investment and tourism, which has treated investment and tourism from these regions as overseas Chinese sources. During the main period examined here, the 1980s and 1990s, these regions were not part of the PRC, and scholars of Chinese emigration conventionally treated residents of Hong Kong, Macao, and Taiwan as part of the Chinese diaspora.[7] Hong Kong reverted to the PRC in 1997, and Macao returned in 1999, after which scholars ceased to consider the mainland-born in these places Chinese diaspora. However, the national government of the PRC guaranteed that Hong Kong and Macao, as special administrative regions (SARS), would enjoy separate economic, social, and political systems for fifty years. The PRC continues to categorize visitors and investments from these regions as separate from domestic sources. Figures on foreign direct investment include coethnic investments, what I call EDI, originating from these places.

A Brief Overview of Chinese Immigration

Chinese emigrated over the years for different mixes of economic and political reasons. During different historical periods, some Chinese immigrants played important roles in their homelands. Historically, there were two main types of émigrés, elites and laborers. Elite émigrés influenced reform initiatives of the Chinese government. This was true already during the so-called strengthening movement launched by the Qing court (1860s to 1890s) and during the Republican era (1910s to 1930s). Laborers, by contrast, during neither period influenced government reforms.

The exodus unleashed by the revolution in 1949 involved both types of Chinese, from the same regions of China as the earlier migrations. Overseas Chinese predominantly came from Guangdong and Fujian, and secondarily from Shanghai, Zhejiang, and Jiangsu. They built on earlier immigrant networks, amplifying the networks where they settled. However, in the exodus of 1949, the divide between the elite and the rank-and-file was murkier. Even elite émigrés to Hong Kong and Taiwan experienced economic hardship.

When industrialization took off where the émigrés who fled the revolution resettled, both sets of immigrants prospered. Although they continued to be anticommunist, they resumed homeland ties, following leadership changes in China in the late 1970s. They visited China with increased frequency. However, while migrant laborers shared some of their new earnings with family who remained in China, they tended to do so in the form of remittances, which their Chinese families used to upgrade their material living standards.[8] Entrepreneurial immigrants often provided their mainland families with remittances, but they also invested in businesses on the mainland, and they established ties with officials through which they influenced the FDI policies of the PRC and spurred export-oriented industrialization. Many of the high-ranking officials who assumed power following Mao Zedong's death, including the new top leader, Deng Xiaoping, had been victims of Mao's revolutionary policies, as had many who had fled the communist takeover in 1949. Given their shared experiences, the leadership that took over after Mao died removed political hurdles to the return of overseas Chinese.

In the changed political environment, Chinese émigrés came to have an unprecedented impact on China. The enormous economic gap between the wealthy immigrants and the impoverished population on the mainland who had suffered from Mao's destructive economic policies, led the new leadership to be receptive to immigrant influence. Anxious to develop the economy, state officials recognized that overseas Chinese had skills and capital to offer. Meanwhile, immigrant entrepreneurs who had developed globally competitive industries where they resettled faced rising production costs and were keen to relocate their businesses elsewhere, where their costs would be lower. China provided a possibility. Under the circumstances both the state and immigrants, driven by mutual interests and enhanced by social ties, put their political differences aside. In close collaboration with the Chinese government, overseas Chinese oversaw the "Chinese miracle" that began in the 1980s.

To some extent premigration differences among the Chinese who fled the revolution influenced how they related to their homeland from where they resettled. Chinese of different socioeconomic and political backgrounds relocated in different places. The business class fled mainly to Hong Kong, while the prerevolutionary political class typically followed the nationalist government to Taiwan. Those who moved to Hong Kong had less political enmity toward the PRC than those who relocated in Taiwan. Consequently, even though the PRC offered similar investment incentives to all overseas Chinese, emigrants to Taiwan were less receptive. They invested later and less than émigrés who settled in Hong Kong. Ultimately, however, Taiwanese investment proved crucial to the development of the computer hardware sector in the PRC, especially in Shanghai and Kunshan.

Foreign Direct Investment in China and the Contribution of Overseas Chinese

The PRC's success in attracting direct foreign investment since initiating its economic reform has been well documented. Before the reforms, it had received almost no FDI. Then, between 1979 and 1984, it received

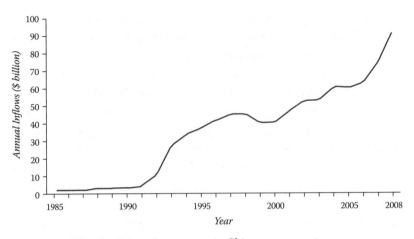

FIGURE 3.1. Foreign Direct Investment in China, 1979–2008

Source: China Statistical Yearbook (1985–2010), http://chinadataonline.org

over $4.1 billion, and another $2 billion in 1985. Figure 3.1 demonstrates how rapidly FDI rose thereafter. Between 1991 and 1992 FDI more than doubled, and doubled again between 1992 and 1993. By then China became the largest recipient of FDI in the developing world, and by the turn of the century the largest in the world. Foreign direct investment increased throughout the 1990s, except between 1997 and 1999, the years of the Asian financial crisis. In 2001, when China joined the World Trade Organization (WTO), the government opened many more sectors of the economy to foreign investors, such that by 2008 the country had attracted a total of $853 billion in foreign capital.

Foreign direct investment was the most important factor behind China's export boom. The Chinese government offered incentives to attract export-oriented FDI in special zones it established. While in 1992 it allowed FDI to be directed also to the domestic market, most FDI continued to focus on international markets, largely because overseas Chinese investors were already competitive exporters before China's economic opening. Since the 1990s, FDI has been involved in over half of exports in the country's booming export economy.

Foreign direct investment focused mainly on manufacturing, first in low-tech but increasingly in high-tech production.[9] Foreign investors took advantage of the country's cheap labor. According to the Chinese National Statistics Bureau, 56 to 70 percent of FDI went to manufacturing between 2000 and 2008. China became the third largest trading

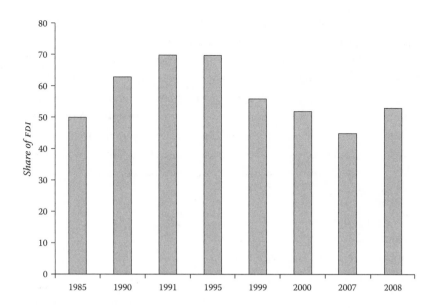

FIGURE 3.2. Overseas Chinese Contribution
to Foreign Direct Investment in China (percent)

1 The data refer to investments from Hong Kong, Macao, Taiwan, and Southeast Asia,
home to many Overseas Chinese. Investments by companies headquartered
elsewhere, but operating in Hong Kong, are not included.

Sources: China Statistical Yearbook (1979–2008), http://chinadataonline.org

nation in the world, and FDI became fundamental to 80 percent of the
high-tech exports.

China became the "world factory," and overseas Chinese the main
force behind it. As indicated in figure 3.2, overseas Chinese were the
largest investors in the PRC between 1985 and 2008. Between 1991 and
1995, overseas Chinese from Hong Kong, Macao, Taiwan, and Southeast Asia accounted for as much as 70 percent of FDI. Its share subsequently declined somewhat, first because of the Asian financial crisis
and, after 2001, because of increased FDI from other places. Nonetheless, in 2008, overseas Chinese still accounted for more than half of FDI.

In sum, overseas Chinese were central to the industrialization of the
PRC, including its industrial export boom. They contributed financial
resources, manufacturing technology, and excellent world market trade
networks. The technological upgrading of overseas Chinese investment
provided a foundation for the PRC's success in expanding its export

niche from low-tech to high-tech products. In turn, overseas Chinese investors paved the way for the entry of other foreign investors.

The Chinese government, at both the national and local levels, played a key role in creating conditions that induced Chinese who had emigrated in opposition to the communist revolution to put their political differences aside and prioritize their economic interests. The government initiated reforms that made the country an attractive place to invest, once reformers gained political influence after Mao Zedong died. In this changed context, overseas Chinese influenced the new leadership to institute reforms.

Overseas Chinese and the Liberalization of Foreign Investment Opportunities

When Chairman Mao died, he designated Hua Guofeng as his successor. Although Hua was pragmatic in his economic outlook, overseas Chinese remained wary of the intent of the communist regime. After a domestic power struggle between Hua and Deng Xiaoping, an economic pragmatist, ended in late 1978 with Deng's becoming the paramount leader, officials associated with Mao were replaced by persons he and his followers had purged. Deng Xiaoping himself had on two occasions challenged Chairman Mao's policy and was demoted as a consequence. His illustrious, but checkered, political career under Mao earned him tremendous credibility and legitimacy among Chinese, both domestically and abroad. His rise to the pinnacle of power implied that the communist regime had taken a pragmatic turn.[10]

The new government launched policies attractive to overseas Chinese. Official newspapers began to publish editorials that praised the achievements of Chinese abroad.[11] The national and local governments founded, reinvigorated, and gave new mandates to Offices of Overseas Chinese (oocs) that under Mao had carried out tirades against overseas Chinese. Ties with overseas Chinese that had been extensive in southern China shifted from being viewed as a liability to an asset for economic development. To lure back overseas Chinese, local governments showered them with perks and praise. Overseas Chinese watched these changes and visited the mainland in growing numbers. The timing was opportune. Overseas Chinese manufacturers in East Asia, facing rising labor costs, wanted to relocate their production, and the mainland seemed attractive in light of the changes under Deng, and the cheap labor there.[12] They proceeded to cultivate ties with mainland officials at both the local and national levels, to influence their thinking about foreign investment and policy initiatives.

Overseas Chinese Policy Networks

Overseas Chinese in Hong Kong had especially extensive ties to Beijing. Under Mao's rule, only in Hong Kong did the PRC set up offices that sold Chinese products in order to earn much-needed foreign exchange. Business representatives in Hong Kong thereby built important connections both with major state-owned enterprises (SOEs) and with industrial ministries in the PRC. These representatives visited China and met with Deng after he took over, and with other high-ranking officials. Convinced of the new government's economic commitment, other Chinese immigrants also returned. They developed ties promoting economic reforms in the PRC, most notably an opening of the economy to foreign investment.

Lee Kashing, who fled from the mainland to Hong Kong as a penniless teenager, became the wealthiest overseas Chinese. He exemplifies how Chinese immigrants responded to the mainland government's changed stance. He cultivated relations with PRC officials, including with business-oriented family members in top political positions, and with China's SOEs operating in Hong Kong, such as with China Venturetech, Citic Pacific, and Shougang Hong Kong, typically managed by high-ranking mainland officials.[13] Lee also made a generous donation in 1981 to found a new university in his birthplace, in Guangdong, that earned him respect and helped him establish good political connections there. Building on these ties, Lee's family invested in various infrastructure projects in Guangdong and in SOEs.

Another important overseas Chinese, Y. K. Pao, came from a prosperous family in Zhejiang Province. He had a successful business career in Shanghai before the revolution, and after the communists took power he moved his financial assets to Hong Kong. There he built the largest shipping empire in Hong Kong, and in all of Southeast Asia, and diversified into real estate, banking, and trading by the late 1970s.

But in the post-Mao era, Pao put his political differences aside and forged what became a long-term relationship with Deng Xiaoping.[14] In the early 1980s, he frequently visited Beijing as a national guest, and occasionally dined with Deng at his private residence.[15] Deng consulted

Pao about major economic issues, including about building up China's shipping industry. By the mid-1980s, Pao had invested extensively in shipping, as well as in real estate, hotels, roads, education, and other social programs, and in business ventures with several ministries on the mainland. And, like Lee, he donated funds to build a university in his birthplace, Zhejiang.

Pao also exemplifies how overseas Chinese developed ties with PRC ministries of industry, and influenced their stance regarding FDI.[16] For example, the Ministry of Machine Building recognized its need for additional investment to expand its operations, and the Ministry of Ship Building its need for overseas markets for its ships. Both ministries forged partnerships with Pao. Pao provided the Ministry of Machine Building with investment capital, and he purchased two ships for the ministry. Although originally wary of working with foreign investors, the two ministries developed confidence in Pao, and by 1984 they and other national bureaucracies became increasingly receptive to the liberalization of FDI.[17] They went out of their way to attract foreign partnerships, often preferring to work with overseas Chinese over other foreign investors.[18]

The ties that overseas Chinese established or reestablished with China under Deng led the government to adopt increasingly FDI-friendly policies. In November 1978 the Chinese Communist Party (CCP) had convened a Central Committee Work Meeting to decide a grand strategy for development. They agreed on an industrialization plan called socialist rationalization, which built on the experiences of Yugoslavia and Japan.[19] The plan approved of foreign borrowing and the promotion of industrial exports, but not of FDI. Most participants at the meeting argued that FDI should be limited, in order not to undermine government control over the domestic economy.[20]

The socialist rationalization plan quickly ran into difficulties. First, the SOEs that relied on foreign loans to develop products for export failed to generate sufficient export revenue for loan repayments. As a consequence, continued foreign borrowing became untenable. Second, technological and financial collaborations with foreign firms were strained by distrust. Early joint projects with foreign companies, especially with those not headed by overseas Chinese, were not successful. This was true of Baogang Steel, which involved Japanese investors, and of the Oil Exploration Project, involving Americans. By contrast, fledgling joint ventures with overseas Chinese proceeded more smoothly, with interpersonal relationships developing rapidly between Chinese immigrants and mainland officials. Coethnic ties became decisive in the creation and build-up of four important Special Economic Zones (SEZs) in southern China.

Local Governments, Overseas Chinese, and the Formation of Special Economic Zones in 1980

Positive changes in national policies toward overseas Chinese led to the resumption of long-standing relations between émigrés and local officials. Because most Chinese immigrants traced their ancestral roots to Guangdong and Fujian, in southern China, local officials in these provinces were at the forefront of forging industrialization based on collaboration with overseas Chinese. The formation of four SEZs, three in Guangdong and one in Fujian, built on remarkable and important coordination between local officials and overseas Chinese.

Only the narrow Pearl River separates Guangdong and Hong Kong. Even before 1949, many from Guangdong had moved to Hong Kong. Then, during the famines of the 1960s, many in Guangdong followed their predecessors and fled to the then still-British colony. However, they maintained extensive family ties with the mainland. Because of long-standing ties, local officials in Guangdong had greater knowledge of Hong Kong's capitalist-based prosperity than did officials elsewhere in China. And in 1979 they were encouraged to seek out overseas Chinese and were given autonomy to devise their own regional economic policies. Interpersonal ties between local officials and Chinese immigrants burgeoned and became an important catalyst for industrialization in southern China. Putting their political differences aside, local officials lobbied national leaders to liberalize their foreign investment policy, in anticipation that overseas Chinese, especially in Hong Kong, would take advantage of the investment opportunity and thereby help develop their local economy.

As early as 1977, three years before national approval of SEZs, Guangdong officials lobbied to relax Deng Xiaoping's FDI restrictions. At the military commission meeting in Guangdong in October 1977, local officials reported that they hoped to develop Bao'an (today's Shenzhen) and Zhuhai as export zones. They hoped, especially, to attract investment from Hong Kong and Macao, and to export to both places. The following year, local officials reiterated their desire for overseas Chinese investment to a delegation from the Central Economic Planning Commission and Ministry of Foreign Trade and Economic Cooperation, which visited the province. Despite national policies that at the time opposed FDI, the local government in Guangdong and overseas Chinese began to collaborate.

Chinese immigrants in Hong Kong took the lead in promoting China's opening to foreign investment, in special zones. Upon convincing local authorities in Guangdong of the merits of such an opening, they together convinced central authorities to shift from opposing to embracing such investment. In January 1979 Guangdong-born Yuan Geng, president of the Hong Kong Merchants' Group, proposed the establishment of an export processing zone in Shekou (a section of Shenzhen, Guangdong) both to the Guangdong government and the national Ministry of Transportation. Meanwhile, some overseas Chinese businessmen proposed that the Shekou zone be expanded to encompass property development and tourism, and suggested the name *special economic zone*.[21] In the zone, a corporate tax rate of 15 percent was applied, comparable to the rate in Hong Kong.[22]

Perceiving prospects of high economic returns, Guangdong officials enthusiastically lobbied central leaders for the project. The Guangdong-born minister of transportation lent his support to the project, and the Guangdong party boss, Xi Zhongxun, asked Beijing to authorize SEZs.[23] At the same time, overseas Chinese worked with a range of national authorities that had strong personal ties in Guangdong, including with Deng Xiaoping, Ye Jianying, and Yang Shangkun, who either were born or had worked extensively in the province, to support a new industrialization model that included SEZs. Hong Kong businessmen directly approached Deng, the top leader. In a letter, they solicited his authorization to establish factories in Guangdong, which they promised would benefit the local economy.[24]

Despite opposition in the CCP to foreign investment, expressed at the November 1978 Central Committee meeting, Deng Xiaoping acceded to the request of the Hong Kong businessmen and, with his backing, the government proceeded to pass the Joint Venture Law in June 1979. Even before it went into effect, overseas Chinese had signed agreements with Guangdong authorities to establish 100 merchandise assembly projects, in conjunction with which they agreed to invest $33.5 million. Accordingly, Chinese immigrants, together with local officials, took the lead in establishing a bedrock for the opening to foreign investment, to which central authorities were responsive. Only in August 1980 did the National People's Congress approve the SEZ proposal that detailed incentives to encourage investment of overseas Chinese.[25]

Fujian province, in southern China, also had strong ties to overseas Chinese before the national government officially embraced liberalization of the economy. Thirty million Fujian had emigrated to Hong Kong, Macao, Taiwan, and countries in Southeast Asia before 1949. Under Mao, some of them returned to their homeland to invest. For example, 12,000 overseas Chinese invested 70 million renminbi (RMB, equivalent to $41 million in 1981) in sixty-two firms in twenty-seven Fujian cities between 1952 and 1967.[26] Overseas Chinese also invested in education, roads, and other infrastructure in Fujian during these years. Overseas Chinese involvements stopped, however, in 1967, when Mao launched the Cultural Revolution and severed international ties.

Thus, when national policies changed in the late 1970s, local officials in Fujian built on earlier experiences and courted overseas Chinese to invest, especially in export and light industries. The Fujian government approved several joint ventures with foreign firms, including with Hua Fu (Japan, United States), Fu Ri (Japan), and Hua Mei (United States), in which overseas Chinese were involved. The Hua Fu Bank, the first bank to open up to foreign investment, is a case in point. A Hong Kong banker who had invested in the state-owned Fujian Bank arranged loans from U.S. and Japanese banks, which led to the creation of the Hua Fu Bank.

In 1980 and 1981 ties between Hong Kong, Beijing, and southern China intensified. Authorities in Beijing came to view the SEZs as great successes. The central government incurred no costs in the operation of the SEZs; they were profitable, and they generated substantial foreign exchange.[27] The State Council proceeded, in 1980, to offer incentives for the formation of joint ventures between overseas and mainland Chinese. The national government allowed overseas Chinese, for example, to transfer equipment worth as much as 100,000 RMB (equivalent to $59,000 in 1981) to mainland Chinese without having to pay customs duties.

Overseas Chinese became early and key investors in the SEZs established in Guangdong and Fujian. In 1981, Hong Kong businessmen provided 90 percent of the foreign investment in the Shenzhen SEZ. Other overseas Chinese provided an additional 6 percent of the investment. Non-Chinese accounted for only 4 percent of the capital. Businessmen in Hong Kong built the three largest projects there. Three years later, Chinese in Hong Kong accounted for 92 percent of foreign investment in the Guangdong Zhuhai SEZ.

Overseas Chinese provided information and technology, as well as capital.[28] But they quickly extended their economic involvements beyond the SEZs, for example, to Dongguan, also in Guangdong province.[29] Meanwhile, local officials from places other than Guangdong set up 50 Beijing-approved trading companies in Hong Kong and another 300 without central government authorization between 1979 and 1981, to attract overseas Chinese investment.[30]

The economic opening, nonetheless, faced opposition. While the reformist political faction argued for bolder and more liberal economic policies, the so-called conservatives opposed the liberalization of FDI, antithetical, they believed, to socialist precepts. Moreover, in southern China, when FDI rapidly increased, smuggling, corruption, and other illicit economic activity surfaced, contributing to political opposition in Beijing to the construction of the SEZs.[31] The "conservative faction" in the national government made the case that FDI had eroded the socialist moral fabric in southern China, in response to which the national government, in 1981, initiated a rectification campaign against "ideological dissolution," and the CCP Propaganda Department launched an "anti-spiritual-pollution" campaign that targeted the SEZs, and then another campaign against "bourgeois liberalization."[32] In response, the national government introduced more restrictive policies, to counter earlier reform efforts. It emphasized recentralization, resumed control over finances, and designated a larger share of investment for heavy industry.[33] Although initially supportive of SEZs, Deng cautioned against the negative effects of FDI.[34]

Against this backdrop, non-Chinese foreign investors became more reluctant to enter China. They had already been frustrated with obstacles they faced in the newly established SEZs. In contrast, overseas Chinese were undeterred. Having built local relations and ties to reformists in the national government during the process of SEZ policymaking, they continued to invest. Local officials in southern China remained committed to local economic development and to the increased revenue FDI made possible. Despite the opposition in Beijing, they continued to promote and facilitate the activity of overseas Chinese in the SEZs.[35]

Reformists, together with local officials, appealed to Deng Xiaoping not only to continue but to deepen FDI liberalization.[36] In turn, overseas Chinese, in contributing to the development of SEZs, helped strengthen the reformist faction. They demonstrated to national leaders that FDI helped develop infrastructure and manufacturing industries, boost exports, and improve living standards in southern China. In so doing, they convinced the top leadership to open an additional fourteen coastal cities to FDI.

The Expansion of Foreign Investment Opportunities

Amid the political and policy divide, Deng Xiaoping conducted a highly publicized twenty-seven-day tour to the special zones, in early 1984. The tour dispelled any misgivings he may have had. He strongly endorsed each SEZ. He publicized to potential foreign investors that he supported the SEZs, and FDI in general, and he emphasized to the domestic populace that foreign investment, and SEZs in particular, very effectively fueled economic growth. Most important, in his tour he highlighted how important overseas Chinese were to the industrial success of the SEZs.[37]

THE ESTABLISHMENT OF COASTAL CITIES

After Deng's tour the central government announced the opening of fourteen coastal cities, from north to south, to foreign investment.[38] It sponsored a high-level forum on Open Coastal Cities (OCCs) in Beijing in April of 1984, and the Symposium on Investing in China's Open Cities later that year in Hong Kong, where both overseas Chinese investors and bankers, and local and central government officials from the mainland, discussed collaborative business opportunities.[39] Overseas Chinese agreed to invest $2.2 billion in the new OCCs.[40]

Like the SEZs, with two exceptions, the OCCs were located in provinces that had experienced substantial out-migration. Aside from Guangdong and Fujian, they were located in Zhejiang, Shanghai, Jiangsu, and Shandong, where overseas Chinese had informally and covertly been involved in business ventures before the central government had formalized the OCC policy.[41] The two provinces Tianjin and Dalian, which never experienced significant out-migration, had, however, attracted visitors and tourists from Hong Kong before 1984, and after the founding of OCCS overseas Chinese in Hong Kong invested heavily there.[42] In 1985, for example, Hong Kong investors signed contracts with the Dalian government worth $100 million for the construction of six hotels.[43]

During the 1980s, municipal and provincial governments, as well as national ministries, sought to attract foreign investment through both the SEZS and OCCS. They established their own offices and guesthouses in Shenzhen, and proceeded to set up their own "foreign investment open areas," whether or not they attained central government endorsement for such investment.[44] Overseas Chinese typically responded earlier than other foreign investors to the new business opportunities. They felt less constrained by legal restrictions.[45]

However, the student-led protest in Tiananmen Square in 1989 sparked countrywide urban unrest, and led to a reassertion of the influence of antireformists at the national level, in Beijing. At the local level, officials associated with the reformist faction were disadvantaged, and economic liberalization toward FDI slowed down. Nonetheless, local governments in southern China remained eager to remain open to FDI, having benefited from it throughout the 1980s, and state officials in other regions were in the process of modeling their policies after southern China. Deng Xiaoping continued to support the local-level economic openings. He launched another historic tour to the south, in early 1992, which helped to mobilize local and overseas support for liberalization of FDI. As figure 3.1 demonstrates, his tour was followed by a surge in FDI inflows, particularly from overseas Chinese.

Political Crisis and Reconsolidation of Support for Foreign Investment

In late spring, 1989, college students in Beijing gathered in Tiananmen Square to mourn the death of Hu Yaobang, a former party leader famous for his liberal thinking, who had been popular among intellectuals. The gathering quickly turned into a demonstration against government corruption and hyperinflation in the country and a call for political liberalization. As news spread, unrest erupted in other cities across China. The student demonstration quickly incorporated workers and businessmen as it expanded nationwide.

Within the national government, the reform and "conservative factions" divided on how to respond to the protests. The reformers, led by the CCP general secretary Zhao Ziyang, sought to appease protestors by introducing some political changes, while "conservatives" argued for a forceful crackdown. Initially, Deng Xiaoping appeared to side with the conservatives in ordering the People's Liberation Army to quell the protests, at the same time that CCP leaders launched another rectification campaign to undermine the reformers. Zhao Ziyang was ousted and placed under house arrest, and many national and local level bureaucrats associated with him were forced to resign. Official documents and pronouncements criticized economic liberalization.[46]

Beijing's crackdown on reformers led Western investors to pull out. However, Chinese abroad were unfazed. Thus, between 1989 and 1991, in Guangdong, U.S. investment decreased from $306.7 million to $64 million, while Hong Kong investment increased from $1.8 billion to $4.2 billion and Taiwanese investment more than doubled.[47] Despite the national-level crackdown, local governments continued to promote foreign investment. Guangdong officials, for example, showcased the province's "golden era" of economic development in the *Renmin ribao* (People's Daily) in September 1989. It boasted that the GDP of the province had grown 312 percent, and Shenzhen's GDP, in particular, to have grown forty-two-fold in the decade since the opening to foreign investment.[48] In the same publication, Fujian publicized that its GDP had increased six-fold, its industrial output seven-fold, and its savings fourteen-fold, since the opening to foreign investment.[49]

Although Deng Xiaoping backed the political crackdown, to restore order, he remained committed to economic reform. During his southern tour in early 1992, he made numerous speeches in defense of FDI and a deepening of economic reform, and he asked for stepped-up investment contributions by overseas Chinese. His tour and his multiple speeches were reported by major newscasts in communities of overseas Chinese. Overseas Chinese responded by increasing their investments, as demonstrated in figures 3.1 and 3.2.

Even before Deng Xiaoping's southern tour, local governments sought to replicate the development success of Guangdong and Fujian. Shanghai, designated an OCC in 1984, stepped up its efforts to attract foreign investment after the Tiananmen crisis. In 1990, the Shanghai municipality designated the massive, undeveloped land east of the downtown area as the Pudong New Development Zone and constructed bridges to connect the two areas of the city. Shanghai, the country's historic commercial center and home to countless entrepreneurs and financiers who fled the revolution in 1949, became economically vibrant anew, with the help of overseas Chinese. Between 1990 and 1994, overseas Chinese accounted for most foreign investment in the city.[50] Although Shanghai subsequently attracted more FDI from other sources, overseas Chinese contributed to essential infrastructure development and improved the investment climate in these transformative years.

Taiwanese small businesses have become ubiquitous in Shanghai, underreported in statistics but evident to visitors to the city. These businesses include restaurants, cafes, beauty salons, and boutiques. They have imbued old Shanghai with a modern lifestyle, making the city attractive to foreign investors and tourists. Because many of the Taiwanese were originally from Shanghai, they easily reintegrated. Their businesses reenergized entrepreneurship in the city, which became the mainland's main locus of foreign investment, beginning in the 1990s.[51]

Although much Taiwanese investment is small in scale, some is large and central to the city's foreign-investment boom. Returning Taiwanese provided the infrastructural foundation for the city's economic "take-off." Jiang Binxian, a Shanghai-born Taiwanese businessman, leased the first industrial land in the city, in 1990, and built a massive industrial complex.[52] The Thompson Group, based in Taiwan, whose founder, Tang Junnian, was also born in Shanghai, returned in 1991, and the following year agreed to invest billions of dollars in twelve major projects. Two years later Tang built a financial center in Shanghai's main financial district, a trade center near the Customs, a commercial center in downtown Shanghai, 230 mansions for sale to rich Chinese and foreigners, large factories and residential buildings, and the first five-star hotel in Pudong.[53]

Just as Hong Kong was indispensable to early infrastructural development in Guangdong, Taiwan was pivotal to Shanghai's resurgence in the 1990s. Compared to Hong Kong, Taiwan had different manufacturing strengths. In the 1980s it developed rather sophisticated high-technology sectors and mass-produced computer parts and components for the world market. In the 1990s, however, production costs in the hardware industry rose in Taiwan, to the point that manufacturers and exporters sought cheaper production sites. In light of the economic opening and new attractive investment conditions, and long-standing homeland ties, they relocated on the mainland.

Over 90 percent of Taiwanese come from Guangdong, Fujian, Shanghai, Zhejiang, and Jiangsu. Those from the last three regions, in particular, fled China in opposition to the revolution in 1949. The first-generation immigrants maintained especially strong ties to Shanghai and the two neighboring provinces. They put their deep political differences with the mainland government aside in the 1990s to pursue their economic interests. In particular, the Taiwanese computer-hardware industrialists created successful production enclaves near Shanghai that manufactured and exported computer parts and components to the world market.

The high-tech export zone in Kunshan, located in Jiangsu Province, north of Shanghai, produces over half of the world's computer components. Taiwanese investors have been among the largest manufacturers and exporters there. The local government constructed the export-processing zone in 1988, without central government authorization. Taiwanese businessmen, in close collaboration with local authorities, provided most of the capital, technology, and foreign orders for the products.[54]

Taiwanese have been instrumental in helping China move up the "industrial value chain" within the global economy. Chinese export-based industrial growth, in which overseas Chinese have been instrumental, began with exports of textiles and toys, then included appliances and electronics, and, most recently, computer hardware. Moreover, increasingly, Chinese are studying and getting work experience in the United States that they are applying in China, shaping the domestic development of science and technology and, thereby, deepening domestic human capital development.[55]

In turn, the gamut of overseas Chinese have indirectly as well as directly fueled the "Chinese miracle." Indirectly, the example they set attracted other foreign business, for example, from the United States, Japan, and Europe. As a result, overseas Chinese have come to account for a declining portion of foreign investment (see figure 3.2), especially after China joined the WTO and the Chinese government opened more sectors to foreign investment in 2001.

CHINESE IMMIGRANTS WERE shown to be central to China's economic boom, most notably immigrants who had fled the country in opposition to the revolution and to the dire economic conditions under Mao. They have been responsible for most foreign capital invested in the country, especially in manufacturing, and in conjunction with investing they have infused ideas, information, and technology that mainland Chinese have drawn upon to deepen the country's economic transformation. Overseas Chinese were the first to invest; they helped develop physical, social, and institutional infrastructure that provided bedrock for the "economic miracle." And their success induced other foreigners also to put their personal politics aside and invest in the communist country.

Overseas Chinese did not, on their own, transform the Chinese economy. The Chinese government, at the national level and, in certain places, at the local level, was instrumental in creating conditions that made homeland investment attractive to Chinese abroad. But only under Deng, in the post-Mao era, did officials come to power who were supportive of foreign investment and relations with Chinese who had rejected the revolution. The Chinese experience thus suggests that governments may, but do not necessarily, play a critical role in inducing economic development, including in establishing conditions attractive to foreign private investors. This is true of liberal democratic states, as well as those dominated by a communist party. The Chinese experience also suggests that communist states are not necessarily so autocratic that the political class is united in their stance on economic policy. There were reformist and antireformist factions in the government and communist party, with the reformist faction ultimately getting the upper hand. Also, the central government was not so autocratic as to determine economic dynamics and policies at the local level. Especially in southern China, local governments established, on their own, ties with immigrants from their areas, and created, independently of Beijing, conditions that welcomed the immigrants and encouraged them to invest.

The Chinese experience further demonstrates that not all immigrants are equally likely to establish from their new land relations that spur economic development in their homeland. Successful entrepreneurial immigrants were the main investors in productive ventures on the mainland, and it was this group of immigrants who established relations with homeland officials that influenced policies attractive to their investing. Labor migrants from China (as from most other countries worldwide) had no comparable homeland impact. They sent remittances that helped their families upgrade their living standards, fueling consumption, not investment. The entrepreneurial immigrants developed vested interests in investing in their homeland once conditions there became propitious, lowering their production-related labor costs. They accordingly began to live their lives across borders, enjoying the benefits that both their homeland and new land had to offer. They illustrate the types of immigrants that Alejandro Portes notes in his chapter may have a development impact in their homeland.

The comparison between the impact of immigrants from China and from India, as described by Kyle Eishen in his chapter in this book, highlights how immigrants with somewhat different backgrounds and somewhat distinctive overseas experiences, and from countries where governments have implemented somewhat different policies, may significantly spur economic development in their homeland, in somewhat different ways. Indian immigrants have contributed to India establishing an important niche as an exporter of information-technology-based software services that build on their skills, networks, and capital acquired in the United States. These immigrants capitalized on those acquired assets when they returned to India. Because of the capital-intensive and export-oriented nature of the service activity, a far narrower segment of Indian than Chinese society has thus far benefited from the economic growth that Indian immigrants have helped set in motion. The Indian government, like the Chinese, contributed to the creation of conditions facilitating the immigrant-based economic transformation by expanding the technical training of selective Indians that U.S. firms in information technology covet. The Indian government also facilitated the founding of investment zones, but directed to software activity, not to industrial manufacturing, as in China. As a result, the two countries have established somewhat complementary niches within the global economy.

Notes

1 For a comprehensive analysis of these issues, see Lawrence Ma and Carolyn Cartier, *Chinese Diaspora: Space, Place, Mobility, and Identity* (New York: Rowman and Littlefield, 2003).

2 See Gary Hamilton, *Business Networks and Economic Development in East and Southeast Asia* (Hong Kong: University of Hong Kong, 1991); Gary Hamilton, "Overseas Chinese Capitalism," in Tu Wei-ming, ed., *Confucian Traditions in East Asian Modernity: Moral Education and Economic Culture in Japan and the Four Mini-Dragons* (Cambridge, MA: Harvard University Press, 1996); and Gary Hamilton, ed., *Cosmopolitan Capitalism: Hong Kong and the Chinese Diaspora at the End of the Twentieth Century* (Seattle: University of Washington Press, 1999).

3   John Kao, "The Worldwide Web of Chinese Business," *Harvard Business Review* 71 (March-April 1993): 24–36.

4   Robin Cohen, *Global Diasporas: An Introduction* (Seattle: University of Washington Press, 1997).

5   In contrast, the first émigrés who fled the revolution in Cuba adamantly opposed investing in their homeland. See Susan Eckstein's chapter on Cuba, in this book.

6   See Ma and Cartier, *Chinese Diaspora*.

7   Sen-dou Chang, "The Distribution and Occupation of Overseas Chinese," *Geographical Reviews* 58, no. 1 (1968): 89–107.

8   For an analysis of the community-level impact overseas Chinese have had through remittances, see Anita Chan, Richard Madsen, and Jonathan Unger, *Chen Village under Mao and Deng* (Berkeley: University of California Press, 1992). Recipients use the money from family abroad for consumption, rather than investment.

9   Overseas Chinese initially invested in low-tech footwear and clothing manufacturing. Today, domestic Chinese mainly operate these companies.

10 *Deng Xiaoping yu qiaoqu* [Deng Xiaoping on overseas Chinese affairs] (Beijing: Central Compilation Publisher, 2000).

11 C. Y. Chang, "Overseas Chinese in China's Policy," *China Quarterly* 82 (1980): 281–303.

12 Many overseas investors reported that production costs in Hong Kong rose rapidly in the 1970s, making relocation to the mainland attractive for labor-intensive manufacturing. See *Renmin ribao* [People's Daily], July 21, 1989, 4.

13 Lee's more publicized relations included those with Deng Xiaoping's son, Deng Zhifang, and son-in-law, Wu Jianchang, and with the Chinese vice president Yang Shankun's son, Larry Yang. C. Lever-Tracy et al., *The Chinese Diaspora and Mainland China: An Emerging Economic Synergy* (Basingstoke, UK: Macmillan, 1996).

14 X. Yu, *Deng Xiaoping yu bao yugang* [Deng Xiaoping and Y. K. Pao] (Beijing: Chinese Cultural Publisher, 2000).

15 Ibid.

16 *Renmin ribao*, May 23, 1978, 2; *Renmin ribao*, June 4, 1978, 2; *Renmin ribao*, July 3, 1978, 1, 3.

17 See *Renmin ribao*, November 17, 1984, 2.

18 Li Lanqing, *Breakthrough* (Beijing: Foreign Language Teaching and Research Press. 2008).

19 Min Ye, "Diasporas and Chinese Foreign Direct Investment," in *China Today, China Tomorrow*, ed. Joseph Fewsmith (New York: Rowman and Littlefield, 2010), 129–47.

20 M. Gu, "Zhongguo duiwai kaifang de fengfeng yuyu" [Winds and rains of China's open-door policy], *Ban yue tan* [China comment] 15 (1980).

21 S. Ho, *China's Open Door Policy* (Vancouver: University of British Columbia Press, 1984), 49.

22 Yun-Wing Sung, *The China–Hong Kong Connection: The Key to China's Open-Door Policy* (New York: Cambridge University Press, 1991), 13.

23 *Renmin ribao*, July 21, 1989, 4.

24 D. Xiao, "1979–1984 nian zhongguo jingji tizhi gaige silu de yinjin" [Reformist thinking on China's economic system, 1979–1984], in *Deng Xiaoping yu gaige kaifang* [Deng Xiaoping and China's reform and openness] (Beijing: CCP History, 2005).

25 D. Lu, "Guangdong de duiwai kaifang yu jingji tizhi gaige" [Guangdong's openness and economic structural reform], in *Deng xiaoping yu gaige kaifang.*

26 G. Ren, *Huaqiao huaren yu guogong guanxi* [Overseas Chinese and the CCP and KMT] (Wuhan: Wuhan, 1999).

27 E. Vogel, *One Step Ahead in China: Guangdong under Reform* (Cambridge, MA: Harvard University Press, 1989), 134.

28 Y. Zheng, *Duochong wangluo de shentou yu kuozhang* [Multiple networks' mutual penetration and expansion] (Beijing: World Knowledge, 2006).

29 *Renmin ribao*, March 20, 1983, 2.

30 *Hong Kong jingji ribao* [Hong Kong economic times], Oct 4, 1988.

31 S. R. Schram, "Economics in Command? Ideology and Policy since the Third Plenum, 1978–1984," *China Quarterly* 99 (1984): 417–61.

32 See Victor Shih, *Factions and Finance in China: Elite Conflict and Inflation* (New York: Cambridge University Press, 2008); L. Dittmer, "China in 1981: Reform, Readjustment, Rectification," *Asian Survey* 22, no. 1 (1982): 39.

33 Shih, *Factions and Finance in China*, 35.

34 Dittmer, "China in 1981," 43.

35 See a series of publications in *Renmin ribao*, January 11, 1983, 4; January 15, 1983, 4; February 4, 1983, 4; March 15, 1983, 2; March 20, 1983, 2.

36 Ibid.

37 "Wang Zhen Gives Impressions on Tour of Special Economic Zones in the Company of Deng Xiaoping," *Liao wang* [Outlook] 16 (1984).

38 Ministry of Foreign Economic Relations and Trade, *Guide to China's Foreign Economic Relations and Trade: Cities Newly Opened to Foreign Investors* (Beijing: Economic Information Agency, 1984), 74.

39 D. Jin, *Congratulatory Speech at the Opening of the Symposium on Investment Guide to China's Foreign Economic Relations and Trade* (Beijing: Economic Information Agency, 1984).

40 *Renmin ribao*, November 17, 1984, 2.

41 "Shadow trade" with overseas connections contributed to the growth of early entrepreneurs in Wenzhou, Zhejiang, for example.

42 Y. Yeung, *China's Coastal Cities: Catalysts for Modernization* (Honolulu: University of Hawai'i Press, 1992).

43 Yeung, *China's Coastal Cities*, 34.

44 Vogel, *One Step Ahead in China*, 141.

45 In 1990, although overall conditions for FDI deteriorated, overseas Chinese investment in OCCs remained steady. In that year, for example, Taiwanese investment accounted for over one-third of foreign invested firms. Taiwanese investment began only two years prior. See *Renmin ribao*, October 31, 1990, 2.

46 See Jiang Zemin, speech at the Fourth Plenum of the Thirteen Party Congress, June 24, 1989, in *Major Documents since the Thirteen Party Congress* (Beijing: People's Publisher, 1991); see also articles in *Renmin ribao*, September 1989 to November 1989.

47 *Zhonguo duiwai jingji tongji daquan* [Statistics on China's external economic relations, 1979–1991] (Beijing: China's Statistical Publisher, 1993), 401–7.

48 *Renmin ribao*, September 11, 1989, 4.

49 Ibid.

50 Some Taiwanese investment entered via subsidiaries in Hong Kong. It thus registered as Hong Kong investment.

51 Shanghai is one of the most pro-FDI areas in the PRC, according to Yasheng Huang (*Capitalism with Chinese Characteristics* [New York: Cambridge University Press, 2008]). In the early 1990s, it was mainly overseas Chinese investment that contributed to the development of Shanghai.

52 Hong Kong, *Lian he bao* [United daily news], July 16, 1993.

53 Ibid.

54 Kunshan originated its construction of industrial areas in 1984, and began to develop export processing zones in 1984. For a detailed study of Kunshan's high-tech export zone, see Min Ye, "EDI vs. FDI in China and India," presented at the American Political Science Association, September 2–6, 2009, Toronto. See also *Renmin ribao*, July 22, 1988, 2.

55 See David Zweig, "Globalization and Transnational Human Capital: Overseas and Returnee Scholars to China," *China Quarterly* 179 (2004): 736–57.

4

Immigrants' Globalization of the Indian Economy

KYLE EISCHEN

At the beginning of the 1980s, Prime Minister Rajiv Gandhi initiated measures to open the Indian economy to foreign investment and trade, bedrock for the establishment of what today we recognize as the information technology (IT) industry.[1] The process of globalization and development accelerated a decade later following the dramatic financial shifts that swept through India following the Soviet Union's collapse. Indian engineers and entrepreneurs who had worked and studied in the United States played a key role in shaping the structure, pioneering successes, and continued evolution of India's IT transformation. Building on the IT industry in the United States, especially in California's Silicon Valley, so-called nonresident Indians (NRIS) transformed their home country into a global site of high-technology work. They established networks that sustain global markets, and defined the model that enabled Indian industry (and thus enabled India's global opening) to thrive and expand over time.

The successes of Indian immigrants in Silicon Valley and in information technology as an industry are well documented.[2] The importance of the story of India's economic opening rests less on the transfer of wealth and government policy and more on the creation of norms, relationships, and networks that provide structure in the global economy. Nonresident Indians established practices that laid the groundwork for new economic patterns and migration that supported India's global opening, rooted in and reinforcing deep ties between India and the United States.

Indian Migration to the United States

Indian migration to the United States and, in turn, its impact back home, is relatively recent. It involves both permanent and temporary resettling. Between 1970 and 2010, Indian migration to the United States had two broad phases. The first two decades of migration mainly involved permanent migration to the United States. In the 1990s and 2000s this permanent migration continued, but it was increasingly supplemented with temporary stays, on temporary work visas. The shift rested on changes in government policy, particularly U.S. visa policy. However, on closer analysis, the shift also rested on the creation of new linkages between the United States and India that NRIs established.

By 2010, more than 1.4 million Indians had obtained permanent-residency status in the United States.[3] Most of them had emigrated since 1970 (following U.S. immigration reform in the mid-1960s, which eliminated country quotas that favored Europeans), and especially since 1990. Annually, an average of 35,000 Indians immigrated in the 1990s, and 60,000 during the first decade of the 2000s.[4] Although the numbers are substantial, they are relatively small, both from the host-country and home-country perspective. Indians account for only slightly more than 4 percent of all immigrants to the United States since 1970, and for less than 10 percent of the approximately 20 million nonresident Indians who currently live outside India.[5] Permanent-resident NRIs make up less than a half percent of the total U.S. population, and less than a tenth of one percent of the total Indian population.

Given their small numbers, how can one explain the outsized impact NRIs have had in both the United States and India? For one, they come from highly selective backgrounds. Most emigrants who have moved to the United States (and to other advanced economies) are from India's top socioeconomic strata.[6] Thirty percent of Indians in the United States are from the wealthiest urban classes, which make up only 3 percent of the Indian population.[7] The top three socioeconomic groups, which represent 14 percent of the Indian population, account for almost 73 percent of Indian immigrants to the United States. Nearly all of the Indian immigrants to the United States were urban, highly educated, and very globally connected before they left India.

Over the years, increasing numbers of Indians have emigrated for temporary stays. They have come to the United States on student, employment, and business visas (see table 4.1). H1-B employer-sponsored visas grant three-year stays for professionals to work in the United States, with the possibility of one three-year extension. Similar in structure, L-1 business visas allow foreign firms to bring employees to work for them in the United States, also for three-year stints.

Temporary entrants have special significance for the global IT industry and for India in particular. Technology firms in the United States developed the practice of using H1-B visas to staff their U.S. operations since the 1990s. On average, 40 percent of recipients of H1-B visas were in computer-related fields. The increasing number of Indians who come to the United States on H1-B visas partly reflects the increased importance of Indian professionals to the global IT industry and to U.S. firms in particular. However, it also reflects the increased desire of Indian firms to work in the United States with Indian professionals. Indians employed both by U.S. and Indian firms accounted for one-third of all H1-B entrants between 2000 and 2009.[8]

Bases of migration to the United States differ among Indians and non-Indians. Among non-Indians who come to the United States on temporary visas, student entrants predominate over business entrants (H1-B or L-1). For Indians, the ratios are reversed. For each student, approximately two professional and business visas are issued, and the numbers are substantial. More than 217,000 Indians came to the United States on H1-B and L-1 visas in 2008, and 177,000 in 2009.[9]

What accounts for the distinctive pattern of Indian migration? It is explained by the nature of India's economic development since the mid-1980s and the country's increased integration with the global IT industry. The temporary work visas contribute to a continuous movement of highly skilled individuals between India and the United States in information-intensive, specialized technology industries. The fact that both Indian and U.S. firms make use of temporary migrants suggests a structural feature of the global industry. Nonresident Indians based in the United States were essential in initially creating this structure, and in shaping how India has become integrated into the global IT industry.

TABLE 4.1. Total Indian Temporary Visitor Entry by Type,
1996–2009 (Select Years)

	1996		1999	
	Number of Visas	Percentage of All Such Visas	Number of Visas	Percentage of All Such Visas
Academic Students (F-1)	17,354	4%	28,335	5%
Specialty Occupations (H-1B)	31,417	14%	88,391	19%
Intra-company Transferee (L-1)	2,255	2%	6,160	3%

The emigration of high-skilled labor has increased at the same time that opportunities for high-skilled labor in India have increased. The two developments are intricately related, and have been fundamental to India's high rate of economic growth in recent years.

Visa policy in the United States is not specifically focused on IT or India, and it did not in itself induce the migrant flows between India and the United States. Rather, changing demands within the global IT industry induced individuals and firms to make use of visa possibilities. Accordingly, the migrant flows reflect a very specific way in which India has integrated into the global economy, an integration influenced by NRIS. The success of NRIS in information technology in general, and in Silicon Valley in particular, created an opportunity for Indian immigrants to spur economic development in their homeland that rested on ongoing India-U.S. migration.

Indians, Silicon Valley, and Information Technology

Nonresident Indians have been central to Silicon Valley's cutting-edge development within the global IT industry. By 2000, at the peak of the IT boom in the United States, Indian immigrants led 972 technology firms in Silicon Valley, which had over $5 billion in sales and employed nearly 26,000 persons. These firms represented 6 percent of all sales and 7 percent of all employment in the region.

Those born in India work as managers in established firms, and build new companies through entrepreneurship. Their rate of entrepreneur-

	2004		2008		2009
Number of Visas	Percentage of All Such Visas	Number of Visas	Percentage of All Such Visas	Number of Visas	Percentage of All Such Visas
51,191	8%	85,067	10%	95,332	11%
123,567	43%	154,726	38%	123,002	36%
23,134	7%	63,156	17%	54,556	16%

ship is extraordinarily high in Silicon Valley. While Indian Americans accounted for less than half of 1 percent of the U.S. population, during the first decade of this century they accounted for 16 percent of entrepreneurs in the valley, up from 3 percent in the early 1980s and from 10 percent in the late 1990s.[10] As immigrants, nonresident Indians have not been narrowly focused as engineers and technicians. They have been fully integrated into the Silicon Valley career and business cycle, succeeding as engineers, managers, executives, entrepreneurs, and venture capitalists. They have been central to the success story of Silicon Valley exactly because of their individual success across all the skills required in an entrepreneurial region.

The economy in Silicon Valley, in which NRIs have become deeply entrenched, is structured to support entrepreneurial innovation. It supports innovative ideas and technologies that can be readily combined with skilled labor and risk capital to quickly bring new products to market. Many organizational practices make this possible, including practices that enable firms to manage and retain talented people central to innovation and successful operations. Stock options, for example, allow firms to motivate and lock-in smart individuals into multiyear commitments, to compete for talent where skilled labor is the central resource, to operate with minimal capital, and to promise outsized returns for outsized efforts. Information technology firms also thrive on minimal layers of internal hierarchy, at the same time that engineers are given clear pathways to greater responsibility and involvement in challenging projects. Companies have set up corporate campuses that offer free gourmet food, onsite healthcare, childcare, transportation, and sports facilities—embedded with their own subculture, attractive to their workforce. These features have sustained Silicon Valley's global leadership in information and communication technologies.

Thus, the success of NRIS is rooted in involvement in a globally unique environment premised on high risk, innovation, and potentially high rewards in a dynamic market. This entrepreneurial mindset fit extraordinarily well with the unique opportunities and challenges India presented in the 1980s.

India and the Global IT Industry

Today, India plays a central role in the global IT industry. However, its emergence as a key location of global IT software and services took time and initiative.

Well into the 1990s, India had the reputation for having an inhospitable work and investment environment, and an unimpressive workforce. Although Prime Minister Rajiv Gandhi had opened the IT sector in the 1980s to foreign investment and participation, the quality of the country's physical infrastructure (power, telecommunications, transportation) and its educational system remained poor, and the regulatory environment, for example, licensing and capital requirements at both the state and federal levels, was unattractive to investors. Although following the financial crisis in 1991, Prime Minister Rao and Finance Minister Singh removed regulatory obstacles, they failed to address adequately core infrastructure and educational needs. The initiative expanding the Indian Institutes of Technology (IITs) and the Software Technology Park (STP) remained insufficient to spur self-sustained growth in the IT industry.[11] Foreign firms continued to perceive India as not worth the risk of investment, and local companies had no means to prove their worth or link to the global economy.

While India's main asset became its human capital, obstacles to accessing it had to be overcome. Nonresident Indians played a key role in overcoming these obstacles. They knew how significant the talent pool in India could be, and their personal success offered proof of the country's potential talent. More important, they had the managerial skills, along with the local knowledge, to access that talent, to shape it into a globally competitive resource, and to overcome difficulties in the Indian work environment.

Nonresident Indians helped multinational corporations (MNCs) open IT subsidiaries in India, subsidiaries that demonstrated the country's value to the industry. They established groundwork whereby IT-related businesses could thrive, and created a pathway for NRI entrepreneurs to establish Indian operations tied to start-up initiatives in Silicon Valley. Some of the new start-ups were founded or supported by NRIs associated with the early MNC investments, who built on their connections and knowledge about the Indian political and business environment. Then, as India developed its own entrepreneurs and IT leaders, the bases of cross-border business-induced migration became two-way. Indian businesses set up U.S.-based operations, and imported Indian personnel to access U.S. markets, technologies, and people. Each wave in the development of the Indian IT industry reinforced U.S.-Indian ties, linking success in each country with success in the other.

The developments in which the NRIs were intricately involved contributed to India's becoming a central site of the global IT industry. The country established an important global niche in IT service-provisioning. It has become responsible for half of the international IT services market, more than any other country.[12] Almost nonexistent in the early 1980s, IT rose from accounting for 1.2 percent of India's GDP in 1998 to 5.8 percent in 2009. Software services and business-process outsourcing account for approximately $60 billion of the $71 billion IT industry in India and involve some of the most skilled, human-capital-intensive work in the global technology industry. By 2009, IT generated nearly $47 billion in exports, nearly one-fifth of all Indian exports, and it employed 2.23 million people (while indirectly generating an additional 8 million jobs, through multiplier effects).

Impact of NRIS on the Early Indian IT Industry

Looking at the leading firms in the evolution of the Indian IT industry from the mid-1980s to 2000, the impact of NRIs comes to the fore. By the year 2000, there were 128 MNCs operating within India's IT sector, where they accounted for 11 percent of revenue and 16 percent of employment.[13]

The timing of the MNC investments was important. Four corporations invested before 1985, twenty-four between 1985 and 1991, eighty between 1992 and 1999, and twenty in 2000 and 2001.[14] Each wave of investment laid the groundwork for the next, with NRIs advocating for, leading, and supporting the investments that were pivotal for success and growth. As AnnaLee Saxenian noted, "Although US-educated engineers rarely returned to India permanently . . . , many used their positions in large corporations to champion India as a location for a software development center or to promote the use of Indian firms as outsourcing partners. Along with the process of market liberalization that began in 1991, these early successes changed the world's perception of the Indian business environment."[15] Success in the IT industry, and in Silicon Valley in particular, created a unique resource upon which India's new global opening built.

Individual experiences highlight how the involvement of NRIS in Silicon Valley served as a springboard for building up the Indian IT economy.[16] In 1985, for example, Radha Basu, a U.S.-educated Indian-born manager of Hewlett-Packard and adviser to the Indian Department of Electronics on the development of the local IT industry, pioneered the involvement of multinational corporations in India. Together with Texas Instruments, Hewlett-Packard established one of the first software development centers in India. Basu played a vital role in the development and success of the center, which provided a model for subsequent government-MNC collaboration. The operational challenges were monumental. They included a lack of electrical power and telecommunications, hostility toward NRIS, suspicion of multinational corporations, and apprehension about dealings with the infamous Indian bureaucracy. In promoting the Indian Hewlett-Packard venture, Basu took on professional risk and personal hardship. India at the time was an unproven, backwater location that could have derailed his corporate career.

Despite the challenges, early successes paved the way for other NRIS to lead initiatives for their firms to invest in India. Kailash Joshi, for example, led IBM's entry into India, in 1991. He contracted the first government-approved foreign-Indian joint venture (involving Tata Consultancy Services (TCS) and IBM). In turn, Nimish Mehta helped establish the Oracle-India center in Bangalore in 1991, and Ranga Puranik started Motorola's India Software Center the following year, after promoting the location to senior management and promising to relocate with two other nonresident Indian managers to lead the venture. The center's early success depended on securing contracts from Indian-born managers in diverse divisions of Motorola.

Nonresident Indians continued to play a key role throughout the

1990s, as the industry expanded to new places in India and established itself globally. In 1999, Microsoft established its first Indian development center, in Hyderabad, Andhra Pradesh. Its managing director, who held a bachelor's degree in engineering from Andhra University and a master's degree in computer science from a U.S. university, had worked for Microsoft for a decade before transferring to the company's new Indian subsidiary. At the time, the 4 percent of software developers at Microsoft's headquarters who were Indian worked mainly in product development leadership positions. The core transition team to India drew upon skilled managers and software developers experienced in specific product lines, personnel who were deeply embedded in the Microsoft system as well as deeply familiar with the Indian work environment.[17]

Each investment affirmed the possibility of working in India, and, combined, solidified India's reputation as a world-class technology location. Bangalore, the site of many of the original investments, became a model for other regional IT centers in India. U.S.-based NRI managers took direct responsibility for advocating, locating, and shepherding the success of Indian operations, while thousands of additional NRIs spent time directly on the ground in India, establishing operations and ensuring their success.

A Virtuous Cycle Involving Silicon Valley Start-up Investment

The early on-the-ground successes in India signaled the beginning of a U.S.-India transnational virtuous cycle. The success of nonresident Indians in building and managing cutting-edge U.S. technology companies gave them the clout to push for the first Indian investments and partnerships. Their success with these efforts reinforced their reputations, and furthered their success as entrepreneurs, venture capitalists, and policy advisers, both in Silicon Valley and India. As "reputational intermediaries" they fostered the development of new generations of Indian entrepreneurs in Silicon Valley and the expansion of investments and markets in India for Indians.[18]

Basu and Joshi returned to Silicon Valley with enhanced reputations. They started new firms and contributed to important network-building institutions in Silicon Valley, including The Indus Entrepreneurs (TIE). The enterprise promoted Indian entrepreneurship that confirmed Silicon Valley as the benchmark of Indian success, while deepening transnational U.S.-India ties.

Once MNCs established India as a viable, human-capital-rich region for IT work, Indian entrepreneurs based in Silicon Valley soon added another wave of investment that reinforced the overall cycle. The initial successes in India established networks that supported additional MNC investments and India as a bedrock for Silicon Valley start-ups. By 2001, Indian entrepreneurs established fifty-eight firms that they incorporated in the U.S., with almost all their ground operations in India. One of India's top software exporting firms, iGate, was founded by nonresident Indians in this way.[19] Such ventures firmly established India as a key Silicon Valley partner, no longer merely an outpost of multinational corporations.

A Representative Story of an NRI Entrepreneur

The history of a NRI entrepreneur illustrates how intricately interconnected IT developments in the United States and India became and how NRIs played a key role in establishing a niche for India within the global IT economy.[20] The NRI is Sridhar Bathina, who became a managing director of a leading global telecommunications research lab in Hyderabad, Andhra Pradesh. Born and raised in Andhra Pradesh, Bathina began his career with a local electrical engineering degree and training at the Electronics Corporation of India Limited in Hyderabad. Following his brother, a medical doctor, he emigrated to the U.S. Midwest, where he obtained a master's degree in computer science, and then worked for AT&T in Chicago. In 1993 four of his former Indian classmates, three from the same family and all from Andhra Pradesh, presented him with a business plan for a start-up firm in Silicon Valley that focused on networking and internet access products for homes and small businesses. Thinking, at thirty-five, that this might be his only chance to push his abilities, he joined the firm as a founder.

The five partners established the company, Ramp Networks, in a garage in Silicon Valley. They financed the venture through the sales of their homes and the capital Bathina's brother invested. While developing the hardware team in Silicon Valley, the firm established a software-development center in Hyderabad, which Sridhar returned to India to manage. The Hyderabad venture became the eighth firm to locate in the local software technology park.

Almost from the beginning, six or seven people worked in the Silicon Valley and Hyderabad offices, through a 9.6 kilobyte data connection.

The relation between the Silicon Valley and Hyderabad offices involved not only hardware and software. It also involved a split between market requirements, namely, marketing and fundraising in the United States, and firmware requirements, design and development in India. Their California operations maximized client access and time to market, while their India operations provided access to high-quality, low-cost development efforts.

The firm went through the classic start-up phases. After slowly attracting venture capital funding, it went public in 1999 on NASDAQ. It became the industry leader in small-scale internet access solutions, and expanded into proprietary firewall products, increasing its staff to thirty-five. However, realizing that the slow market expansion of high-speed Internet access limited the firm's growth, the partners sold the company in 2000 to a foreign mobile-telecommunications firm that sought to expand its Internet offerings. Bathina and the Hyderabad office were incorporated into a new division of the telecom firm that focused on corporate-security research and development. While the end result was a major investment by a leading international MNC in a research and development lab in Hyderabad, NRI networks underlay the investment process.

Although Ramp Networks and its immigrant entrepreneurs represented a pioneering effort in 1993, a decade later its Silicon Valley–India operations became standard industry practice. Nonresident Indians contributed to IT development in the United States and India, and in India to regional IT development, structurally integrated into global networks and the global economy.

Temporary and Cyclical Indian Immigration and Industry Growth

While NRI managers and entrepreneurs built networks in the United States that extended to India, networks that combined access to markets with access to talent, managers and entrepreneurs in India followed the same transnational model, in the opposite direction. Native-born Indians, often U.S.-educated and with professional experience in the United States, moved to establish their new Indian firms as global players through new transnational linkages. Firms like TCS and Wipro Technologies illustrate this aspect of India's growth as well as their role in strengthening India's importance within the industry globally.

TCS is one of India's first-formed and largest IT firms. F. C. Kohli, an electrical engineer with graduate degrees from MIT and the University of Waterloo, attained TCS's first outsourcing contract on a trip to New York for a board meeting of the Institute of Electrical and Electronics Engineers, the main international professional engineering association. A few years later S. Ramadorai, a University of California graduate and CEO of TCS, established a New York office for the firm.[21]

Another example involves Wipro Technologies, also one of the first and most important Indian IT firms. Vivek Paul, a U.S.-educated Indian executive who worked for General Electric, was recruited to manage Wipro. His first major decision, in 1999, was to move the firm's headquarters to Silicon Valley, to be closer to customers, after which the firm's sales rose from $150 million to $1.5 billion in five years.[22]

The figures cited in table 4.1 reflect not merely the surge in temporary migration from India to the United States but also the growth in the number of Indian firms with U.S. offices that make use of Indian labor. The number of Indians who entered the United States on L-1 visas, involving foreign firm transfers to the United States, increased twenty-four-fold between 1996 and 2009.

As Indian firms sent skilled personnel to the United States, they deepened cross-border ties in new ways at the business level. In 1993 Sanjay Anandraram moved to Silicon Valley to manage projects for Wipro. Within a decade, he helped launch JumpStartUp, a venture-capital firm "specializing in early-stage, cross-border technology start-ups in India and the United States."[23] The mixed transnational model that combined U.S. and Indian operations became the standard for individuals and organizations in both countries. Nonresident Indians fostered IT-based growth in India that eventually fueled new developments in both countries and expanded and transformed the IT sector internationally.

Broader Homeland Impacts

Developments both in Silicon Valley and India reinforce the overall patterns of investment, migration, and management that have become standard in the global IT industry. They have become embedded in new undertakings in IT, including those in new regions of India.

Firms in India increasingly structure their operations to include the best international practices, for which Silicon Valley serves as model. For example, Six Sigma, the management strategy and process that has been widely adopted throughout India, was first introduced by Motorola when it initially invested in India. Also, technical quality and process standards, such as Capability Maturity Model (CMM) and various ISO designations, have been widely adopted in India as industry benchmarks of global quality—not only in IT but in other economic sectors as well.[24]

Furthermore, the organizational innovations developed in Silicon Valley to retain employees have also been adopted in India, to retain talented individuals who might otherwise transfer to foreign firms or emigrate to the United States. Indian firms have duplicated the Silicon Valley "campuses" that offer such amenities as free food, transportation, and recreation. Cross-border similarities extend to work practices that offer seamless transitions between development centers in India and the United States—in feel, organization, and culture.[25] Indian firms invest in education and training, issue stock options and bonuses, and institute clearly defined internal management career paths, as do Silicon Valley firms. Even when the practices in India have failed to enable firms to retain employees, they have served to embed Silicon Valley norms and structures. Suma Athreye found that 20 percent of the 279 founders of 125 software start-ups in India previously worked for MNCs.[26] This mirrors the situation in Silicon Valley, where individuals routinely move among firms, both small and large, start-ups and established, circulating ideas and practices within the IT sector.

The expansion of the IT industry to new locations beyond Bangalore also illustrates how these broad patterns shaped the geography of India's development. The same process that overcame obstacles to establishing India as a leading global technology location is evident in the emergence of new economic growth poles elsewhere in the country, such as in Andhra Pradesh.

Microsoft and Ramp Networks clearly illustrate NRI influence upon the timing and location of investments in India. Moreover, the transnational business model in which NRIs have become intricately involved has also been applied to a growing number of new lines of business activity. It has been replicated in business processing, and, more recently, in legal process outsourcing, and in health care ventures such as medical transcription, drug development, clinical trials, and fertility treatment.[27] In addition, efforts to address problems of corruption and poverty alleviation at the national level, and to expand e-governance (for example, digital programs for land records and drivers licenses) at the state level, have incorporated management approaches and expertise, as well as technology, developed within the IT sector.[28]

NONRESIDENT INDIANS WHO lived and worked in the United States helped initiate and frame Indian globalization and economic development. They have done so in different ways over the years.

Initially, NRIs promoted the investment in India and then led the on-the-ground establishment of multinational firms' subsidiaries in India. Building on their professional experience and country knowledge, they demonstrated how an India-based IT industry could thrive. They, in turn, created a pathway for entrepreneurs to establish Indian operations tied to Silicon Valley start-ups, again building on their professional expertise and home-country knowledge. Then, as India developed its own cluster of entrepreneurs, many of whom had studied and worked in the United States, Indians followed the proven pathways in reverse. They established U.S.-based outposts, to access markets, technologies, and people. Each wave strengthened the Indian economy while deepening the country's niche within the global IT economy. High-skilled Indian immigrants who emigrated to the United States temporarily as well as permanently helped make the transformation of India possible.

The Indians who shepherded the transformation were not run-of-the-mill immigrants. Coming from India's well-educated, urban, upper and middle classes, they were able to take advantage of opportunities for advanced technical and business studies in the United States and to qualify for jobs in the leading-edge sector in the United States. Shifts in U.S. policy, beginning in the 1960s, allowed for increased Indian immigration, on a permanent and, more recently, temporary basis. However, the success of NRIs in the IT industry, especially in Silicon Valley, was not a planned or even anticipated outcome. The very success of Indian immigrants and the Indian IT sector fueled continual migration between the United States and India. This migration took on a dynamic of its own, rooted in Silicon Valley and Indian developments, independent of U.S. immigration policy.

Changes in Indian governmental policy created an opportunity for the IT boom in which NRIs played a central role. Amid financial and economic problems in the 1980s and early 1990s, the Indian government opened the economy to foreign investment and eased trade restrictions. However, the policy shifts were centered neither on NRIS nor on capturing the benefits of global networks, as came to be the case in Silicon Valley. India sought to replicate the successful electronics industry, development-based export model of newly industrialized Asian countries, though without understanding the specific possibilities inherent within its global diaspora. Only beginning in the late 1990s did the government begin to understand and specifically build on the contributions of nonresident Indians and specifically promote measures to develop the IT industry as we now understand it.

The development of India's globally competitive IT sector has not rested merely on what might be called host-to-home-country social, cultural, and economic remittances. India has become a source of ideas, networks, and capital that has influenced IT developments in the United States as well. In very different contexts, José Miguel Cruz and Rhacel Parreñas, in their chapters on Salvadoran and Philippine immigrants, respectively, and Susan Eckstein in her introductory chapter, have similarly demonstrated immigrant-based home-to-host-country, along with host-to-home-country, social and cultural influences. Developments in the IT industry illustrate the two-way economic influences as well.

Nonresident Indians have played a central role in the development of knowledge-intensive work both abroad and at home. They pioneered a model that fostered economic growth across India while defining patterns of production that now are essential features of the global economy in general and in Silicon Valley in particular. Key to this success has been the movement of individuals, continuously reinforcing the cycles of immigration and return that is at the heart of the process. These patterns are robust, supported by policy, economics, and culture, and they are likely to continue to play a central role in the evolution of the Indian economy in the coming decades.

Notes

1   I am grateful to Susan Eckstein for her insights and reviews of earlier drafts of this chapter. Her generosity with her time and knowledge was invaluable. All errors and omissions are, of course, mine alone.

2   AnnaLee Saxenian, *Silicon Valley's New Immigrant Entrepreneurs* (San Francisco: Public Policy Institute of California, June 1999), http://www.ppic

.org/content/pubs/report/R_699ASR.pdf; AnnaLee Saxenian, *Local and Global Networks of Immigrant Professionals in Silicon Valley* (San Francisco: Public Policy Institute of California, April 2002), http://www.ppic.org/content/ubs/report/R_502ASR.pdf; Ashish Arora and Alfonso Gambardella, eds., *From Underdogs to Tigers: The Rise and Growth of the Software Industry in Brazil, China, India, Ireland, and Israel* (Oxford: Oxford University Press, 2005); Kyle Eischen, "People, Places and Practices: The Evolution of the IT Services Industry in India," *Comercio Exterior* (September 2005): 764–74.

3 Department of Homeland Security, *Yearbook of Immigration Statistics: 2010*, http://www.dhs.gov/files/statistics/publications/yearbook.shtm.

4 Ibid.

5 Department of Homeland Security, *Yearbook of Immigration Statistics: 2010*; Susan Eckstein, "Immigrants from Developing Countries: Their Homeland Impacts: An Overview," this volume.

6 Devesh Kapur, *Diaspora, Development, and Democracy: The Domestic Impact of International Migration from India* (Princeton, NJ: Princeton University Press, 2010), chapter 3.

7 These socioeconomic groups are defined in terms of the education and occupation of the chief wage-earner within a family. See Kapur, *Diaspora, Development, and Democracy*, for more details.

8 Department of Homeland Security, "Nonimmigrant Admissions (I-94 Only) by Class of Admission and Country of Citizenship: Fiscal Year 2009," *Yearbook of Immigration Statistics: 2009*, http://www.dhs.gov/files/statistics/publications/yearbook.shtm.

9 Ibid.

10 AnnaLee Saxenian, "The Silicon Valley Connection: Transnational Networks and Regional Developments in Taiwan, China and India" in *Global Software Industry: Innovation, Firm Strategies and Development*, ed. Anthony P. D'Costa and E. Sridharan (New York: Palgrave Macmillan, 2004), 181; Vivek Wadhwa, AnnaLee Saxenian, Ben Rissing, and Gary Gereffi, "America's New Immigrant Entrepreneurs: Part I," *Duke Science, Technology and Innovation Paper* 23 (January 4, 2007) (http://ssrn.com/abstract=990152).

11 As one example, the first five IITs were established by 1961. The sixth campus was established only in 1987, and the seventh campus in 2001. During the forty years in which the two most recent IITs were established, India's population grew from 450 million to over a billion.

12 NASSCOM, *IT-BPO Sector in India: Strategic Review 2009*, http://www.nasscom.org.

13 Suma Athreye, "The Indian Software Industry," in *From Underdogs to Tigers*, ed. Arora and Gambardella, 26.

14 Ibid., 27.

15 AnnaLee Saxenian, *The New Argonauts: Regional Advantage in a Global Economy* (Cambridge, MA: Harvard University Press, 2006), 275.

16 The following section is drawn from Saxenian, *The New Argonauts*, chapter 7, 274–89.

17 Kyle Eischen, "The Limits of Rationalization: Work Practice, Industry Structure and Spatial Organization in the Software Industry" (Ph.D. diss., University of California, Santa Cruz, 2004), 262–63.

18 Devesh Kapur and John McHale, "Sojourns and Software: Internationally Mobile Human Capital and High-Tech Industry Development in India, Ireland and Israel," in *From Underdogs to Tigers*, ed. Arora and Gambardella, 250–52.

19 Arora and Gambardella, "Bridging the Gap: Conclusions," in *From Underdogs to Tigers*, 283.

20 This section comes from Eischen, "The Limits of Rationalization," 242–43.

21 Saxenian, *The New Argonauts*, 275–76.

22 Ibid., 274.

23 Ibid., 4.

24 Athreye, "The Indian Software Industry," in *From Underdogs to Tigers*, 28.

25 Ibid., 35–36.

26 Arora and Gambardella, "Bridging the Gap: Conclusions," in *From Underdogs to Tigers*, 283.

27 Mari Sako, "Globalization of Knowledge-Intensive Professional Services," *Communications of the ACM* 52, no. 7 (June 2009): 31–33; "High-tech India Contrasts with Rural Ways," interview with Sirisha Gummaregula, chief operating officer, QuisLex, Newshour, PBS, April 8, 2009.

28 See, for example, the central government's unique identification program (http://uidai.gov.in) led by Nandan M. Nilekani, a founder and former chief executive of Infosys Technologies.

5

How Cuban Americans Are
Unwittingly Transforming Their Homeland

SUSAN ECKSTEIN

Between the time Fidel Castro assumed power, in 1959, and the first years of the new millennium, approximately one million Cubans emigrated to the United States.[1] They account for nearly 90 percent of Cuba's diaspora, and for 9 percent of the Cuban population.[2]

What impact have they had on their homeland from their new land, and how does one account for it? Their impact changed in the 1990s, when the country experienced a deep economic recession following the collapse of the Soviet Union and the Soviet bloc, and the consequent termination of Soviet aid and trade. The crisis shattered most Cubans' belief in their country's utopian, revolutionary, socialist project. Cubans became pragmatic as they struggled to subsist in the new milieu, and their views changed toward those who emigrated. Instead of perceiving the diaspora as enemies of the revolution, they came to see their fellow compatriots who left as sources of dollars to supplement domestic earnings that were no longer sufficient. In the post-Soviet era, the diaspora, in turn, became more willing to share their new country earnings. In the context of the crisis even the stance of the Cuban government toward the diaspora changed. It shifted from obstructing to facilitating islander ties with émigrés, and it created conditions that encouraged émigrés to send remittances.[3] Cuban émigrés came to share their overseas earnings with friends, and especially with family, they left behind. They did so because they felt morally committed to helping loved ones in economic duress who wanted their assistance, and because institutional conditions where they settled, and especially in their homeland, made it possible. Governments in developing countries, and Cuba is no exception, have developed their own interests in attracting remittances to their country. State and societal interests in remittances may converge, but so too may they conflict, and the interests of each may change over time. Neither state nor society is static in their needs and wants.

In turn, the impact remittances have hinges on the political economy in which they become embedded. Remittances may generate consequences distinct from the reasons immigrants share earnings and the reasons homeland people and their government seek them. The impact of remittances may be far greater than the parties involved want or even comprehend.

In the post-Soviet era, ordinary Cubans came to covet diaspora remittances to address their subsistence needs and then also their consumer yearnings, while the government sought the hard currency to address its own fiscal concerns. Meanwhile, the émigré community became increasingly made up of Cubans willing to share their foreign earnings.

Although the remittance interests of ordinary Cubans and the government initially converged, and the government implemented reforms to encourage the diaspora's dollar-sending, the government quickly began to exploit émigré generosity to its own advantage, at recipients' expense. Under the circumstances, Cubans covertly as well as overtly, illegally as well as legally, and indirectly as well as directly, evaded state regulations to maximize the portion of remittances they accessed to use as they so chose. Subaltern studies alert us to how and why even the politically weak may engage in pilfering, hoarding, sabotage, absenteeism, desertion, foot-dragging, black-marketeering, sideline activity, and the like, activities that undermine what those in dominant positions, such as agents of states, can accomplish.[4]

In the process, state control over the economy and the social order eroded and socialism ceased to function as Cubans for decades had known it. Remittances proved a double-edged sword. The state became weaker and society, transnationally grounded, stronger—contrary to conventional portrayals of communist regimes as strong states with weak societies.[5]

Transnational Social-Capital Formation and the Role of the State in Remittance-Sending

Transnational social-capital formation provides the bedrock on which immigrant remittance-sending rests, but it does not form in a social vacuum. Governments can create conditions conducive to its build-up, and influence (even if not determine) its impact.

During the Soviet era, few of the three-quarters of a million Cubans who then had emigrated sent remittances to Cuba, even after they became one of the wealthiest foreign-born groups in the United States. At the time of the break-up of the Soviet Union and Soviet bloc, remittances to Cuba totaled a mere $50 million. Even as remittances rose in the 1990s, and came to total more than $1 billion annually by the first years of the new millennium, few Soviet-era émigrés sent remittances.[6] Mainly only post-Soviet-era émigrés sent them.

The Cuban immigrant experience points to the role transnational social-capital formation plays in remittance-sending, namely, the development of benefit-generating relations that span national borders. Such relations are not an automatic by-product of emigration. They are contingent on the degree to which those who do and do not emigrate value bonding, trust one another, possess resources the other covets, and share norms supportive of mutually beneficial ties.[7] Only after the crisis that ensued when Soviet aid and trade ended did Cubans consider cross-border ties an asset rather than a liability, a source of social capital grounded in an exchange of material for symbolic reward. In the context of the crisis, norms changed and became supportive of such ties.

THE ROLE OF THE STATE

States have their own institutional, economic, and political interests. Remittances may address those interests, should they help finance imports and foreign debt repayments, stimulate economic growth, raise living standards, and strengthen regime legitimacy.[8] For such reasons, a government may try to encourage remittance-sending by encouraging its diaspora to maintain homeland ties, by promoting conditions that give its people reason to want remittances (for example, for investment, savings, and consumption) and by facilitating cross-border income transfers. Conversely, a government that believes it has sufficient alternative sources of capital, or that believes the negative effects of remittances outweigh gains, may use its powers to prevent, discourage, and obstruct remittance-sending. State economic and political interests in remittances may even conflict. Policies designed to direct remittances to the central government treasury, to address fiscal and other economic exigencies, may erode state capacity to maintain law and order, if people attain or use money from abroad in impermissible ways.

State and societal interests in remittances may also conflict. Governments may directly and indirectly tax transnational people-to-people income transfers in ways that increase the portion of remittances they appropriate for their own use. Or the transfers may benefit recipients while undermining state control over the economy, state-sanctioned bases of stratification, and the state-sanctioned normative order. Furthermore, states may be faced with societal tensions resulting from unequal citizen access to asset-generating transnational networks.

Accordingly, the very vibrancy of transnational social capital formation may be socially, culturally, economically, and even politically destabilizing from a state's vantage point. In the aggregate, ordinary people's cross-border ties may be so consequential as to transform society, values, economic structures, politics, and policies.

CUBAN REMITTANCES IN THE POST-SOVIET ERA

The Cuban government modified its stance toward remittances when the island economy contracted over 30 percent between 1989 and 1993, following the dissolution of the Soviet bloc and then the Soviet Union, and the abrupt ending of Soviet aid and trade. It modified its stance toward remittances also because it needed to reintegrate into the global, capitalist economy, based on hard currency, once Soviet bloc ties were terminated. Hard currency became essential to financing imports and investment, and to qualifying for (and repaying) foreign loans.

So traumatic was the impact of the bloc's collapse that within four years the total value of trade fell to about one-fourth the level in 1989.[9] With trade having accounted for around half of the island's gross national product, the plunge in exports played a key role in the economic downturn.

Cuba's problems were compounded by debts incurred in the Soviet era, which continued afterward to mount. At the end of the Soviet era, Cuba had the second highest ratio of hard-currency debt to hard-currency export earnings in Latin America, and by 2008 its hard-currency debt (other than to Russia) had tripled.[10] Meanwhile, Russia, which took over Soviet debt claims, argued that Cuba owed it $20 billion.[11]

Under the circumstances, the Cuban government creatively developed hard currency, generating tourism. By 2008 tourist revenues were 1,410 percent greater than in 1989.[12] Even more impressive, after the turn of this century the government secured international contracts for the provisioning of medical and other services, which, as of 2006, reportedly generated nearly half of island hard-currency earnings, more than tourism.[13]

Before securing hard-currency service contracts, and while tourism had yet to offset export losses, the government reversed its stance toward remittances. During the Soviet era, the government had made the possession of dollars illegal, and penalized Cubans with (known) diaspora ties, on which remittances hinge. Portraying those who fled the revolution as worms, social degenerates, and unpatriotic, the government encouraged loyal revolutionaries not to associate with them. Cubans with such ties were denied membership in the Communist Party and job promotions.

Under the circumstances, Cubans had reason to distance themselves from family who fled the revolution. They understood that ties with the diaspora were a political and economic liability. Also, if they internalized the values of the new society-in-the-making, they, on principle, wished no dealings with those who rejected the revolution. Some of them also resented mothers and fathers, sisters and brothers, and the like, who put politics above family and emigrated. Psychological wounds were deep, and stood in the way of cross-border bonding.

Despite the constraints on diaspora ties, and the illegality of dollar possession, Cubans reached out to family abroad for help when the economic crisis left them desperate. Scarcities had fueled a black market both in goods and dollars. Although the dollar and peso remained officially on par, the "street" exchange rate surged to around 130 pesos to the dollar, in 1993. As a result, goods became affordable with dollars but no longer with pesos. Items that the government continued to provide through the ration system, part of the cradle-to-grave, revolution-linked welfare state, remained affordable, but insufficient to cover more than one-third to one-half of a family's monthly needs.

Amid the crisis, Cubans came to see émigrés as a potential economic asset, no longer as a liability. Very quickly the crisis broke down social barriers between family members who did and did not emigrate. Reflecting on the crisis-induced change, a child psychiatrist explained: "During the moments of most extreme hardship . . . it was really remarkable . . . There was a feeling of . . . being rescued by those abroad . . . This is when there was a sudden change in perceptions of, and relations with, family abroad."

Although the initial impetus for the change in relations with the diaspora came from ordinary Cubans, remittances surged once the government intervened to create conditions more conducive to the diaspora's dollar-sending. In 1993 it legalized dollar possession, which ended fear of government confiscation of dollar-holdings and of arrest for breaking the law. The government proceeded to open dollar stores and expand their stock. At the stores, Cubans could obtain goods with hard currency, goods that either were not otherwise available or not in sufficient quantity. Cubans, thus, had growing reason to want diaspora dollars. Sales in these stores rose from $870 million in 1998 to more than $1.3 billion five years later.[14] Remittances accounted for an estimated 80 percent of the foreign currency islanders accessed and financed most dollar-based consumption.[15]

The government even facilitated the growth of the diaspora predisposed to sending remittances. After prohibiting emigration during the Soviet era, except periodically to defuse domestic political tensions (for example, in the first years of the revolution, and then again in 1980 and 1994), in the mid-1990s the government signed accords with the United States that permitted the exodus of at least 20,000 Cubans annually.[16] In comparison to the first who fled the revolution, émigrés in the post-Soviet era were about two and one-half times as likely to send remittances, and to send more money. More of them sent money because they remained committed to family members they left behind.

Soviet-era émigrés had never sent remittances of any scale. Perceiving themselves as exiles and exiled, they opposed dealings of any sort with Cuba under Castro. They advocated for what they called a personal embargo, namely a ban on home visits and remittance-sending, along with a state-level embargo.[17]

In contrast, most émigrés in the post-Soviet era had very different perceptions of themselves, different reasons for uprooting, and different views toward friends and family who stayed in Cuba. Although typically far poorer than earlier émigrés, they remitted more because they, in the main, envisioned themselves as economic immigrants who had uprooted with a mission to help family they left behind. The practices and expectations of immigrants so changed that one-fifth of Cubans interviewed in a 2008 survey believed relatives moved abroad mainly to remit money.[18] Cubans came to view the emigration of their most employable relatives as a "family project," with the assumption that those who left would send remittances.

The Cuban leadership further created bedrock for remittance-sending in publicly reimagining the diaspora. Amid the crisis, it began to portray previously stigmatized "worms" and "traitors" as the "Cuban community abroad," equivalent to what Nina Glick-Schiller and Georges Fouron refer to as long-distance nationalists.[19]

The government also removed Soviet-era restrictions on the number of émigrés it permitted to visit the island. As a result, the number who visited yearly surged from 7,000 in 1990 to over 120,000 in little over a decade.[20] The step-up in visiting reflected not merely the government's new permissive stance, but also the changing makeup of the diaspora. The Cubans who emigrated in the post-Soviet era spearheaded the massive increase in homeland visits, as well as remittance-sending.[21] As of 2007, Cubans who emigrated in the post-Soviet era were about twice as likely as the first who fled the revolution to have ever made a return trip to Cuba, even though they lived in the United States far fewer years.[22]

The new Cuban yearning for dollars and the new state initiatives, plus the new bonding across borders, account for the surge in remittance-sending after 1990. The diaspora came to infuse more hard currency into the economy than all but tourism and international service contracts, and more than foreign governments infused in the form of aid and more than foreign businesses in the form of investment and new bank loans.[23] Remittances soared even though the Clinton and George W. Bush administrations capped the amount Cuban Americans could remit, typically at $1,200 annually, and limited remittance-sending to immediate kin, at a time when Latin American immigrants, on average, remitted two to three times Washington's yearly cap for Cuban Americans, and sent money to whoever in their homeland they wished.[24] Only in 2009 did the United States, under Barack Obama, lift restrictions on remittances sent by Cuban Americans, along with restrictions on travel. The pre-Obama regulations had restricted transnational income transfers by Cuban Americans who wished to comply with U.S. law. However, those who prioritized family over politics found ways to evade regulations that stood in their way by remitting money informally, on visits and via private couriers.[25]

Given the new interest of both ordinary Cubans and the state in remit-tances, how did they each fare? Initially they both benefited.

The state, for one, accessed remittances recipients spent on con-sumption at the newly established dollar stores. The very name of these state stores, Tiendas de Recuperación de Divisas (TRDs), or Shops for the Recovery of Hard Currency, highlighted their key function from the state's vantage point.[26] By the early 2000s, Cubans spent an estimated 75 to 80 percent of their remittances at these stores.[27] Thus, while store purchases enabled hard-currency holders to upgrade their standard of living, most diaspora dollars flowed to the state sector.

Dollar store purchases, in turn, increased demand for domestically manufactured goods, which stimulated production and economic growth, and generated employment. The percentage of sales at dollar stores involving domestically produced items rose from 18 percent in 1995 to more than 50 percent a decade later.[28]

The government also set up new state-run currency exchange out-lets, Cajas de Cambio (CADECAS), whereby remittance recipients could easily and legally convert money from abroad into domestic currency for purchases that remained peso-based. Dollar-holders stood to gain in that the CADECAS honored the informal "street" exchange rate, not the official one-peso-to-the-dollar rate that remained for official transac-tions. Although the peso recouped value from its black market low of 130 pesos to the dollar, in 1993, the dollar continued to trade informally at considerably above the official exchange rate (at twenty-one pesos to the dollar at the turn of the century). But the government, in principle, also benefited from accessing foreign currency not spent on dollar store purchases. And in honoring the street exchange rate it could rein in black-market dollar-dealing.

In addition, the government expanded the bank system to allow for dollar deposits. Cubans could thereby acquire a safe place to keep the foreign currency they did not spend immediately on consumption, and earn interest on their deposits, while the state could access the savings to finance investments and profit from interest charges on loans.[29]

At the end of the 1990s, the state even became a transnational hard-currency transfer agent. State-owned enterprises entered the remittance business. They partnered with international money-transfer companies.

Accordingly, the government facilitated cross-border income-sharing in a manner that allowed it to profit from service charges, while Cubans could quickly and securely acquire money from family abroad. In the early 2000s, the government annually took in over $100 million in wire service fees. Western Union, for example, worked with a government agency. The two institutions split the service charges, which ranged from 10 to 30 percent of the value of money wired, with the Cuban firm receiving a proportionally larger share of the total.[30]

State Benefits from Remittances Increasingly at Recipients' Expense

Although both recipients of remittances and the government benefited from the generosity of the diaspora, the government soon manipulated émigrés' goodwill to its own institutional advantage, at remittance recipients' expense. It did so in several ways.

The government, for one, profited from TRD sales, and increasingly at consumers' expense. Not only did it tax the profits of, and hold dividends in, the state-run stores, but it also set prices high at the stores (in contrast to prices it charged for items distributed through the ration system).[31] Authorities justified what they claimed was an ideal mark-up at the stores, 240 percent above cost, on equity grounds: a tax on hard-currency consumers to fund programs for Cubans not fortunate enough to have family abroad who shared earnings (or who were unable to access dollars by other means, for example, through tourism). While the official discourse claimed the mark-up allowed for distributive justice, the government provided no guarantee that retail sales revenues were channeled to the peso-dependent population.

In periodically raising TRD prices, the government further advanced its economic interests at the expense of those holding dollars. For example, price hikes in 2002 contributed to an 8 percent inflation in consumer prices, and those in 2004 raised consumer costs, on average, an additional 15 percent.[32] Although Cuban authorities partially retracted some of the price increases of 2004 when confronted with consumer anger, they never fully restored prices to previous levels.

The government also profited from money wired from abroad, at recipients' expense. Service charges for money-wiring were higher to Cuba than to other Latin American countries.[33] As of 2006, money transfer companies (in which the Cuban government partnered with foreign firms) charged, on average, nineteen cents for every dollar transferred to Cuba, whereas the average transaction cost to the other countries by then had dropped to about 6 cents per remitted dollar.

Also, beginning in 2004 the government ruled that Cubans could no longer use dollars as domestic currency (although dollar possession remained legal). The new regulation enabled it to profit even more at remittance recipients' expense. It required Cubans to trade their hard currency for so-called Cuban Convertible Pesos (CUCs), promissory notes with dollar value on the island. Because the government charged a 20 percent surcharge for the conversion of dollars (and a 10 percent surcharge for the conversion of other hard currencies), recipients of remittances from the United States were doubly taxed at a steep rate, through currency exchange costs as well as the high mark-ups at state stores, and triply if they received remittances through the wire services. Consequently, the government increased its access to hard currency both by removing foreign currency from informal circulation in the economy and by taxing currency conversion.[34]

The government went on to alter the exchange rate in a manner disadvantageous to dollar-holders. In 2005 it lowered the dollar-peso exchange rate to 22 pesos, and the dollar-convertible peso exchange rate from 1:1 to 1:0.93.[35] Island authorities claimed that the readjusted rates improved the value of the peso, to the benefit of the peso-dependent population. While that is true, the changed exchange rates also bene-fited the government, in that it could release less local currency for every dollar remittance recipients turned in.

The government, in addition, introduced new taxes on self-employed workers, whose entrepreneurial ventures often made use of remittances from family abroad. The tax lowered earnings of the self-employed, consistent with the egalitarian thrust of the revolution, but in a manner intended to increase state revenue at entrepreneurs' expense. It first introduced such taxes in the latter 1990s, and more extensively in 2010 when officially permitting more private economic activity.

State-Incurred Costs Associated with the Remittance Economy

Remittances appear to be a cost-free source of hard currency. However, from the state's vantage point they proved a mixed blessing. While generating funds essential for financing imports, for developing the economy, and for maintaining the cradle-to-grave welfare benefits on which regime legitimacy had rested, they simultaneously contributed to social, political, ideological, normative, and even economic problems that eroded state political and moral authority and state control over the economy and society. Remittances also undermined precepts of the revolution. Remittances were not the only source of the problems the regime faced. However, in that they accounted for about 80 percent of the hard currency Cubans attained, they were a key source of the havoc informal dollarization of the economy caused.

ECONOMIC COSTS

The remittance-based informal dollarization of the economy adversely impacted state-sector productivity and the delivery of services central to the government's socialist base of legitimacy. With few state jobs paying more than the equivalent of $20 per month, far less than the average amount remittance recipients received without any work effort whatsoever, the incentive to labor at peso-paying state jobs declined, including jobs in education and health care that were central to the revolution-linked welfare state. The quality of education, in particular, suffered. The government faced problems attracting and maintaining qualified, motivated teachers.

Under these circumstances, Cubans without access to remittances sought peso-paying state jobs that provided informal and illegal access to dollars (and CUCs). This contributed to a domestic brain drain. Professionals left their jobs, especially for work in tourism.[36] State jobs in tourism did not offer higher salaries, but they provided opportunities to access hard currency informally, especially through tips. Cubans also left state jobs to pursue private ventures that catered to tourists, operating on both sides of the law. Cubans with suitable housing opened up bed-and-breakfasts and small restaurants.[37] Some room-renters earned more in a day than state-sector employees earned in a month. And Cubans who catered to new tourist demand for prostitution earned more in an hour than in a month at a state job. The gravitation to tourism, consequently, left the government with a deteriorating return from its investment in schooling, along with new social problems.

The cash-strapped government also initiated some worker-incentive reforms, both in hard currency and in pesos, to stimulate productivity, to convince labor to continue to toil in state sector jobs, and to reduce differences in income and living standards among Cubans with and without access to remittances. These reforms benefited the peso-

dependent populace, whose living standards had dramatically deteriorated in the post-Soviet era, especially relative to the living standards of
dollar-holders, but at considerable cost to the state. State enterprises in
key sectors began to feed and clothe their workers, to offer performance
bonuses, and to pay employees a portion of their salary in hard currency
(and then in CUCs, special pesos that had dollar value in Cuba). At the
beginning of the twenty-first century, hard-currency bonuses cost the
state $228 million in scarce foreign exchange, one-fourth to one-third
the value of remittance intake at the time (and a higher percentage,
according to the most conservative remittance estimates).[38] Then, in
2005 the government raised base wages, which had declined in real
value. It more than doubled the minimum wage, a 1,800-million peso
expenditure.[39]

SOCIAL COSTS

The government also met up with societal resistance that not only limited its access to remittances but eroded its authority. For one, dollar-
holders were sparing in the money they exchanged at CADECAS during
the years when the dollar served as legal tender. They preferred to hold
on to the hard currency they did not spend at state stores, rather than
exchange it for pesos. Cubans are estimated to have exchanged at
CADECAS only about $10 million in 1996 and $20 million four years
later, in years when estimated remittances totaled about $500 million
and one billion dollars, respectively.[40]

Cubans also preferred to attain remittances informally, especially
from visiting émigrés, rather than via the wire services that channeled
diaspora funds to state transfer agencies. Compared to immigrants
from other Latin American countries, Cubans abroad wired less of the
money they remitted.[41] They thereby evaded the higher costs imposed
on wiring money to Cuba.

Moreover, the number in the labor force who registered as self-
employed declined when the government initiated taxes on entrepreneurial activity in the 1990s.[42] The tax drove private activity underground, if not out of existence.

Few Cubans, in turn, deposited dollars in the state bank system. In
1998, they deposited a mere $50 million.[43] Ten years later a survey in
Cuba found that 60 percent of remittance recipients did not have bank
accounts. Half of them mentioned they distrusted the state-controlled
banking system.[44] With dollar-holders spending $870 million in 1998

and over $1 billion in the first years of the new millennium at dollar stores, the government found it needed to rely far more on consumption than savings to access remittance revenue. While consumption, in part, stimulated domestic production, as noted above, it also drove up the hard currency import bill.

MORAL ORDER

The state's consumer-based accumulation strategy also had the unintended effect of fueling the black market and other illicit activity. In the process, state moral authority eroded, at the same time that its control over consumption and distribution deteriorated and its capacity to profit from consumption suffered.

The state's official near-monopoly of permissible dollar-based consumption (and, after 2004, commerce in CUCs), especially of nondurables, contributed to black marketeering. Anyone who priced goods below dollar store rates created a market for the items they offered. The black market opportunities led state employees to steal goods from their work centers to vend privately and illegally.

By the first years of the new millennium, crime, pilfering, and corruption had become so rampant that Castro announced that they could destroy the revolution.[45] Against this backdrop, both the government and Communist Party launched initiatives to try to halt the wrongdoing. In 2001 the government established the Ministry of Audit and Control. In the following few years it sacked state employees not only for their own illegal dealings, but also for failing to prevent theft by subordinates, and in 2007 the Ministry of Labor stepped up penalties for bureaucrats found guilty of corruption and pilfering.[46] The interventions revealed how agents of the state had become part of the problem, not the solution. Then, in 2008 the government announced yet another large-scale crackdown on illegal private activity and a tightening of financial oversight that included replacing the five-year-old Ministry of Audit and Control with the new Office of the Comptroller General.

No available data documents the scale of crimes and misdemeanors, but ordinary Cubans, as well as officials, complain about the problem.[47] Illicit activity continued despite government efforts to rein it in, because its root cause remained unaddressed: Cuban yearnings for improved living conditions insufficiently obtainable through legally sanctioned means.

Remittances, in turn, contributed to ordinary Cubans' transforming island norms and values in ways that defied principles on which the revolution had been premised. The diaspora infused individualistic, materialistic yearnings that contradicted the nonmaterialistic, collectivistic morality that Che Guevara had advocated and symbolized.

Although Cubans had initially turned to family who emigrated to address subsistence needs, they quickly developed new wants, for electric fans, furniture, televisions, VCRs, iPods, such prestige-label shoes as Nikes, clothing, and the like. They began to identify with the materialistic culture visiting friends and family had taken on for themselves upon emigrating. Cuban awareness of U.S. brand names became among the highest in non-English-speaking countries.[48] Lifestyle differences between families on the two sides of the Florida Straits came to hinge more on differences in earnings than on differences in values. In promoting the consumer strategy to access diaspora dollars the state even became party to the new materialism.

An earlier taboo of American-style consumerism broke down to the point that Cubans flaunted materialism in their everyday lives. Pointing to the change, a man I interviewed noted, "The Miami Cuban culture promotes Lycra, puffy hair, lots of make-up, and gold." With remittances from one sister who left in 1980 and from another who left in 1998, he lived in a freshly painted house that he fenced in and furnished with a TV, VCR, CD player, stereo, computer, wireless phone, and beautiful artwork. His home renovations revealed a new Cuban desire for materialistic consumption. In this vein, a city planner also noted to me: "Whereas it used to be taboo to show that you were living better than others, now people want to show that they live better . . . They put up fences and paint the outsides of their houses." Given that remittances were associated with values antithetical to precepts of the revolution, government and party functionaries viewed diaspora dollars with ambivalence.[49]

Popular culture even parodied the new materialism. The film *A Paradise under the Stars* captured the decadence of the materialistic turn. The film depicts an immigrant who returns from Spain to attend a funeral. The Cubans were so excited about the gifts the returnee brought that they forget about the funeral.

Because Cubans lacked equal access to overseas networks of material worth, remittances, in turn, eroded egalitarian precepts of the revolution. Under Castro, Cuba had become the most egalitarian country in Latin America, as land reform, new wage policies, and the nationalization of the ownership of most of the economy radically reduced prerevolution inequities. However, between 1986 and 1999 the Gini coefficient is estimated to have worsened, from 0.22 to 0.41, and more if dollar earnings and income in convertible pesos (CUCs) were taken into account. Remittances were not the only factor contributing to the new inequality, but they were an important contributing factor.[50] Cuba's new poor involved those dependent on peso earnings.

The new income inequality had a range of ramifications. It resulted, for one, in new dietary inequality. Almost all islanders could afford the portion of their diet rations covered. However, prices at private farmers' markets, permitted since 1994, and at the state hard-currency stores, were ten to one hundred times as much as their price-regulated equivalents.[51] As a result, remittance recipients enjoyed dietary options unavailable to the population dependent on peso income.

Remittances also fueled race-based inequality that defied another precept of the revolution. Studies estimated the average annual per capita remittance earnings of nonwhites to be half that of whites, and only 10 percent of blacks, and slightly more for mixed-blood *mestizos*, but 40 percent of whites, to have received remittances between 1996 and 2002.[52] The diaspora, on whose generosity Cubans depend for remittances, is overwhelmingly white. Because nonwhites benefited immediately from the revolution, few of them had emigrated.[53] As a consequence, the racial accomplishments of the revolution had the unintended effect of contributing to new race-based income inequality in the post-Soviet era. Making matters worse, blacks faced difficulty attaining jobs in tourism, the main alternative source of hard-currency earnings. Without dollars, blacks have difficulty attaining medicine, clothing, and a nice place to live, as well as nonrationed food.[54]

The new remittance-linked inequality also eroded the initial commitment of the revolution to the reduction of rural-urban disparities. During Castro's first decade of rule, the government promoted "a maximum of ruralism, a minimum of urbanism."[55] The rhetoric reflected an effort to reduce the country's prerevolutionary urban bias. But by the beginning of the twenty-first century, Havana, with 20 percent of the island's population, received approximately 60 percent of remittances.[56] New rural-urban disparities came to be embedded in ordinary Cubans' geographically rooted, unequal access to transnational ties of economic worth.

The Transformation and Transnationalization of Bases of Esteem

Remittances also transformed and transnationalized Cuban bases of esteem. With nothing material to offer émigrés in return for their generosity, remittance recipients reciprocated in kind, symbolically, and in ways that gave émigrés ongoing reason to share earnings.

Remittance-sending, for one, raised immigrants' social standing in Cuba, in a manner that turned the status schema in place from 1959 to 1989 on its head. Cubans reenvisioned as heroes the émigrés whom the national leadership previously portrayed pejoratively. Cubans do not care how émigrés earn a living. "They could be trash collectors. It didn't matter," a Havana resident explained. What mattered was that émigrés lived a better material lifestyle, and that in sharing earnings, Cubans could improve their material lifestyle as well.

Cubans also came to treat émigrés with new respect. In this vein, a woman recounted to me how she experienced "almost a civil war" in her neighborhood and workplace when her family fled in the 1960s. She was stigmatized, and had eggs thrown at her. She was also subject to so-called repudiations when she attempted to leave the country in 1980, the year that some 125,000 Cubans fled from the port of Mariel. She marveled, though, at how the same people treated her "like a señora," with dignity, when, after finally emigrating, she visited Cuba in the 1990s. Similarly, another woman who successfully emigrated in 1980, and who visited Cuba yearly, beginning in the 1990s, with thousands of dollars and gifts for island family, felt like a distinguished guest on visits.

Income-sharing émigrés even gained new authority in Cuba. An unemployed woman, estranged from her mother who abandoned her when joining the Mariel exodus, reenvisioned her mother in the 1990s as "the matriarch." The change came when her mother became the primary breadwinner for the island family. New transnationally embedded authority also became patriarchal, and, on occasion, extended to relations that had previously ended in divorce. An island-trained doctor who works as a factory laborer in Miami, for example, felt that the money he sent his ex-wife and child in Cuba gave him decision-making power over her household that divorce had denied him before emigrating.

The emergent informal, transnationalized status schema eroded valuation of the previous schema grounded in the socialist political economy. The most educated Cubans, with what were formerly the most prestigious state jobs, cannot afford the same material lifestyle on their official salary as can remittance-receiving Cubans with less prestigious, poorer-paying peso jobs. Status on the island has come to rest less on what you do, on human capital, than on who you know, abroad. A Cuban whom I interviewed astutely spoke to the point. "Class distinctions have become more noticeable. There is now a new class . . . a disjunction . . . Many of those who [recently] migrated and their island families are lower class with limited education. But they have access to a lifestyle that is inaccessible to the professional class loyal to the revolution."

Remittances undermined the socialist hierarchy because their value is unrelated to the status of Cuban recipients and because even humble laborers abroad could transfer more money than high status islanders earned as a result of years of professional training and hard work. Indicative of the new stratification schema, Cubans began to calculate their peso paychecks in terms of their CUC, hard-currency worth, with once prestigious doctors, for example, earning the equivalent of $20 to $30 a month in the post-Soviet era. Accordingly, those who stayed in Cuba and worked their way up the socialist status hierarchy experienced, de facto, downward mobility, to the extent that they relied on their official salary.

CUBAN IMMIGRANTS HAVE contributed to a transformation of the Cuban economy, to a transformation of Cuban values and norms, and to a transformation of Cuban society. But for the most part only émigrés in the post-Soviet era fueled these changes. They had such impact not because they became rich and powerful in the United States or because they deliberately tried to initiate the changes. Rather, the changes are an unintended consequence, in the aggregate, of commitments these émigrés maintain to family they left behind.

The Cuban experience reveals, however, that such impact is not an inherent by-product of emigration. Only in the post-Soviet era did Cubans emigrate who bonded across borders, in ways that had far-reaching consequences. The Cuban experience suggests that for the most part émigrés who uproot for economic reasons, and who remain committed to family in their homeland, provide the bedrock for the build-up of transnational remittance-generating social ties. The Cuban experience also reveals that the build-up of cross-border ties is most likely when macroinstitutional and normative conditions are supportive. These conditions only took hold in Cuba in the post-Soviet era.

The Cuban experience, in turn, reveals that the homeland impact immigrants have hinges on the political economy in which transnational ties become embedded. Immigrant ties with Cuba simultaneously strengthened and subverted socialism as Cubans had known it for three decades. Immigrant remittances infused hard currency that helped keep the regime afloat. However, they concomitantly eroded the egalitarian, collectivistic, nonmaterialist premises of the revolution, fueled black market activity, and undermined motivation to work in the state economy. In the process, they weakened state power, authority, and control.

The Cuban experience further demonstrates that both a government and its people may share interests in remittances, but their interests in remittances may also conflict. In Cuba, the government increasingly intervened to try to access remittances at recipients' expense. However, it faced resistance. Even in a country with as seemingly a strong state and weak society as Cuba under Castro, where formal power was highly centralized, the populace pursued ties to the diaspora for their own advantage, informally, covertly, and illegally. Governments face constraints in directing remittance economies as they so choose.

Remittances, in essence, generate contradictions. The consequences of immigrant generosity are complex and multifaceted. From the vantage point of U.S. policy, the Obama administration's decision, in 2009, to lift the so-called personal embargo on visits and remittance-sending, was not only a humanitarian gesture consistent with rights extended to other U.S. immigrants. It also provided the bedrock for improving cross-border relations at the people-to-people level and deepening the infusion of U.S. values in Cuba.

When comparing Cuba and China, another country dominated by a communist party, we see how varied immigrant impacts and homeland government relations with their diasporas may be. Although government policies regarding their diasporas changed over the years in both countries, China has established more economically consequential ties with its émigrés, including those who fled the country in opposition to the revolution. Cuban immigrants, and almost exclusively those who left in the post-Soviet era, mainly only fueled consumption. In contrast, Min Ye shows in her chapter that Chinese immigrants have also provided investment capital, and on a scale that has served as an engine of large-scale homeland economic development. For Cuban émigrés to play a comparable role, not only will wealthy Cubans abroad need to develop an interest in and commitment to investing in their homeland and the Cuban government need to create attractive investment conditions, but the U.S. government also will need to remove the embargo that prohibits American (including Cuban American) investment in Cuba. In essence, changes will be necessary at the individual and institutional levels, and in the United States as well as in Cuba.

Notes

1 Susan Eckstein, *The Immigrant Divide: How Cuban Americans Changed the U.S. and Their Homeland* (New York: Routledge, 2009), graph 1.1, page 11. See also Felix Masud-Piloto, *From Welcome Exiles to Illegal Immigrants: Cuban Migration at the End of the Millennium* (Oxford: Clarendon, 1996).

2 José Alejandro Aguilar Trujillo, "Las remesas desde exterior," *Cuba: Investigación económica* (Havana: Instituto Nacional de Investigaciones Económicas, 2001), 71–104; Eckstein, *The Immigrant Divide*, 203.

3 For a discussion of my interview and other data sources, see Eckstein, *The Immigrant Divide*, 8, 9, Appendix.

4 See James Scott, *Weapons of the Weak: Everyday Forms of Peasant Resistance* (New Haven, CT: Yale University Press, 1985) and James Scott, *Domination and the Arts of Resistance* (New Haven: Yale University Press, 1990).

5 Joel Migdal, *Strong Societies and Weak States: State-Society Relations and State Capabilities in the Third World* (Princeton, NJ: Princeton University Press, 1988).

6 Eckstein, *The Immigrant Divide*, 179. Estimates of remittances to Cuba vary substantially, in the absence of adequate officially available data.

7 On social capital, see James Coleman, "Social Capital in the Creation of Human Capital," *American Journal of Sociology* 94 (1988): supplement, 95–120; and Pierre Bourdieu, "The Forms of Capital," in *Handbook of Theory and Research for the Sociology of Education*, ed. J. G. Richardson (New York: Greenwood, 1986), 241–58. On social capital in transnational context, see, for example, Peggy Levitt, *Transnational Villagers* (Berkeley: University of California Press, 2001), 62, 200.

8 See Sharon Stanton Russell, "Remittances from International Migration: A Review in Perspective," *World Development* 14, no. 6 (1986): 677–96; Jorge

Durand, Emilio Parrado, and Douglas Massey, "Migradollars and Development: A Reconsideration of the Mexican Case," *International Migration Review* 30, no. 22 (1996): 423–44; and Massey et al., *Worlds in Motion: International Immigration at the End of the Millennium* (Oxford: Oxford University Press, 1998).

9　William LeoGrande and Julie Thomas, "Cuba's Quests for Economic Independence," *Journal of Latin American Studies* 34, part 2 (May 2002): 330.

10　Susan Eckstein, "Diasporas and Dollars: Transnational Ties and the Transformation of Cuba" (Working Paper 16, Center for International Studies, Massachusetts Institute of Technology, Cambridge, 2003), 247; and Eckstein, *The Immigrant Divide*, 209.

11　Economist Intelligence Unit (EIU), *Cuba Country Reports* (CCR), August 2006, 29.

12　Carmelo Mesa-Lago, "The Cuban Economy in 2008–09" (paper presented at El Caribe en su Inserción Internacional, San José, Costa Rica, February 2009), 9.

13　Jorge Sánchez-Egozcue, "Economic Relations Cuba-U.S.: Bilateralism or Geopolitics?" (paper presented at the Latin American Studies Association Congress, Montreal, September 2007), 7.

14　EIU, CCR, August 2001, 20; and EIU, CCR, June 2000, 19; Lorena Barberia, "Remittances to Cuba: An Evaluation of Cuban and U.S. Government Policy Measures," in *The Cuban Economy at the Start of the Twenty-First Century*, ed. Jorge Domínguez et al. (Cambridge, MA: Harvard University Press, 2004), 372–73.

15　Paolo Spadoni, "The Role of the United States in the Cuban Economy," *Cuba in Transition 13* (Washington, DC: Association for the Study of the Cuban Economy, 2003), 10. Cubans also accessed hard currency through tourism, black marketeering, overseas work, and supplementary payments in state-sector jobs.

16　For a description of Cuban emigration and U.S. and Cuban government immigration policies, see Masud-Piloto, *From Welcome Exiles to Illegal Immigrants.*

17　Eckstein, *The Immigrant Divide*, table 6.2, chapter 6; Florida International University (FIU), Institute for Public Opinion (IPOR), *FIU/Cuba Poll* (Miami: FIU-IPOR, 2004 and 2007).

18　Manuel Orozco, "The Cuban Condition: Migration, Remittances, and Its Diaspora" (paper presented at El Caribe en su Inserción Internacional, San José, Costa Rica, February 2009), 4.

19　Nina Glick-Schiller and Georges Fouron, *Georges Woke Up Laughing: Long-Distance Nationalism and the Search for Home* (Durham, NC: Duke University Press, 2001).

20　Eckstein, *The Immigrant Divide*, graph 4.1; Susan Eckstein and Lorena Barberia, "Grounding Immigrant Generations in History: Cuban Americans and

Their Transnational Ties," *International Migration Review* 36, no. 3 (fall 2002), 814.

21 On changes in Cuba and Cuban lived experiences, see Eckstein, *The Immigrant Divide*, and Silvia Pedraza, *Political Disaffection in Cuba's Revolution and Exodus* (New York: Cambridge University Press, 2007).

22 While fewer earlier émigrés than recent émigrés had close family in Cuba to visit as of the early 2000s, the former rarely visited in the years when they had more close kin in Cuba.

23 Eckstein, *The Immigrant Divide*, 209.

24 For a discussion of U.S. remittance policy, see Eckstein, *The Immigrant Divide*, chapter 6.

25 U.S. restrictions also did not constrict the sending of remittances by Cubans who, in growing but still small numbers, immigrated to countries other than the United States, countries over which Washington had no jurisdiction. Orozco, "The Cuban Condition," 6.

26 Various state enterprises, including CIMEX, TRD-Caribe (affiliated with the Ministry of the Revolutionary Armed Forces), Cubalse, and Caracol, established dollar stores.

27 United States Department of State (USDS), Bureau of West Hemisphere Affairs, *Commission for Assistance to a Free Cuba, Report to the President* (May 2004), 35.

28 Barberia, "Remittances to Cuba," 375; EIU, *CCR, May 2005*, 26.

29 Barberia, "Remittances to Cuba," 370.

30 Ibid., 380–82.

31 In contrast, the government charged low prices for goods allotted through the ration system.

32 EIU, *CCR*, February 2003, 9; ibid., August 2004, 19.

33 Orozco, "The Cuban Condition"; Inter-American Dialogue, "Making the Most of Family Remittances" (Washington, D.C.: Inter-American Dialogue, Task Force on Remittances, May 2007), 5, 7; USDS, *Commission for Assistance to a Free Cuba, Report to the President*.

34 The government also imposed a greater surcharge on the dollar exchange than on other hard currency exchanges to offset new transaction costs the Bush administration imposed on third-country banks that dealt with Cuban dollars (EIU, *CCR*, May 2005, 10).

35 EIU, *CCR*, May 2005, 10.

36 Miren Uriarte, "Social Impact of the Economic Measures," in *Reinventing the Revolution: A Contemporary Cuba Reader*, ed. Philip Brenner et al. (Boulder, CO: Rowman and Littlefield, 2008).

37 Ted Henken, "Condemned to Informality: Cuba's Experiments with Self-Employment during the Special Period (The Case of the 'Bed and Breakfasts')," *Cuban Studies* 33 (2002): 1–39.

38 U.S.-Cuba Trade and Economic Council (UCTEC), "Economic Eye on Cuba" (March 17, 2002), 12.

39 EIU, *CCR*, August 2005, 21.The average annual wage in 2005 adjusted for infla-tion was, however, 77 percent below what it was in 1989 (Mesa-Lago, "The Cuban Economy in 2008–09," 6).

40 Barberia, "Remittances to Cuba," 370; Eckstein, *The Immigrant Divide*, table 6.1, 179.

41 Ibid., 195–96.

42 The number declined by 23 percent during the first four years the tax was in effect (EIU, *CCR*, May 2001, 18).

43 Ibid., August 2001, 20; ibid., June 2000, 19.

44 Orozco, "The Cuban Condition," 12.

45 On rent-seeking, corruption, theft, and employer bribery to access jobs offer-ing illicit money-making opportunities, see Sergio Díaz-Briquets and Jorge Pérez-López, *Corruption in Cuba: Castro and Beyond* (Austin: University of Texas Press, 2006); and Archibald Ritter, "Economic Illegalities and the Un-derground Economy in Cuba," in *Focal* (Ottawa: Canadian Foundation for the Americas, 2006).

46 EIU, *CCR*, August 2006, 20; ibid., November 2006, 15.

47 For descriptions of the illegal economy, see Díaz-Briquets and Pérez-López, *Corruption in Cuba*; and Ritter, "Economic Illegalities and the Underground Economy in Cuba."

48 *New York Times*, May 26, 2002, section 3, p. 4.

49 LeoGrande and Thomas, "Cuba's Quests for Economic Independence," 352.

50 Claes Brundenius, "Whither the Cuban Economy after Recovery? The Reform Process, Upgrading Strategies and the Question of Transition," *Journal of Latin American Studies* 34, part 2 (May 2002): 365–96; Mesa-Lago, "The Cuban Economy in 2008–09," 7.

51 Viviana Togores and Anicia García, "Consumption, Markets, and Monetary Duality in Cuba," in *The Cuban Economy at the Start of the Twenty-First Cen-tury*, ed. Domínguez et al., 245–96.

52 Alejandro de la Fuente, "Recreating Racism: Race and Discrimination in Cuba's Special Period," in *Reinventing the Revolution*, ed. Brenner et al., 320.

53 Rodrigo Espina Prieto and Pablo Rodríguez Ruiz, "Raza y desigualdad en la Cuba actual," *Temas* 45 (January–March 2006): 47.

54 Mark Sawyer, *Racial Politics in Postrevolutionary Cuba* (Cambridge: Cam-bridge University Press, 2004), 81, 85.

55 Susan Eckstein, *Back from the Future: Cuba under Castro* (Princeton, NJ: Princeton University Press, 1994), chapter 6.

56 UCTEC, "Economic Eye on Cuba," 12; see also Espina Prieto and Rodríguez Ruiz, "Raza y desigualdad en la Cuba actual," 47.

6

Immigrant Impacts in Mexico
A Tale of Dissimilation

DAVID SCOTT FITZGERALD

The study of Mexican migration has never neglected the homeland altogether, as influential works by Manuel Gamio and Paul Taylor in the 1920s, the surveys of Wayne Cornelius beginning in the 1970s, and the work of Douglas Massey and Jorge Durand since the 1980s demonstrate.[1] Yet, most migration studies have overwhelmingly focused on immigrants' assimilation into the host country. They address how quickly different groups of immigrants lose their foreign qualities to resemble natives. Since the early 1990s, a transnational perspective has revived attention to migrant homelands, highlighting processes encompassing all poles of a migration circuit. Authors writing in this framework emphasize that those who move abroad are not definitively immigrants or emigrants, but rather human agents who lead lives that span international borders. Whether migrants physically move back and forth between their homeland and new land or participate vicariously in the lives of their places of origin through remittances and phone calls, their experiences cannot be understood from the perspective of the destination country alone. Indeed, the more postmodern inflections of transnationalism reject altogether the dichotomous categories of origin and destination, emigrant and im-

TABLE 6.1. Taxonomy of Migration Studies Perspectives

Analytic Perspective	Assimilation	Dissimilation	Transnationalism
Phenomenon	Immigration	Emigration/return migration	Real or virtual circularity
Reference Country	Destination	Origin	Origin and destination
Trajectory of change	Convergence	Divergence	Reproduction

migrant, and even the geographic spaces of here and there—arguing for a convergence of a single community, social field, or third space across international borders.[2]

Building on the literatures of assimilation and transnationalism, the concept of *dissimilation* offers a third perspective that too often falls out of existing accounts (see table 6.1). Dissimilation, the process of becoming different, is the forgotten twin of assimilation, the process whereby groups and individuals become similar. As Mexican immigrants and their children become similar to other Americans, they become dissimilar from the nonmigrant Mexicans they leave behind.[3] The differences that develop between migrants and those who stay in Mexico are often much greater than the small differences upon which scholars of assimilation focus their microscopes.[4]

For example, policymakers and scholars have viewed some immigrants' adoption of urban and gang-inflected youth culture in the United States as a failure of assimilation.[5] The same set of facts is viewed in Mexico as evidence of Americanization. When young men who left for the United States as children or U.S.-born children of Mexican immigrants visit their ancestral homes in rural Mexico, they often stand apart from their peers who never left. The tattoos, body piercings, baggy pants, shaved heads, and fondness for gothic letters of *cholo* youth telegraph their transformative U.S. experience. Nonmigrants commonly claim that migrants *no son de aquí ni de allá* (are neither from here nor from there). In other words, migrants have dissimilated from the Mexican mainstream, but they do not belong in the U.S. mainstream either.[6]

As with assimilation, dissimilation can be parsed into different domains of social life.[7] Migration may dramatically open opportunities for exogamy, for example, while doing little to change some aspects of the cultural content encountered in the place of destination. Spanish-language music is as widely available in the United States as English-language music is in Mexico. Because heterogeneous cultural influences are felt on both sides of the border, independently of migration (through cross-border flows of media, goods, and tourists), it is challenging to gauge migration's independent effect on cultural change in the homeland. Migrants become different from those who stay behind, while those who stay behind are also changing, as Mexican society undergoes myriad transformations only partly attributable to migration.

The dissimilation perspective shares the transnational perspective's attention to the country of origin and the possibility of migrants' new and ongoing ties across borders, but the dissimilation perspective differs in important ways. Against the transnationalism literature's focus on the reproduction and *similarity* in a community spread across international borders, the concept of dissimilation focuses attention on the creation of *difference* between populations divided by the border. Dissimilation questions the very concept of community by highlighting negotiations over who is a legitimate member of the community, what kinds of behavior are acceptable, and struggles over where the boundaries of the community begin and end.[8] In contrast to skeptics of Mexican assimilation, such as the political scientist Samuel Huntington, who mistakenly saw "deviant" social practices of Mexicans as failures of Americanization, the same practices reflect Americanization from the dissimilation perspective of the country of origin.[9] Vis-à-vis the scholars of transnationalism, who highlight the ongoing connections between migrants and their homeland, and the newly institutionalized possibilities for dual nationality and cultural pluralism, the dominant pattern in Mexican migration is still one of migrant dissimilation.

Mexican Emigration

Emigration from Mexico is exceptional for its large volume and concentration in a single major country of destination. In 2011, roughly 12 million Mexicans, making up 11 percent of Mexico's population, lived in the United States. They accounted for 98 percent of all Mexican emigrants. More Mexicans live in the United States than the total number of immigrants in any other country in the world. Another 16.8 million people of Mexican origin were born in the United States.[10]

Mass migration from Mexico has a centenarian history and con-

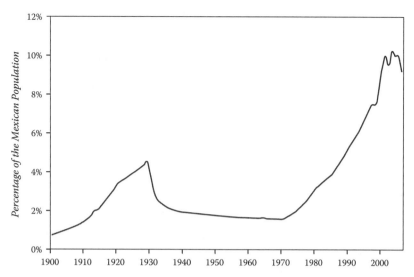

FIGURE 6.1. Mexican Emigrants to the U.S. as a Percentage of the
Mexican Population, 1900–2006

Source: David FitzGerald, *A Nation of Emigrants: How Mexico Manages
Its Migration* (Berkeley: University of California Press, 2009), p. 5.

tinues at high levels that affect those who go and those who stay behind
(see figure 6.1).[11] A quarter of the Mexican adult population has visited
or lived in the United States, and 60 percent have a relative there.[12]
Beginning in the 1960s, and accelerating with the passage of the U.S.
Immigration Reform and Control Act of 1968, emigration from Mexico
shifted from a primarily male-led, circular migration to a permanent,
family migration to the United States.[13] Still, a considerable degree of
circulation continues.

In 2008, however, migration to the United States slowed down. More
than 400,000 Mexicans in the United States returned to Mexico.[14] In the
wake of a downturn in the U.S. labor market, increased U.S. border enforcement, and increased deportations, the population of unauthorized
immigrants from Mexico fell from 7 million in 2007 to 6.1 million in
2011. The authorized population grew slightly over the same period,
from 5.6 to 5.8 million.[15]

Both return migration and permanent emigration are vehicles for
social change. Even migrants' engagement with their homeland highlights to those who stay behind how migrants have been changed by
their U.S. experiences.

TABLE 6.2. Mexican Communities Studied, 1999–2009

Community	2005 Population	2005 County Under-development Index[1]
Arandas, Jalisco	46,099	Low
Agua Negra, Jalisco	486	Low
Tlacuitapa, Jalisco	1,264	Medium
Tunkás, Yucatán	2,812	High
San Miguel Tlacotepec, Oaxaca	1,696	High
Sahuayo, Michoacán	59,316	Very low

[1] Counties with a high score on the underdevelopment index have low levels of education, low levels of access to health care, poor housing infrastructure, and low levels of refrigerator ownership.

[2] Sahuayo is rated as a "medium" migration intensity county by CONAPO, based on the

Methods

This chapter draws on research in six migrant-origin communities in four Mexican states. These six communities were selected to represent a broad range of migration contexts. They vary in size, level of economic development, levels of out-migration, length of community-emigration history, and ethnic composition (see table 6.2).[16]

Cultural Dissimilation

As with assimilation, dissimilation may be segmented. Segmented assimilation refers to the fact that migrants associate with distinctive groups within their destination country that differentially affect the values and behaviors they adopt. Dissimilation refers to the differences in cultural and other practices between the migrants and the groups in their places of origin. Migrants are more likely to dissimilate from rural, conservative, and deeply religious populations than from urban, more socially liberal, and secular populations. Other things being equal, migration to a highly heterogeneous or culturally distinctive milieu will create greater dissimilation than migration to a more familiar context.

According to a common view in Mexico, the local economic benefits of emigration come at a steep cultural cost. For example, attitudes to-

Percent of Adult Population with Migration Experience	Generations of Mass Migration	Ethnic Composition
20%	4	Mestizo
30%	3	Mestizo
50%	4	Mestizo
25%	1	Maya (indigenous)
37%	2	Mixteco (indigenous)
NA[2]	4	Mestizo

2000 census. http://www.conapo.gob.mx/publicaciones/intensidadmig/anexoC.pdf. Unlike the other communities in Table 6.2, I did not conduct a survey in Sahuayo that would provide comparable data on the percentage of adults who have migrated to the United States at least once.

ward economic impacts in my survey of household heads in the county of Arandas, conducted in 2003, were generally positive. Among the Arandenses who had ever migrated, 88 percent said emigration had a positive local economic impact, while 77 percent of nonmigrants said the same. The migrants (a term I use in the Mexican context to refer to anyone who has had migration experience) and nonmigrants interviewed were equally likely to report that migration had a negative impact on the community's customs and morals. They both disapproved of migration-induced cultural changes. Just as nonmigrants feared what they saw as the corrupting influence of American culture on their hometown, migrants feared its corrupting influence on their own children, when living both in the United States and in Mexico.[17]

Negative views of the cultural impacts of migration in the Los Altos region of Jalisco, where all three Jaliscan communities I discuss in this chapter are located, concur with national surveys that show that twice as many Mexicans say U.S. cultural influence is negative than say it is positive.[18] However, the level of nationalism directed against the United States is mitigated when Mexicans look northward for a model of modernity. The suspicions of Mexican elites are "often allied to a sneaking admiration" that has become more pronounced with the advent of the North American Free Trade Agreement (NAFTA) in 1994 and a generation of technocrats schooled in top U.S. universities.[19] Widespread ambivalence toward the effects of migration to the United States reflects ambivalence toward the northern neighbor in general. Cultural nationalists, who already feel beset by pervasive American cultural and economic influence, denigrate migrants. In a process of normative inversion, cultural nationalists flip the geopolitical hierarchy to assert Mexico's moral superiority over the United States. The drugs, criminality, and disease that North Americans often blame immigrants for importing to the United States are seen in Mexico as exports from the United States to their home country brought by emigrants. The dissimilation of migrants is viewed as a cultural threat particularly in the areas of religion, education, public comportment, and work.

Religion

The strongest sentiment against emigration has come from the Catholic Church, an influential voice in a country where more than 99 percent of the population identified as Catholic in 1900 and which remained 88 percent Catholic in 2000.[20] The Church initially opposed mass emigration, in large part because of fears that migrants would convert to Protestantism and then spread Protestantism to Mexico when they returned, but also because it saw migrants as a source of foreign cultural pollution and family disintegration.[21]

Fears that migrants are a Trojan horse for Protestant conversion in Mexico waned over the last century, even though Protestants increased from less than 0.4 percent of Mexico's population in 1900 to 7.6 percent in 2010. Few Mexicans converted to Protestantism in the historic heartland of Mexican emigration in central-west Mexico, which is the most Catholic part of the country. Protestantism in Mexico is strongest in the southeastern, indigenous states where foreign missionaries have been most active.[22] Studies have found that the few non-Catholics who live in rural, central-west Mexico often converted to other faiths while they were working in the United States.[23] However, according to a diocesan survey conducted in 1993 in the Los Altos region, less than 1 percent of return-migrants in the region had left Catholicism for another religion.

Nonetheless, migrant religiosity has declined. My survey of 860 adults in 2007 from the historic migrant-source community of Tlacuitapa, Jalisco, who were living either in Tlacuitapa or its major U.S. satellite destinations, in the San Francisco Bay Area and Oklahoma City, confirmed this decline. Seventeen percent of migrants reported that they did not attend church in the previous month, compared to only 8 percent of nonmigrants. After controlling for age, sex, education, wealth, and marital status in a multinomial logit regression, each additional year spent in the United States was associated with a 1 percent decrease in church attendance.[24]

In the much more heterogeneous religious environment of Tunkás, Yucatán, a new community of emigration, in which 23 percent of the population is Evangelical, more than 40 percent of Catholics and Evangelicals said they attended church less frequently after migrating.[25] In short, migrants appear to be becoming less religious by the conventional measure of church attendance, **but they** are not responsible for much of the growth of Protestantism in Mexico.

Contemporary policy of the Catholic Church in Mexico makes familiar claims about the negative effects of emigration on family life and the social order. Church officials lament the U.S. street fashions introduced by returning migrants and their U.S.-born children. Clergy in the diocese of San Juan de los Lagos also argue that marital separation creates mutual suspicions of infidelity and greater opportunities for bigamy and cohabitation. They say that when men emigrate, their children often become "virtual orphans" in the absence of male role models. The head of the diocese's migrant outreach program in the Los Altos region describes emigration as changing "values typical of our towns," values such as fidelity, solidarity, honor, and sacrifice for the common good. Despite these problems, internal diocesan documents say that "in general, family customs have not suffered significant changes" due to emigration. Similarly, while warning of "the scarce social control of a plural culture" in the United States, official diocesan policy states that cosmopolitan environments should not be "a source of division or conflict, but of mutual enrichment."[26]

In an effort to institutionalize its pastoral plan for migrants in the late 1990s, the diocese of San Juan produced a 119-page migration policy book for local priests. The book provides a sophisticated sociological understanding of the causes and effects of Mexico-U.S. migration and templates for celebrations of the return of the *hijos ausentes* (absent children). During these celebrations, the Church has conducted purification rituals in which migrants confess the sins they committed in the North. Leslie Reese describes a processional float during a patron saint fiesta depicting the depravity of the U.S. drug culture.[27]

In short, the Catholic Church stopped trying to dissuade emigration in the mid-twentieth century, as it realized that return-migrants were not conduits for mass conversion to Protestantism. Yet, clergy remain deeply concerned about the effects of emigration on family stability and conservative social values.

Education

Emigration presents a multifaceted challenge to public education in Mexico. Teachers often blame migration for elevating dropout rates. In a "culture of migration," children in general, and boys in particular, grow up expecting to migrate as a rite of passage into adulthood.[28] Of all the state employees and policymakers I have interviewed, teachers were the most fearful of the effects of migration on cultural change, as they feared that migrants would be a transmission belt for foreign influences undermining national homogeneity.[29]

Studies differ in their assessment of migration's effects on schooling. The quantitative evidence for the common perception that emigration induces children to drop out of school is mixed. Gordon Hanson's 2002 census-based study found that youth from migrant households completed more schooling than those from nonmigrant households, presumably because remittances financed schooling costs and supplemented household budgets, in lieu of child labor. The positive effect of migration was found to be particularly strong among girls whose parents were poorly educated. In turn, William Kandel's and Douglas Massey's and Kandel's and Grace Kao's surveys of youth in the state of Zacatecas, with the highest per capita emigration levels in Mexico, found that respondents' intent to one day migrate negatively correlated with their educational aspirations, but students from migrant households had higher levels of schooling than students from nonmigrant households. In the Oaxacan town of San Miguel Tlacotepec, my 2007 survey found no relationship between remittance income and educational attainment, but receipt of remittances correlated positively with high school attendance. Remittances help pay for the high costs of high school studies. However, David McKenzie and Hillel Rapoport's survey found, in 2006, that living in a migrant household lowered the odds that boys would complete junior high school by 22 percent, and lowered the odds that boys and girls would complete high school by 13 to 15 percent.[30] The diversity of findings suggests that additional longitudinal research is needed to disaggregate the effects of levels of emigration and remittances on educational outcomes at the elementary, junior high, and high school levels.

Return-migrant students and U.S.-born students whose parents take them to Mexico are an understudied challenge to the Mexican educational system. Based on surveys in the low-emigration state of Nuevo León and the high-emigration state of Zacatecas, Victor Zuñiga and Edmund Hamann estimated there were 200,000 students in Mexican elementary and junior high schools with experience in the United States. While these students represented only about 1 percent of the national elementary and junior high student population, they were concentrated in particular schools, due to the highly networked nature of Mexican emigration.[31] The teachers the authors interviewed who worked with children with U.S. experience expressed ambivalence about how to manage migrant students. Teachers wanted to be helpful, but found it difficult because of students' cultural differences.[32] Teachers whom I interviewed in Jalisco in 2003 and 2004 saw return-migrants as conduits for the infusion of U.S. music and the use of English and Spanglish (a mixture of English and Spanish) that they believed threatened Mexican music and "high" Spanish. Although the teachers considered proficiency in English to be an enviable accomplishment, they felt the loss of Spanish to be a moral failure and rejection of Mexican identity. Thus, the same linguistic shift from Spanish to English that is perceived as "assimilation" from a U.S. perspective is seen as national "dissimilation" and betrayal from the vantage point of Mexican educators.

Law and Order

Migrants returning to their homeland with new practices can threaten established mechanisms of social control. Officials in Mexico often blame migrants for the introduction of illegal drugs and the increased consumption of alcohol. According to a study conducted in 1997 by the government of Jalisco in rural communities with high levels of emigration, migrants were eleven times more likely than nonmigrants to have used drugs. In a similar vein, a report in 2003 on the condition of migrants, commissioned by the government of Jalisco, warned of "the presence of mental health problems and addictions originating in the loss or alteration of their original customs and the necessity to adopt new ways of life."[33] This is the country of origin perspective on what some call "segmented assimilation" in the United States, in which a large subset of immigrants assimilate into the "counterculture" of an "underclass" rather than into the national mainstream.[34]

The prevailing folk theory of why young male returnees are so disorderly in Mexico is that they "let loose" after being subjected to police constraints in the United States. Residents I interviewed often said that migrants behave worse in Mexico than they do in the United States. The director of the secondary school in Agua Negra, Jalisco, for example, explained that migrants suffer humiliations, privations, and discrimination in the United States. "Everything they repress there, they come here to vent." Male migrants also refer to the sense of freedom they feel in Mexico, owing largely to less state surveillance and regulation over their lives. In Mexico, they can drive without seatbelts, play their music at the volume they choose, and engage in informal commerce, all without fear of intervention from police and code enforcement. Mexicans who had lived in the United States illegally felt especially free upon their return. They complained of feeling "locked up" and fearful of the immigration authorities while in the United States.

Deported migrants create policing challenges, especially if they were associated with gangs in the United States. Criminal returnees learned new organizational models abroad. Nonetheless, while some Mexican migrant sending-communities have experienced significant problems with returned gang members, the police officers I interviewed said problems in their communities were limited to graffiti and noise, rather than violence.[35] In general, Mexico has not experienced the gang problems on the scale of El Salvador, described by José Miguel Cruz in his chapter in this volume. However, the rising number of deportations of gang members from the United States and the escalation of the drug wars in Mexico since 2006 may lead Mexico to replicate some of the Salvadoran experience even if the relatively stronger Mexican state is better able to restrain gangs.

Attitudes toward Work

Many scholars long assumed, and policymakers hoped, that return-migrants would "modernize" their home communities because of their exposure to the United States. Scholars also believed that migrants would return to Mexico as better workers.[36] Accordingly, in the context of work, cultural dissimilation has often been viewed as a positive source of change.

I found that perceptions of the impact of U.S. experience on returnees' work performance vary. While I know of no longitudinal studies that trace the impact of emigration on work habits, the views of Mexican employers and the rank-and-file are telling. Three quarters of household heads surveyed in Arandas and Agua Negra, Jalisco, in 2003, said that migrants returning to their hometowns from the United States did not work as hard as they did before they left. Only 14 percent said returnees worked harder. There was not a statistically significant difference between return-migrant and nonmigrant views. Clearly, returnees have higher expectations of pay and work conditions than nonmigrants. The migrants have what the labor economist Michael Piore calls a "dual frame of reference." Their assessment of their options in one labor market is based on their experience in another.[37] Even if most Arandenses are on the bottom of the U.S. labor market, earning dollars makes the work preferable to comparable work in Arandas.

Employers whom I interviewed said that returnees generally shun manual work, especially in agriculture. The employers described this as unprincipled laziness, rather than a rational decision by workers to avoid low-paying work in Mexico when better-paying work is available in the United States. At the same time, they also perceived workers who had labored many years in the United States as more disciplined and reliable than nonmigrants. The owner of several businesses, for example, praised the quality of his returnee employees: "They're people who come back accustomed to a schedule in which one has to earn his salary; . . . You don't have to spend half your time watching them or pressuring them. That is to say, they come back with a mentality that they will work eight hours, but they will be eight hours of real work—not simply time passed."

Other Mexican employers I interviewed believed returnees work harder to earn more money to meet consumer aspirations acquired in the United States. In Arandas, for example, the owner of a tequila distillery with 460 employees noted that not only had returnees at his factory "acquired culture" in the United States, which led them to be more responsible and to have a better understanding of the importance of punctuality and machine-work, but also that "they want to live more comfortably, and so they act more responsibly."

Most employers of agricultural workers, in contrast, saw little difference in the work ethic of nonmigrants and return-migrants they hired. However, one employer felt that the U.S. experience teaches Mexicans how to be better workers. He noted that when his day laborers do not come to work, he tells them, "Go to the United States, you bastards, so you'll know what it's like. There, if you're ten minutes late, you come on time the next day, and if not, you're fired!" In general, though, employers found the disciplining of the U.S. labor market useful for improving the quality of factory employees, not fieldworkers.

Mexicans thus differ in their views about the cultural price of economically driven migration. The Catholic clergy has lamented the effects of migration on family separation, secularization, and youth culture, while schoolteachers have blamed migration for encouraging students to abandon their studies, and police have blamed youth violence and disobedience on the U.S. influence. Farmers, in turn, generally believe returnees to be too lazy to work in the fields, but manufacturers, who offer higher wages, believe U.S. experiences make for more disciplined workers. Whether perceiving changes positively or negatively, most agree that migrants are becoming different from nonmigrants.

Politics

The transnational perspective has underscored how migrant activists and governments of migrant-sending countries are institutionalizing new forms of political ties that link migrants to their homelands.[38] These scholarly narratives emphasize laws, organizations, and discourses that enlarge a national community beyond its geographic borders. But they inadequately address how migrants become politically dissimilar from those they leave behind, and how they often distance themselves from home country politics.

As the Mexican political system became more competitive in the late 1980s, the main political parties began to perceive migrants as a potential base of support. Around the same time, the government perceived Mexicans in the United States as potential Washington lobbyists for pro-Mexico and pro-Mexican policies.

The contemporary period of cross-border political engagement began with the presidential campaign in Mexico in 1988, when the center-left candidate, Cuauhtémoc Cárdenas, campaigned among Mexicans in California and Illinois. He urged the migrants to influence the vote of their families back in Mexico.[39] After losing the election, he formed the Party of the Democratic Revolution (designated with the Spanish acronym *PRD*), which continued to press for migrants' political rights. Eight years later, the longstanding ruling Institutional Revolutionary Party (designated with the Spanish acronym *PRI*) amended the country's constitution to allow Mexicans to vote for president from outside their districts of residence.[40] The amendment, in principle, allowed Mexican citizens to vote from abroad. However, the initiative proved mainly symbolic, in that it did not include enabling legislation for the Federal Electoral Institute to organize elections outside the country. In July 1999 the opposition-controlled federal Chamber of Deputies passed the enabling legislation, but the senate, controlled by the ruling PRI, blocked the measure.[41] The PRI had merely wanted to incorporate emigrants symbolically, so as to subvert opposition party efforts to reach out to Mexicans abroad.

The electoral reform, meanwhile, inadvertently paved the way for the formation of a Mexican emigrant lobby in Mexico City. Various emigrant groups that began with a PRD base, but expanded to include activists from across the political spectrum, formed the Coalition for the Political Rights of Mexicans Abroad. The coalition successfully lobbied for a bill that enabled Mexicans to vote from abroad by absentee ballot in the presidential election in 2006.

Ironically, the migrant vote in 2006 proved inconsequential in the closest official election count in modern Mexican history. Three million out of the 10 million Mexicans in the United States were eligible to vote in the election. However, only 57,000 U.S.-resident Mexicans registered to vote, and less than 33,000 cast valid ballots.[42] The absence of Mexican voter-registration programs in the United States, difficulties in obtaining absentee ballots, the requirement to vote by certified mail weeks in advance of the election, and a new ban on Mexican presidential campaigning in the United States all contributed to the low turnout. A Pew Hispanic Survey conducted in 2006 found that 78 percent of Mexicans in the United States knew that Mexicans could vote from abroad, but 55 percent did not know there would be elections that year.[43] Policymakers from the PRI and their ruling National Action Party (designated with the Spanish acronym PAN) symbolically supported migrant political participation, while limiting it in practice, because they feared voters abroad might contribute to a PRD victory. Against this backdrop, migrant activists reacted angrily. They sensed that the Mexican government was encouraging political apathy in Mexican partisan politics, even as it encouraged the formation of a Mexican lobby in Washington and migrant remittances to Mexico.

Migrant disaffection with Mexican politics contributed to the low voter turnout. According to the same Pew Hispanic Center survey, only 13 percent of Mexican-born adults in the United States viewed Mexican political institutions favorably. Other surveys have found that interest in Mexican politics among Mexican-born U.S. residents declined over time and across generations, indicative of political dissimilation. Nonetheless, a small core of committed migrant activists increased their cross-border political engagement over the years (see the chapter by Alejandro Portes, in this volume).[44]

Meanwhile, the Mexican government began to court emigrants in the United States to lobby for legislation it coveted and against legislation it opposed, although it met with little success. Its strategy was based on emigrants' maintaining enough interest in Mexico to not entirely dissimilate from their homeland, while assimilating sufficiently into the United States to effectively make their political demands. Lobbying is much more effective when migrants become naturalized U.S. citizens, master English, and learn U.S. tactics for exerting political influence through writing letters, signing petitions, making political contributions, and meeting with politicians. Most Mexicans in the United States lacked the combination of interest, legal standing, and economic resources necessary to lobby effectively on behalf of the Mexican government. When Mexicans have pushed for immigration reform, either through conventional lobbying in Washington or through massive street protests, they have done so because they perceived it in their self-interest, not because they acted at the behest of the Mexican government.

The Mexican government first cultivated a lobby in the United States in the early 1990s, to press Congress to pass NAFTA. The measure passed, but without Mexican lobbyists' playing a significant role. Meanwhile, in 1994, Mexican consulates and Mexican American political organizations failed in their efforts to defeat Proposition 187 in California. The proposition restricted unauthorized immigrants, most of whom were Mexican, from a wide range of public services. A federal judge—not Mexican organizations, institutions, and immigrants—ultimately overturned the legislation.[45]

The Mexican congress, in turn, passed a dual nationality law that took effect in 1998, in large part to encourage Mexican nationals to become U.S. citizens, so that they could vote against such measures as

Proposition 187 and against politicians who supported anti-immigrant policies. The dual nationality law applies to Mexicans who take out foreign citizenship. While dual nationals may not vote or run for certain offices in Mexican elections, they may, by law, buy land in their name along Mexico's coasts and borders that foreigners may not. Yet, indicative of political dissimilation transpiring among Mexican migrants in the United States, during the first five years the law was in effect, only 67,000 Mexican-origin foreign citizens applied for dual nationality rights.[46]

Efforts by Mexican political parties and the Mexican government to court emigrants for political purposes have met with little success because most of those who have settled in the United States have distanced themselves from Mexican politics. There is one major exception to migrants' distancing from the Mexican government. It is born of migrants' personal interests. Over 7 million Mexicans in the United States obtained official Mexican *matrícula consular* identification cards between 2000 and mid-2008. Mexicans who entered the United States illegally could not obtain U.S. identification documents, other than driver's licenses in some states. For them, the newly offered cards are especially attractive. The cards may be used for routine transactions that ultimately have assimilatory consequences, such as for enrolling children in U.S. schools, but also for reinforcing ties to Mexico, such as in facilitating the opening of bank accounts through which remittances can be sent to nonmigrant family members.

It is noteworthy that migrant politics among Mexicans in the United States differs from that among Turks in Europe, described by Riva Kastoryano in her chapter in this volume. Turkish migrants are much more engaged in homeland politics. There are at least two reasons for the difference between the two migrant groups. First, almost all Mexican emigrants live in the United States, which is much more politically welcoming of immigrants and their children than most European countries. The United States has low barriers to naturalization and an extremely strong version of jus soli that grants citizenship even to the children of unauthorized immigrants who are born on U.S. soil. Easy political assimilation into the destination country encourages dissimilation from the country of origin. Second, contemporary Mexican migrants come from a country with far less ethnic politicization than Turkey, which faces armed movements from Kurds demanding regional autonomy and even independence. Violent separatist politics thrive on foreign bases of support and refuge. Notwithstanding the ethnic heterogeneity of Mexico, the only contemporary armed, quasiseparatist group is the Zapatista guerrillas, who since 1994 have been confined to a small sliver of jungle in the southern state of Chiapas, a state with little emigration.

Remittances and Hometown Associations

The remittances that Mexicans in the United States send to family they left behind reflect the strength of ties retained across borders. Nationwide, 18 percent of adult Mexicans receive remittances, an average of $350 monthly.[47] Remittances, which have become the country's second largest source of foreign exchange (after petroleum), totaled $26 billion in 2007.[48] Because of the macro importance of remittances, the Mexican government has sponsored several initiatives to lower transaction costs, to channel remittances to community projects, to undertake job-creating investments, and to discourage emigrants' dissimilation.

What impact have remittances had? Scholars disagree. Most Mexican migrants are low-skilled, the type who Portes argues in his chapter in this volume fuel minimal economic development in their homeland. Some scholars also argue that remittances exacerbate income inequality and, in raising consumer expectations beyond the level obtainable with local jobs, fuel further emigration. Other researchers, in contrast, point to ways that remittances have stimulated economic development. In certain settings, remittances supplement the incomes of microentrepreneurs. Furthermore, when cash transfers are spent on household consumption, they may have multiplier effects, creating jobs for workers who produce the goods and services that remittance-receiving households consume.

Survey data from a range of settings reveal that most remittances to Mexico are used for household expenditures, land purchases, and home construction, not for investments that generate jobs and capital accumulation. Nonetheless, economists have estimated that remittances increase Mexican GDP by $2.69 for every $1 sent to urban households, and by $3.17 for every $1 sent to rural households. Remittances that are spent in Mexico also generate fiscal revenues through the value-added tax at the federal level and through property taxes at the county level.[49] And they provide foreign exchange that stabilizes the peso and balances the government's current accounts.[50]

Viewing remittances as a positive economic asset, the Mexican government has actively encouraged remittance-sending. To minimize the costs of international transfers, in the late 1990s the Mexican government began to encourage use of automatic teller machines in Mexico linked to U.S. bank accounts. Mexican consulates in the United States compile weekly lists of the most affordable wire transfer companies and complain vociferously about the high fees some companies charge. The cheaper the transfer costs, the more recipients receive of every dollar remitted from abroad. However, the Mexican government has not effectively used the banking system to capture remittances for the kind of investment projects that the Moroccan government has, described by Natasha Iskander in her chapter in this volume. Remittances are not deposited in Mexico for savings or investment on a large scale. Currently, most banks in the country are subsidiaries of U.S. and Spanish banks, committed first and foremost to their foreign stockholders, not to Mexican development, and over the years most migrants transferred funds to their families in Mexico either through postal-system money orders or private money-transfer companies, such as Western Union, if not on home visits. In the past, when Mexican banks were involved in remittance transfers, they alienated migrants. During the Bracero temporary worker program which operated between 1942 and 1964, U.S. employers withheld ten percent of workers' wages, which were channeled through Mexican banks. Although the banks were charged with returning the money to migrants when they finished their work stints in the United States, many migrants never received their earnings. Legal and political battles over their missing funds continue to the present day. Memories of the experience during the Bracero program may disincline contemporary migrants from using banks to transfer funds to the extent they otherwise might.

The Mexican government has also promoted migrant hometown associations (HTAS) to channel remittances for collective projects, such as for the digging of wells and the paving of roads. The number of Mexican HTAS has risen rapidly from a handful in the 1970s to an estimated 2000 by 2004. And since 2002, municipal, state, and federal levels of government have contributed matching funds for infrastructural improvement projects that HTAS sponsor, through the Three for One (matching fund) program. In 2008, HTAS contributed $33 million, which generated a total investment of $133 million.[51]

Collective remittances are but one way that HTAs reinforce home-land community ties. Hometown associations often sponsor religious processions involving return-migrants during annual patron saints' day festivities. These public events are venues in which migrants, the Church, and the state together display their idea of a proper moral order. One of the main ways that HTAs raise money is through a beauty pageant in which neatly coiffed young migrant and U.S.-born women compete to display their conservative cultural traditions and ties to Mexico. The contestants embody the claim that migrants are still good moral members of the home community, despite their absence.

Hometown association projects enhance migrant stature, by demon-strating not only that they have money, but that they use it for the good of the community and that they remain committed to community val-ues.[52] Concomitantly, though, HTA projects highlight how migrants have changed. They often favor different projects than nonmigrants. In this vein, Robert Smith describes in his study of the Mexican town of Ticuani, Puebla, how residents eager to develop their community ar-gued that HTA money should be raised to pave the town's streets for the purpose economic development, while migrants in New York sought to keep the more rustic cobblestones that made the town a charming place for a holiday visit.[53] The HTA-sponsored pageants and philan-thropic activities contribute to the perception of timeless communities that have not changed or that have only changed in ways migrants initiated, when in fact the communities are transforming independently of migration to the United States. Internal migration within Mexico, higher levels of education, improved communications, and a better transportation infrastructure have also integrated once-remote areas into a broader economy and circulation of ideas.

As temporary return migration has become more difficult, because of the U.S. crackdown on illegal border crossings, many HTA members are re-creating patron saint fiestas where they have settled in the United States. Visiting hometown priests bring replicas of the hometown pa-tron saints to the U.S. festivities. In such instances, even HTAs subtly reflect Mexican dissimilation, and a shift in collective homeland-linked activities to the United States.

From an economic standpoint, collective remittances are modest, and are mostly felt in very small towns and villages with high rates of emigration. In urban areas, municipalities have development budgets much larger than funds HTAS remit. Nonetheless, collective remittances strengthen hometown ties in ways that temper dissimilation and keep massive private transfers flowing.

STUDIES OF IMMIGRANT assimilation focus on intermarriage, educational mobility, English language proficiency, ethnic identity, and involvement in mainstream American life. They point to variation in the immigrant experiences of different nationalities in the United States. Scholars of migrant transnationalism, in contrast, point to cross-border ties at the individual, community, and institutional levels. They address common practices in a single field of social action and a single imagined community that extends across national territorial boundaries.

Left largely unaddressed in transnational as well as assimilation-centered studies, however, are ways that migrants have come to differ socially, economically, culturally, and politically from the people they leave behind. The concept of dissimilation offers an analytic frame to capture these changes. It points to how migrants change even when they maintain homeland ties and even when they assimilate in their new land.

Notes

1 Manuel Gamio, *Mexican Immigration to the United States* (Chicago: University of Chicago Press, 1930); Paul S. Taylor, *A Spanish-Mexican Peasant Community: Arandas in Jalisco, Mexico* (Berkeley: University of California Press, 1933); Wayne A. Cornelius, *Mexican Migration to the United States: The View from Rural Sending Communities* (Cambridge, MA: Migration and Development Study Group, Center for International Studies, MIT, 1976); Douglas S. Massey, Rafael Alarcón, Jorge Durand, and Humberto González, *Return to Aztlan: The Social Process of International Migration from Western Mexico* (Berkeley: University of California Press, 1987).

2 For a review of these debates, see Roger Waldinger and David FitzGerald, "Transnationalism in Question," *American Journal of Sociology* 109 (2004): 1177–95; and Nina Schiller and Peggy Levitt, "Haven't We Heard This Somewhere Before? A Substantive View of Transnational Migration Studies by Way of a Reply to Waldinger and Fitzgerald" (working paper, Center for Migration and Development, Princeton University, New Jersey, 2006).

3 Richard Alba and Victor Nee, *Remaking the American Mainstream: Assimilation and Contemporary Immigration* (Cambridge, MA: Harvard University

Press, 2003); Tomás R. Jiménez, *Replenished Ethnicity: Mexican Americans, Immigration, and Identity* (Berkeley: University of California Press, 2010).

4 Tomás Jiménez and David FitzGerald, "Mexican Assimilation: A Temporal and Spatial Reorientation," *Du Bois Review*, 4, no. 2 (2007): 337–54.

5 Herbert Gans, "Second-Generation Decline: Scenarios for the Economic and Ethnic Futures of the Post-1965 American Immigrants," *Ethnic and Racial Studies* 15, no. 2 (1992): 173–92.

6 David FitzGerald, *A Nation of Emigrants: How Mexico Manages Its Migration* (Berkeley: University of California Press, 2009), chapter 5; Rafael Alarcón, "Nortenización: Self-Perpetuating Migration from a Mexican Town," in *U.S.-Mexico Relations: Labor Market Interdependence*, ed. Jorge A. Bustamante, Clark W. Reynolds, and Raúl A. Hinojosa Ojeda (Stanford, CA: Stanford University Press, 1992), 302–18.

7 Milton M. Gordon, *Assimilation in American Life* (New York: Oxford University Press, 1964).

8 David FitzGerald, *Negotiating Extra-Territorial Citizenship: Mexican Migration and the Transnational Politics of Community* (La Jolla: Center for Comparative Immigration Studies, University of California, San Diego, 2000).

9 Samuel P. Huntington, *Who Are We? The Challenges to America's Identity* (New York: Simon and Schuster, 2004).

10 Jeffrey Passel, D'Vera Cohn, and Ana González-Barrera, "Net Migration from Mexico Falls to Zero and Perhaps Less" (Washington, DC: Pew Hispanic Center, 2012); Instituto Federal Electoral, www.ife.gob.mx, 2000; Consejo Nacional de Población, www.conapo.gob.mx, 2009.

11 For a broad overview of the history of Mexican migration, see Mark Overmyer-Velázquez, ed., *Beyond the Border: The History of Mexico-US Migration* (Oxford: Oxford University Press, 2011); and Douglas S. Massey, Jorge Durand, and Nolan J. Malone, *Beyond Smoke and Mirrors: Mexican Immigration in an Era of Economic Integration* (New York: Russell Sage Foundation, 2002).

12 John Zogby and Luis Rubio, *How We See Each Other: The Cidac-Zogby International Survey of Attitudes in Mexico and the United States of America* (Utica, NY, and Mexico City: Zogby International, 2006).

13 Massey, Durand, and Malone, *Beyond Smoke and Mirrors*, 132.

14 Jeffrey Passel and D'Vera Cohn, *Mexican Immigrants: How Many Come? How Many Leave?* (Washington, DC: Pew Hispanic Center, 2009).

15 Passel, Cohn, and González-Barrera. "Net Migration from Mexico Falls to Zero and Perhaps Less."

16 Mexican emigration has historically been concentrated in such central western states as Jalisco and Michoacán. Levels remain highest in that region, even as emigration has spread to such southern states as Oaxaca, and most recently to the Yucatán. I focus in this chapter mainly on the state of Jalisco, whose

long history of migration to the United States allows for a historicized understanding of how Mexican institutions have attempted to manage migration over the last century. I draw on interviews I conducted with ordinary Mexicans who never migrated and return-migrants, as well as with employers, clergy, and other community leaders.

17 See Leslie Reese, "Morality and Identity in Mexican Immigrant Parents' Visions of the Future," *Journal of Ethnic and Migration Studies* 27, no. 3 (2001): 455–72.

18 Zogby and Rubio, *How We See Each Other*.

19 Alan Knight, "The Peculiarities of Mexican History: Mexico Compared to Latin America, 1821–1992," *Journal of Latin American Studies* 24 (1992): 128.

20 Instituto Nacional de Estadística, Geografía e Informática (INEGI). *La diversidad religiosa en México* (Aguascalientes, Mexico: INEGI, 2005).

21 FitzGerald, *A Nation of Emigrants*, chapter 3.

22 With the exception of the border state of Baja California, all ten states in which Protestants comprise at least 10 percent of the population are in Mexico's southeast. Chiapas was 21.9 percent Protestant in 2000, Jalisco only 2.9 percent Protestant. See J. W. Dow, "The Expansion of Protestantism in México: An Anthropological View," *Anthropological Quarterly* 78 (2005): 827–51.

23 Miguel J. Hernández Madrid, "Iglesias Sin Fronteras. Migrantes y Conversos Religiosos: Cambios de Identidad Cultural en el Noroeste de Michoacán," in *Fronteras Fragmentadas*, ed. Gail Mummert (Zamora, Mexico: El Colegio de Michoacán, 1999), 393–404.

24 Wayne A. Cornelius, David FitzGerald, and Scott Borger, *Four Generations of Norteños: New Research from the Cradle of Mexican Migration* (La Jolla: Center for Comparative Immigration Studies, University of California, San Diego, 2009), 169–70.

25 Wayne A. Cornelius, David FitzGerald, and Pedro Lewin Fischer, *Mayan Journeys: The New Migration from Yucatán to the United States* (La Jolla: Center for Comparative Immigration Studies, University of California, San Diego, 2007).

26 "Archivo de la Parroquia de San Juan de los Lagos," *Boletín de Pastoral* 53 (1986).

27 Víctor M. Espinosa, "El día del emigrante y el retorno del purgatorio: Iglesia, migración a los Estados Unidos y cambio sociocultural en un pueblo de Los Altos de Jalisco," *Estudios Sociológicos* 17 (1999): 375–418; Reese, "Morality and Identity in Mexican Immigrant Parents' Visions of the Future," 464.

28 Wayne A. Cornelius, David FitzGerald, Jorge Hernández Díaz, and Scott Borger. *Migration from the Mexican Mixteca* (La Jolla: Center for Comparative Immigration Studies, University of California, San Diego, 2009), chapter 5.

29 See Eugen Weber, *Peasants into Frenchmen: The Modernization of Rural France, 1870–1914* (Stanford, CA: Stanford University Press, 1976).

30 Gordon Hanson and Christopher Woodruff, "Emigration and Educational At-
    tainment in Mexico" (University of California and NBER, San Diego, 2003);
    William Kandel and Grace Kao, "The Impact of Temporary Labor Migration
    on Mexican Children's Educational Aspirations and Performance," *Interna-
    tional Migration Review* 35, no. 4 (2001): 1205–31; William Kandel and Doug-
    las S. Massey, "The Culture of Mexican Migration: A Theoretical and
    Empirical Analysis," *Social Forces* 80, no. 3 (2002): 981–1004; David John
    McKenzie and Hillel Rapoport, "Can Migration Reduce Educational Attain-
    ment? Evidence from Mexico" (World Bank Policy Research Working Paper
    3952, Washington, DC, 2006); Cornelius, FitzGerald, Hernández Díaz, and
    Borger, *Migration from the Mexican Mixteca*, chapter 5.

31 Victor Zuñiga and Edmund T. Hamann, "Sojourners in Mexico with US
    School Experience: A New Taxonomy for Transnational Students," *Compara-
    tive Education Review* 53, no. 3 (2009).

32 Ibid., 347.

33 Archivo de la Oficina de Atención a Jaliscienses en el Extranjero (2003).

34 Alejandro Portes and Rubén G. Rumbaut, *Legacies: The Story of the Immi-
    grant Second Generation* (Berkeley: University of California Press, 2001), chap-
    ter 3.

35 Robert C. Smith, *Mexican New York: The Transnational Lives of New Immi-
    grants* (Berkeley: University of California Press, 2006).

36 Gamio, *Mexican Immigration to the United States*.

37 Michael J. Piore, *Birds of Passage: Migrant Labor and Industrial Societies*
    (Cambridge: Cambridge University Press, 1979).

38 Eva Ostergaard-Nielsen, *International Migration and Sending Countries: Per-
    ception, Policies and Transnational Relations* (London: Palgrave, 2003).

39 David FitzGerald, "'For 118 Million Mexicans': Emigrants and Chicanos in
    Mexican Politics," in *Dilemmas of Political Change in Mexico*, ed. Kevin J.
    Middlebrook (London: Institute of Latin American Studies, University of
    London, 2004), 523–48.

40 Michael P. Smith and Matt Bakker, *Citizenship across Borders: The Political
    Transnationalism of El Migrante* (Ithaca, NY: Cornell University Press, 2008).

41 FitzGerald, "For 118 Million Mexicans."

42 "Informe final sobre el voto de los mexicanos residentes en el extranjero, di-
    ciembre de 2006," Instituto Federal Electoral, accessed August 21, 2012, http://
    www.ife.org.mx/documentos/votoextranjero/libro_blanco/index.htm.

43 Ibid.; Roberto Suro and Gabriel Escobar, *Survey of Mexicans Living in the U.S.
    on Absentee Voting in Mexican Elections* (Washington, DC: Pew Hispanic
    Center, 2006).

44 See also Roger Waldinger, "Between 'Here' and 'There': Immigrant Cross-
    Border Activities and Loyalties," *International Migration Review* 42, no. 3
    (2008).

45 De la Garza, "Foreign Policy Comes Home," 83.

46 David FitzGerald, "Nationality and Migration in Modern Mexico," *Journal of Ethnic and Migration Studies* 31, no. 1 (2005): 171–91.

47 In the state of Zacatecas, with the highest per capita emigration level in Mexico, a quarter of households received remittances. By way of comparison, 14 percent of Ecuadorian adults and 28 percent of Salvadoran adults receive remittances. Roberto Suro, *Remittance Senders and Receivers: Tracking the Transnational Channels* (Washington, DC: Pew Hispanic Center, 2003).

48 With the U.S. economic recession, and the consequent drop in Mexican immigrant earnings, the value of remittances declined in 2008. By 2012, remittances had almost returned to their 2007 levels.

49 Irma Adelman and J. Edward Taylor, "Is Structural Adjustment with a Human Face Possible? The Case of Mexico," *Journal of Development Studies* 26, no. 3 (1990): 387–407.

50 For a review of these debates, see Douglas S. Massey, Joaquin Arango, Graeme Hugo, Ali Kouaouci, Adela Pellegrino, and J. Edward Taylor, *Worlds in Motion: Understanding International Migration at the End of the Millennium* (Oxford: Clarendon, 1998), 222–43; and International Bank for Reconstruction and Development, *Global Economic Prospects: Overview and Global Outlook* (Washington, DC.: World Bank, 2006).

51 David FitzGerald, "Colonies of the Little Motherland: Membership, Space, and Time in Mexican Migrant Hometown Associations," *Comparative Studies in Society and History* 50, no. 1 (2008): 145–69.

52 Hometown associations are found in international and domestic migration contexts around the world, but as the contribution by Portes in this volume shows, they are unusually strong in the Mexican case. Mexican hometown associations have been promoted "from above" by the Catholic Church and the Mexican government, and they have also grown "from below," due to the highly networked nature of Mexican migration to the United States in which streams of people from the same Mexican towns and villages live abroad, in the same neighborhoods. See FitzGerald, "Colonies of the Little Motherland"; and FitzGerald, *Negotiating Extra-Territorial Citizenship*.

53 Smith, *Mexican New York*.

7

"Turks Abroad" Redefine Turkish Nationalism

RIVA KASTORYANO

Transnational involvements have placed migrants at the core of economic developments, political democratization, and sociocultural transformations in both home and host countries.[1] Through their political, social, and economic activism beyond borders, migrants have become the driving force behind changes in the two sets of countries. Turkish migrants to Europe, on whom this chapter focuses, have consolidated their transstate and transnational activities via economic and political networks that span European countries and Turkey. They diffuse new ideas, introduce new discourses, and initiate new forms of actions. For Turkey, they constitute a new category, referred to as "Turks abroad." A report published by the Research Center on Turkey, in Essen, Germany, concludes with the statement, "Turks living in European Union member states have the responsibility of making a bridge between the European Union and Turkey in civil, economic and political affairs."[2]

Obviously, transnationalism is not new. Migrants have always lived in more than one setting, for one or two generations at least, maintaining ties with a real or "imagined community" that the home country may become. Migrants who expatriate for economic reasons have almost always considered their departure temporary and have maintained ties with their home country. What is new in transnationalism today is its organizational dimension, rooted in the development of networks and the construction of communities beyond borders, and its institutionalization, which requires coordination based on common objective or subjective references and interests.[3] Today, transnationalism is linked to globalization and the "economic uncertainty that facilitates the construction of social relations that transcend national borders."[4] Alejandro Portes calls the phenomenon "'globalization from below' through which poor people seek to mitigate the growing inequalities and lack of opportunity foisted on them by capitalist-driven 'globalization from above.'"[5]

Increased mobility and communication, including frequent trips back and forth between Turkey and Europe, have contributed to the intensification of transnational relations and the elaboration of cross-border networks. Not only do these networks promote cultural, social, political, and even ideological transfers, but they also channel activities that connect Turkey to host countries and give migrants "the illusion of the non permanence" of their exile, all the more so since Turkey is a candidate for European Union (EU) membership.[6] Turkish migrants live, as the Turkish state lives, with the expectation that Turkey will one day become part of the European Union. They therefore feel at home in Europe and, when living in Turkey, they feel as if they were in a European country.

Studies on the emergence of transnational communities emphasize postcolonial migration and the economic relationships individuals maintain with their countries of origin. Transnational actors thus operate in two countries.[7] In the context of the EU, a "transnational community" transcends the borders of the member states, connecting each member state, as well as Europe as a whole, to the home country. Thus, a number of transnational networks that immigrants have formed claim recognition of a collective identity before the host state as well as European institutions, thereby linking the home country at once to the host country and to a broader European space.

The European Union has thus spawned a new type of transnational community. By promoting the free circulation of individuals (and goods) and by encouraging economic activities and political participation across borders, it has led to the creation of interest groups who try to establish their independence vis-à-vis the state, placing their action directly on the European level and defining their activities as transnational.[8] The supranational logic of European institutions produces a European civil society in which transnational networks compete and turn Europe into a "communicational space," to use Jürgen Habermas's phrase. Information and media exchange networks, institutional networks and networks of solidarity and interests—whether presented as economic, political, cultural, or identity-based—constitute the fabric of European political construction. Encouraged by supranational institutions, the actors involved in setting up such networks try to act directly through the European Commission, in Brussels, thereby bypassing nation-states. Thus, a new mode of political participation has emerged, brought about by a space open to demand-making rooted in citizen and resident interests and identities autonomous of the territorially defined state systems. By the same token, transnational activity bolsters the demands of migrants in European countries for equal rights, demands to combat racism and exclusion at the European level.[9] Transnationalism becomes a means to circumvent the homogenizing effects of nation-states. Through greater interaction among actors from different traditions, transnational activities lead to political socialization and training in a new political culture that can truly be called European.

Immigrant associations can be a refuge, sometimes even a sanctuary, where culture, religion, ethnicity, and nation (home) are interpreted, materialized, and asserted in the host country. Such organizations are created by local and national authorities in the host countries and to some extent by European supranational institutions, such as the European Parliament. Adopting the democratic norms of the host societies and those norms diffused by European human rights institutions, these organizations have become a place where identities and interests are expressed and actions are undertaken to achieve representation in the host countries and then transferred for recognition and legitimacy in home countries. From this perspective, the process of transnationalization does not correspond to "globalization from below" as argued by Portes; the actions of organizations, grounded in Europeanization stimulated "from above," affect Turkey. The political activity of Turks abroad, their mobilization and their demand for representation before host states, plays an important role in the recognition of minority identities repressed by the ideology of a unified, homogeneous Turkish state, and challenge the official understanding of Turkish nationalism. In response, the Turkish state has acted as a transnational actor, extending its influence beyond its national borders.

Turks Abroad and the Formation of a Transnational Community

More than 4 million Turkish migrants currently live in Europe. They migrated in large numbers in the 1960s and 1970s, mainly for economic reasons, following agreements between Turkey and European countries, especially Germany. In moving to a variety of West European countries, they differ from postcolonial migrants. In contrast to North African migrants who settled in France, and South Asian Indians who settled in Great Britain, Turkish immigrants, with historical indifference to Europe, settled in all European countries, though mainly in Germany.[10] The development of commercial, cultural, and political networks has introduced Turkey into Europe, subtly outlining the contours of a transnational community.

As a result of political liberalism that privileges ethnic pluralism, cultural activities are encouraged through migrant associations, wherein identities are organized and redefined. Multiculturalism and "identity politics" in Western democracies, since the 1980s, have led migrants to construct communities to claim cultural recognition and political representation within state institutions. When France authorized immigrants to create their own voluntary associations in the name of the "right to be different," these organizations were defined officially as "the expression of national, cultural, and social solidarities and the instrument of their improvement. In that capacity, they constitute a means of breaking the isolation transplanted persons may suffer, of renewing the bonds with the homeland, and of reappropriating a cultural identity."[11] The host country thereby provides legal and political support for their action, which, by definition, leads to political participation in both countries, transplanting political norms and values from one culture to the other.

The creation of associations initially draws boundaries among immigrants that are national. Within national boundaries the full diversity of complex societies appears: social diversity by class, sex, and age as well as cultural diversity, which sometimes is linguistic, such as Turkish or Kurdish, and sometimes ethnic, and often regional. It is as if the anthropological diversity that had been eclipsed by the concern for cultural homogeneity in the native nation-state reemerged, "liberated" in the country of emigration, where each specific feature constitutes an element of distinction. In addition, ideological divisions affecting certain Islamic religious associations have also come into play, along with positions for or against the government in power in the homeland and positions on policies in the country where migrants settled.

The associations have spawned a fragmentation of identity and new allegiances. Identity politics in democratic host countries has brought a cultural heterogeneity to the surface that was present in Turkey but repressed in public life, a heterogeneity based on regional, linguistic, ethnic, and even religious (denominational) diversity. The demand for recognition of these identity fragments brings out differences in the public sphere. Each identity is a differentiating factor from which new cleavages emerge among migrants from Turkey who settled in different European countries. It is within this division that ethnicity is invented and redefined, by way of defining oneself as Turk or Kurd, Sunni or Alevî, or as originally from western or eastern Turkey. As for the Kurds, they pride themselves on their ethnic identity, which has persisted despite the Turkish Republic's assimilationist policy.

Certain ethnic, nationalist movements that developed in Europe have formulated demands that have not only grown out of the immigrant situation but have also been induced by a status of double minority, both in immigrants' homeland and Europe, and they assert an identity that is regional, linguistic, ethnic, and political in their home country as well as in Europe. This is true for the Kurds and the Alevî community, a branch of Islam banned from the public sphere in Turkey and at odds with the official Sunni majority there. The same is also true for Turkish Islamic associations that were banned in secular Turkey but found a democratic terrain in Europe from which to oppose the state in Turkey. Some imams were sent to Germany and France on official missions, and once establishing themselves in Europe, they joined, with a greater power of conviction and ability to mobilize than in Turkey, brotherhoods that were illegal in Turkey but active in Europe.

The actions of these groups were oriented toward the Turkish Republic. Founded by Kemal Atatürk in 1923, the republic was built on a secular, centralized, and indivisible ideology, in place of the Muslim Ottoman Empire. The new urban and Westernized political elite, inspired by the Jacobin ideal of the French, imposed a model of society and politics in which ethnic, regional, cultural, linguistic, and denominational differences were repressed in the name of national unity. The republic also declared itself *laik* (secular) by removing Islam, the official religion of the Ottoman Empire, from state and political activity, as in France. But Turkey represents an interesting path to national unification, focusing at once on Islam and the secularization of Islam. Secularism has led, however, to fusing nationality and religion into a Turkish and Muslim identity, a way of asserting national identity as a basis for nationalism.

The way the identities of Turks abroad and migrant political participation are organized and mobilized reflect multiple belongings, both as migrants and in Turkey. The constituent elements of the transnational community's identity do not necessarily correspond to the "official" identity of Turkey. They often involve "reappropriating" an identity during migration that transcends the territorial borders between Turkey and Europe. Identity formation has brought about new "transnational actors" who have either personally taken on the role or been assigned the task of linking Turkey and Europe.

The new political actors emerging from migration have reorganized their interests and identities, be they social, cultural, ethnic, or political, around associations typically supported by their countries of residence in the name of a democracy increasingly conscientious of recognizing difference. Some of the associations have replaced left- and right-wing military and revolutionary, religious and ethnic, organizations that prevailed in Turkey at the time of the massive migration in the 1970s, associations brought by migrants to Europe. They were originally protest movements against the Turkish government, against the conception of the regime, its understanding of the state and the nation, and its attitude toward ethnic and linguistic diversity and religion. In Europe, these associations, financed by individuals, political opposition parties in Turkey, and international organizations, found a space in which they could take action and express their beliefs in a manner not possible in Turkey.

Other associations have arisen, often with the assistance of host-country authorities, that aim to "integrate" immigrants. Turkey looks favorably on their activities and regards their representatives as the ideal interlocutors between the two countries. Yet other associations have sought to combine the two aspects: militant action *against* the Turkish government and its policies and militant action *for* the integration of Turkish immigrants in the host country. However, irrespective of whether the organizations emanate from political groups that were active in Turkey, from a transformation of workers' movements in Turkey or in Europe, or from host country initiatives, since the 1980s the leadership discourse has placed particular emphasis on culture and identity, national, religious, ethnic, linguistic, regional, or political identity.

The expression of ethnic, religious, and linguistic diversity among Turkish immigrants does not call into question the structure of the Turkish transnational community. On the contrary, the transnational community is characterized by heterogeneity, with conflicts among the networks expressing the hermeticism of the transnational community, not its disintegration. Each division or cleavage contributes to the formation of a "community" that can be described as "segmented," that is, "conflictual," and yet "transnational." Paradoxically, conflicting relationships and internal rivalries reinforce interwoven bonds of solidarity and stimulate identification with the "transnational community" thus created. Despite efforts to distance themselves from one another and their activities that facilitate the "integration" of Turkish families in French or German society, the links between the organizations and their representatives in Turkey establish a relationship among politically active migrants that is determined by their membership in associations, but with one common reference—Turkey—be it geographic, social, political, or culturally defined. This common denominator leads to the "invention" of an ethnicity on which the transnational community is built. It increases the influence of the constituent migrant identities, all the better to influence Turkish political life in a manner redefining the nature of Turkey's political community. Actions targeting Turkey draw the boundaries of a boundaryless Turkish transnational community.

In the European Union, Turkish organizational networks cover Europe. Their goals and activities are closely related to the project of the European Parliament, which between 1986 and 2001 made funds available to immigrant organizations so that they could coordinate their activities. At the time, the "Migrants' Forum" constituted a new transnational structure. Although it owes its origin to the European Union's budget policy, it aimed to become "a place where third country nationals, i.e., migrant populations from countries that are not members of the European Community but established in Europe, can express themselves and across which they can both announce their claims and disseminate information from European authorities."[12] Affiliated associations receive the most support from European host-country welfare states, and their leaders promote equal rights, human rights, and universality in their discourse, and consider transnational mobilization an effective way to fight racism and xenophobia.

Since the creation of the Migrants' Forum, Turkish associations have been the most active, for two reasons.[13] First, Turkish immigrants are spread throughout Europe. Since the 1970s, they have settled in all European countries, with new waves of arrivals nourishing old communities. Some have become citizens of their host country, whereas others are residents who either claim rights to permanent settlement or seek to fight expulsion. Second, Turkish activists are exceptionally mobilized political actors, with regard to Turkey within the framework of voluntary associations in the countries where they settled. Their associations represent Turkish migration at the local, national, and transnational, including European, levels. Public authorities in the host countries typically recognize their activity. The quest for representation has led association leaders to organize into federations of associations that incorporate all ethnic, regional, religious, linguistic, and ideological divisions. At stake is also the representation of Turkey before the European Commission. The organizations promote or obstruct Turkish membership in the European Union, by shaping European public opinion toward Turkey and by urging Turkey to enact the democratic reforms European Union membership requires.

The Migrants' Forum encourages the formation of "national support groups" and "regional support groups," to which "stateless peoples" should be added.[14] It is within this framework that the Kurds—a regional group recognized as stateless—find institutional legitimacy in Europe. Kurds, who are identified only through self-definition, account for 15 to 20 percent of the Turkish population, but for some 30 percent of Turkish immigrants in Europe. They live in diverse European countries. Interests expressed in terms of the identities of populations formed through immigration find an opportunity for action within Europe, leading to new forms and structures of representation and to new negotiations.

Such European supranational institutions as the European Court of Justice and the European Court of Human Rights offer a framework for identities seeking recognition before states. The normative power of these institutions, based mainly on the principle of human rights, affects both home and host states. The transnational actions of Turkish migrants take Turkey as a source of identity and Europe, and its member states, as a source of legitimacy for mobilization and claims-making, at the same time that the different immigration and integration policies of individual European countries shape migrants' modes of political participation and strategies. Even if Turkish-migrant voluntary associations are similar in each country, their demands result from negotiations with their respective states, regarding their collective rights based on their specific identities.[15] Any claim is integrated into the existing institutional structures of each country.[16] Thus, while Turkish immigrants claim citizenship rights in Germany in the context of its restrictive citizenship laws, they associate with immigrants from North Africa in France who seek to claim recognition of Islam in French institutional structures. Accordingly, Turkish identity in state negotiations focuses on citizenship in Germany and on religion in France. Transnational networks, however, aim to act directly at the level of supranational European institutions, to influence collective rights in host state policies. This evolution results both from integration policies and the recognition of differences in host-country policies that directly affect how Turks define themselves and politicize their identity in different European countries.

Redefining Turkish Nationalism

Turkish immigrants circulate between home and host countries and within Europe with political values and norms they acquired abroad, that were institutionalized in associations, and legitimized by European authorities. Through the voice of their militants, the Kurds in Germany, for example, seek recognition as a "Kurdish community" of immigrants whose culture, history, and language are distinct from the "Turkish community." This differentiation, which takes the form of conflicting "nationalisms" in Turkey, situates the Kurds as a "minority" within a minority in Germany and a minority within the Turkish transnational community. Their demand for recognition shows how claims are not only pursued by migrants, but also by people claiming a dual-minority status. Given that they have access to more political resources abroad than in Turkey, they bring their claims before the European Court of Human Rights, the Council of Europe, the European Court of Justice, and the European Parliament, in order to return to Turkey with recognition of minority rights that include cultural and linguistic rights in their homeland.

Nonetheless, the concept *minority* is ambiguous. It even causes uncertainty in defining legal forms of recognition, and the rights that go along with the status. States each have their own understanding of *minority* and work out specific relations with their minorities. Progress in the judicial sphere now involves questions regarding the cultural and religious rights of minorities, regarding all forms of discrimination in all member states and in countries subjected to European norms (EU candidates and neighbor countries). That does not resolve the issue of whether a minority is defined in territorial or nonterritorial terms. Definitions remain ambiguous and differ according to national experiences that define relations between states and minorities.

For Turkey, the concept of *minority* was reserved for the old Millet (ethno-religious communities of the Ottoman Empire, mainly non-Muslims, Armenians, Greeks, and Jews). With the creation of the republic, the Treaty of Lausanne, in 1923, afforded them legal and political status, plus such cultural privileges as the preservation of their languages and institutions (including places of worship and community schools).[17] The status and concept does not apply to the populations subjected to cultural, linguistic, and religious assimilation, for example, to the Kurds and Alevîs. Having been assimilated into the Turkish nation-state by virtue of being Islamic, the majority denomination, other Muslim populations (the brotherhoods, the Alevîs) do not enjoy institutional representation. Their demands for recognition, especially when voiced by the brotherhoods that bring them in opposition to the national community, face the Turkish state that follows the French example of centralization, republicanism, and secularity. Kurds, mostly concentrated in the east of the country and ethnolinguistically defined, are denied any specific identity and expression in the public sphere. Their claims for recognition and their activism in Turkey have caused new ethnolinguistic, religious, and national rifts that have become apparent in present-day Turkey. Thus, the emergence of diversity in political life in Turkey today challenges the official definition of the nation.

Islam, meanwhile, crystallizes the very contradiction of the secular Turkish state. Its manifestation as a political force in Turkey has given rise to a controversy that divides the nation into two antagonistic factions: one laik, the other "Muslim." Furthermore, as an identity, it challenges the official state identity, and casts doubt on the indefinite place granted to Islam in the "national conscience" and in state institutions. The fight against political Islam, which seeks to mobilize passions and emotions, gives rise to a variety of interpretations about the nature of Islam, ranging from national faith to individual faith, from a collective culture to a political force, from recognition of its place in political life to the conquest of power in Turkey. Although the debate intends to establish a separation between religion and politics, it underscores the difficulty of defining a clear borderline between them.

The boundaries between Islam and secularism are thus blurred. Although the function of secularism was to neutralize the state with regard to religion, in the Turkish context it has been translated into a way to unify the nation around Islam. The principle has been institutionalized with the Directorate of Religious Affairs, incorporated into the Office of the Prime Minister and led by a civil servant. Institutionalization of Sunni Islam results more in controlling the directorate than separating it from the state and politics.[18] Since the victory of the religious party (the Party of Prosperity) in 1994, Islam has become a permanent fixture in the Turkish political spectrum and public life. Seemingly reluctant to leave the monopoly of religion to religious parties, secular state representatives kept reminding the populace that 99.9 percent of Turks are Muslim. Since 2002 the party in power (the Justice and Development Party, or AKP) has brought Islam into the official rhetoric, challenging secularism and criticizing its relation to democracy.

Secular Turkey had no official religious representation abroad. Turkish Islam in Europe was first organized on a local level by spontaneous gatherings of Turks abroad. The leaders of such local gatherings were members of brotherhoods banned in Turkey. Since 1970 Turkish Islam has been organized mainly around the formal organization Millî Görüş (National Vision), which brings together the various religious parties in Turkey. This organization, banned in Turkey, benefited from a democratic environment in Europe that allowed the founding of religious associations to help families transmit and perpetuate cultural and religious traditions, and, most importantly, that allowed it to position itself as the main religious representative of Turkish immigrants in different countries. It established twenty-eight foreign offices in Europe, ten of them in Germany. Today it enjoys official status in Turkey as well, since it represents the party in power.

Although the Turkish state and the army have been combating political Islam in Turkey, the president of the Diyanet (the Directorate of Religious Affairs) recognizes the importance of Islam among Turks in Europe and wants to prove that "the state does not neglect Islam." The Diyanet İsleri Türk Islam Birliği, an organization in Europe that represents the Diyanet within the consular network in countries where Turks have emigrated, has, through its task of disseminating Turkey's "official Islam" abroad, influenced the nature of nationalism. The Turkish state established the Diyanet throughout Europe to combat the form of Islam that has developed among migrants through the Millî Görü and the brotherhoods; that is, its aim is to combat a "dissident" Islam spread by political parties opposed to the republic's secular principles. The secular state has thereby explicitly introduced religion into national identification and institutionalized it under the auspices of the consular network abroad. This development has contributed to a redefinition of Turkish nationalism both outside and inside its borders.

The *tarikat* (brotherhoods) that escaped abroad when banned in their homeland, have reestablished themselves in Turkey as civil-society organizations similar to politically active interest groups. Fetullah Gülen, the leader of the *Nurcu* movement, has, in particular, defended the role of the brotherhoods in national politics and the place of Islam in popular culture and beliefs.[19] The charismatic leader has preached the reconciliation of Islam with secularism and its importance in defining "what it means to be Turkish" outside the country's borders. His movement has gained considerable importance in the media and in public opinion, and within the political class and among intellectuals, via the more than 4,000 schools it operates worldwide, from Central Asia to Europe. The schools were founded to teach not only Islam, but also the Turkish language, along with the language of the country where the schools are located. Even more important in the Turkish national context are Fetullah Gülen's declarations regarding Turkish Islam, which have made him a "negotiator of Turkish identity" that binds together the strength of the state, the nation, and religion.

The Alevîs, on the other hand, reentered national politics as friends of the republic, even though the republic has lumped them together with the tarikat and consequently banned them from the public sphere. Their mobilization through associations and the visibility that they have gained since the 1990s has made both the political class and the public more aware of their historical, sociological, and political reality. The entire Turkish population pays attention to their belief system.[20] There is an interesting parallel between the mobilization and representation of the Alevîs among Turkish immigrants in Europe and their increasing visibility in Turkey. Because of their approach to Islam and worship, the Alevîs have attracted the attention of authorities in European cities. While some Sunni families and imams require young girls to wear the Islamic headscarf and prohibit girls to go to swimming pools with their school class, Alevî families promote moderation and tolerance in allowing girls to go to swimming pools and to reject the headscarf. They promote a nondogmatic Islam. To what extent has their nondogmatic approach to Islam (that is, their modern Islam) among migrants and in Turkey changed the political class's views in Turkey? Does the political class recognize the Alevîs, which identify with the secular state, for instrumental reasons, to fight emergent ethnic and religious divisions in domestic politics? In both cases, the parallel developments within and outside national borders are interdependent, and they contribute to a redefinition of nationalism.

There thus is an inversion of the situation. When Turks first emigrated, they turned Europe into an extension of Turkish politics. They transformed class-based political cleavages and ideological conflict in European countries, by turning Europe into an extension of Turkish politics. Today, the organizations of Turks abroad that are recognized and legitimized in European countries affect Turkish politics. Claims for equal rights and full citizenship in European countries have been transferred to Turkey, where they have transformed political action and nationalist discourses.

Changes across borders have also occurred in cultural, economic, and social spheres. These changes have been amplified through new means of communication, in particular through satellite television, used by Kurdish, Turkish, Alevî, and Sunni families of Turkish origin. Indeed, families experience life in Turkey on a daily basis via images broadcast by more than a dozen private and public channels.[21] Because programs are watched at the same time by people in Turkey and in Europe, the link between territory and identity is blurred. While the territory of belonging remains regional, the territory of reference becomes national and religious (albeit negotiable), and the territory of residence French, German, Dutch, or simply European.

Transnational actors, through their action within the institutional structures of host societies and the European Union, in turn have become agents of social and political change in Turkey. They transmit their knowledge of democratic politics acquired in Europe. They now play an important role in questioning official Turkish nationalism based on an ideology that dates from the creation of the republic, claiming the country indivisible, a nationalism considered "natural" until recently, but now defensive in the face of Kurdish mobilization and claims for cultural and Islamic rights with a legal basis in European institutions and European countries. Migrants return to Turkey with the same claims for political recognition. Activists rely on new solidarities formed in the particular countries where they settled and at the transnational (European) level to set a new framework for political action that has changed the understanding of Turkish nationalism.

Transnational Turkey

The Turkish state has also intervened in the formation of the transnational community. It acts as its "regulator." It operates in the countries in Europe where Turks live, through the promotion of "mother-tongue" education, which ensures that the migrants adhere to a national ideology it controls. To defend the official ideology, it promotes the creation of such associations as Atatürkçü Düşünce Derneği (Atatürk's Thought Association), named for the nation's founder. In contrast to associations preaching the virtues of integration, this organization aimed to defend the interests of Turkey. In the organization's inaugural speech, its president spoke of the centrality of Ankara, and added that it was "impossible to dissociate the Turks in Germany from Turkey." He considered it necessary to "remind the Turks in Berlin, and the whole population of Berlin, that the Turkish state is secular." He thus attacked the Millî Görüş, the largest association among immigrants in Germany, which, despite its growing legitimacy in Turkey, is not considered the voice of official Turkish Islam, a role ascribed to the Diyanet. The spokesperson for Atatürk's Thought Association in Berlin declared that his association sees "its duty to make the Turkish nation return to its Kemalist ideal," a unified and secular state. He foresees the establishment of a secular school in Germany as a reaction to the Quranic classes organized by Islamic organizations. In his speech, he rejected any "fragmentation of the national identity" that would allow the resurgence of the ethnic, linguistic, and regional bonds within Turkey.

At the same time, the Turkish government develops relations with social and cultural associations involving Turks abroad that have a local and national impact, and which present themselves as "multicultural," and recognized as such by host states in Europe. Their activities are based on the "ethnic" definition of the group, a definition that seeks its foundation in a "common nationality." As if intended to contribute to the ideal that a national community is a "united community," the Turkish state relates to the different aspects of Turkish identity the groups represent, be they national, religious, or political. It thereby aims to influence the public's image of Turkey and fashion a "representation" of Turks abroad as a "community." It promotes the idea of Turkish citizenship abroad—extraterritorial, outside Turkey's territorial boundaries. In so doing it keeps the nation linked to citizenship, and, conversely, citizenship linked to the nation, in either case deterritorialized or extraterritorial vis-à-vis Turkey. This citizenry does not demand a common identity with the nation, but with the state.

Turkish immigrant political actors respond to these state attempts with efforts to form lobbies that both countries recognize, based on community organizations defined by Turkish politics but situated within the host country's political system, or in opposition to it. They react, for example, to all statements by the German government about Turkey. Their power rests on their economic success. Having organized in many regions of the country into Turkish business associations, they influence national politics in both the host and home country.[22] Simultaneously the large Turkish business associations in Turkey that exert great influence over national politics, have also established a footing in Brussels to influence the European Commission on matters related to Turkey's integration into the European Union. Taken together, they contribute to the evolution of a nationalism that in reality is "transnational." This is also true of the oppositional nationalist movements, such as the Kurdish movement, whose mobilization is both European and transnational.

TRANSNATIONALISM SHAPES A present-day nationalism that differs from the highly territorialized nationalisms of the nineteenth and most of the twentieth centuries. Transnational communities are constructed around shared references that bring to the fore a feeling of belonging to a "deterritorialized nation," with identity claims that are nourished by new expressions of nationalism. This has led to a redefinition of the link between territory, nation, and political space, which challenges the nation-state as well as culturally and territorially defined political structures.

In the case of Turkey, the "deterritorialized nation" has weakened the Turkish state, at a time when it is negotiating its place on the international and, more precisely, the European stage. Despite its heterogeneity, segmented organization, and often conflicting internal relations, the emergent "transnational community" acts as a driving force for political and social change in Turkey because of the "know-how" and democratic political values migrants gained abroad in their struggle for equal rights.

Transnationalism entails dual or multiple citizenship in relation to several countries for social, cultural, economic, and political participation. Multiple citizenship introduces different ways of conceiving moral and political values, including different concepts of civic duties imposed on those who live within the communities.[23] For some, dual citizenship is a source of "democratic influence," a basis for applying Western democratic values in the country of origin.[24]

The interdependence between internal and external nation-state dynamics, and between nation-states and transnational communities, pose both a challenge to, and an opportunity for, Turkey: a challenge in light of its concern with negotiating its identity as a state, and an opportunity in light of its ability to affirm its sovereignty and its integration into the general process of globalization. This is one of the paradoxes of transnationalism: while it questions the relevance of nation-states as political, cultural, and territorial units, it reinforces the role of states. Transnational activities, in essence, aim to influence states from abroad, as became apparent when transnational actors sought to strengthen their representation at the European level to attain recognition at the national level.[25] In the final analysis, activists, even those most involved at the European level, imagine the state as the only "adversary" they need consider.

Notes

1 A version of this chapter was published as "Turkish Transnational Nationalism: How Turks Abroad Redefine Nationalism," in *The Politics of Multiple Belonging: Ethnicity and Nationalism in Europe and East Asia*, ed. Flemming Christiansen and Ulf Hedetoft (Aldershot, UK: Ashgate, 2004), 77–93.

2 *Konsumgewohnheiten und wirtschaftliche situation der türkischen Bevölkerung in der Bundesrepublik Deutschland* (Essen, Germany: Zentrum für Turkeistuden, Institut an der Universität Duisburg-Essen, September 2002).

3 David Held et al., *Global Transformations* (Cambridge: Polity, 1999).

4 Gaspar Rivera-Salgado, "Mixtec Activism in Oaxacalifornia. Transborder Grassroots Political Strategies." *American Behavioral Scientist* 42, no. 9 (1999): 1439–58.

5 Alejandro Portes, "Migration and Development: Reconciling Opposite Views." Annual lecture sponsored by *Ethnic and Racial Studies*, May 8, 2008, 8.

6 Expression used by Myron Wiener in "Labor Migration as Incipient Diasporas," in *Modern Diasporas in International Politics*, ed. Gabriel Scheffer
(London: Croom Helm, 1986), 47–74, cited by Nicholas van Hear, *New Diasporas: The Mass Exodus, Dispersal and Regrouping of Migrant Communities*
(London: UCL Press, 1998), 5.

7 Linda Bash, Nina Glick-Schiller, and Cristina Szanton Blanc, *Nations Un-
bound: Transnational Projects, Postcolonial Predicaments, and Deterritorial-
ised Nation-States* (Amsterdam: Gordon and Breach, 1994); Robin Cohen,
Global Diasporas: An Introduction (Seattle: University of Washington Press,
1997); Akhil Gupta and James Ferguson, eds., *Culture, Power, Place: Explora-
tions in Critical Anthropology* (Durham, NC: Duke University Press, 1997); Ulf
Hannerz, *Transnational Connections: Culture, People, Places* (London: Routledge, 1996); Alejandro Portes, "Transnational Communities: Their Emergence and Significance in the Contemporary World System," in *Latin America
in the World-Economy*, ed. Roberto Patricio Korzeniewicz and William C.
Smith (Westwood, MA: Greenwood, 1996), 151–68; Peggy Levitt, "Local-Level
Global Religion: The Case of U.S.-Dominican Migration," *Journal for the Scientific Study of Religion* 37 (1998): 74–89.

8 Jackie Smith, Charles Chatfield, and Ron Pagnucco, eds., *Transnational Social
Movements and Global Politics: Beyond the State* (Syracuse, NY: Syracuse
University Press, 1997).

9 Research done by the Turkish Center in Essen shows that 39.1 percent in
Belgium, 26.4 percent in Denmark, 27.6 percent in Germany, 47 percent in
France, 64.4 percent in the Netherlands, 40 percent in Austria, 62.2 percent in
Sweden, and 47.1 percent in Great Britain identify with the nationality of their
host country.

10 More than 2 million in Germany; 300,000 in France; 35,000 in the Netherlands; etc. (SOPEMI 1997).

11 Riva Kastoryano, *Negotiating Identities: States and Immigrants in France and
Germany* (Princeton, NJ: Princeton University Press, 2002).

12 Catherine Neveu, "Citoyenneté et racisme en Europe: exception et complé-
mentairté britanniques," *Revue Européenne des Migrations Internationales* 10,
no. 1 (1994): 95–109.

13 Sixteen Turkish associations were represented in the forum, of which ten
were organized in federations of associations.

14 The regions are defined as the Maghreb (North Africa), Sub-Saharan Africa,
Latin America, the Caribbean, and Turkey. Although the regions are defined
as groups of countries reflecting their geographic and cultural proximity, Turkey is represented as a region in its own right.

15 Kastoryano, *Negotiating Identities*.

16 Ruud Koopmans et al., *Contested Citizenship: Immigration and Cultural Diversity in Europe* (Minneapolis: University of Minnesota Press, 2005).

17 In 1926, the Greek, Jewish, and Armenian minorities, former millets, rejected these privileges.

18 See Jean-Pierre Burdy and Jean Marcou, "Laïcité/Laiklik: Introduction," *CEMOTI*, 19 (1995): 34.

19 For a deeper understanding of the Nurcu movement, see Serif Mardin, *Religion and Social Change in Modern Turkey: The Case of Beddiuzzaman Said Nursi* (Albany: SUNY Press, 1989).

20 Since the 1980s, state officials and members of successive governments have participated, with media coverage, in celebrations of pilgrimage that take place each August in Central Anatolia.

21 Altan Gökalp, Riva Kastoryano, and Stéphane de Tapia, *L'immigration turque et kurde: La dynamique segmentaire, la nouvelle donne générationelle, et le nouvel ordre communicationel* (report prepared for the FAS, Paris, January 1997).

22 A report published in Belgium in 1991 estimated the value of Turks' direct and indirect contribution to the economy to be around 57 billion German marks; the amount far exceeded the state's expenses on foreigners, which amounted to 16 billion marks. Among the 1.8 million Turks in Germany in 1992, there were 35,000 entrepreneurs, who ranged from restauranteurs to industrialists. They employed 150,000 Turks and 75,000 Germans, and paid 1 billion marks in taxes. See *The Economic and Political Impact of Turkish Migration in Germany*, Zentrum für Türkeistudien (March 1993). This center regularly publishes reports on enterprises owned by Turkish residents in Germany, including their economic activity, the number of their employees, and their tax payments.

23 Noah M. J. Pickus, ed., *Immigration and Citizenship in the Twenty-First Century* (Lanham, MD: Rowman and Littlefield, 1998).

24 Peter Spiro, "Dual Nationality and the Meaning of Citizenship," *Emory Lax Journal* 1411 (1997): 46.

25 Kastoryano, *Negotiating Identities.*

8

Moroccan Migrants as Unlikely Captains of Industry
Remittances, Financial Intermediation,
and La Banque Centrale Populaire

NATASHA ISKANDER

In 1963 Morocco signed an accord with West Germany to send workers to address the European country's shortage of labor. Morocco soon thereafter signed similar accords with France, as well as with Belgium and the Netherlands.[1] Within a decade, over 200,000 Moroccans were recruited from rural areas in the north and south of the kingdom to work in Europe's factories and mines. Many more Moroccans migrated to Europe as "tourists," securing employment and labor contracts after they arrived.[2]

The work was arduous, and the pace on assembly lines and in mine shafts was relentless. "I didn't even think I would be able to complete my one-year contract, it was so hard," recalls a Moroccan immigrant employed in a mine in the north of France. "It was all just work, then exhaustion, and starting all over again [the next day]."[3] The living conditions were equally difficult. Lodged in employer-supplied barracks where workers were often assigned beds in shifts, in shanty-towns that sprung up on the edge of industrial complexes, in shacks that were, as one resident remembered, "soaked to the nails in water and mud," or in substandard public housing, the immigrants lived segregated by nationality and isolated from the rest of the population.[4] In France, the destination country for most Moroccans, they were subject to intensive policing, both on the street and on the factory floor.[5] French authorities in major cities conducted frequent checks of North African workers' identity papers and work permits. Those unable to prove current employment were detained and deported for being "vagrants." Likewise, immigrants who were injured on the job or who challenged their working conditions were reported to the authorities as "unfit," and many were summarily extradited.[6] In Paris, Moroccan immigrants, at their jobs on factory assembly lines before daybreak, began to call themselves "the tunnel people, those that never see the light of day."[7]

The same workers, whom European employers favored as a source of strong, abundant, and cheap labor, paid in turn, for Moroccan industrialization.[8] From their jobs on Europe's factory floors or in its mineshafts, they were, collectively, one of the most important financiers of Moroccan national development initiatives. From the late 1960s onward, their wages, though consistently lower than their European coworkers, helped bankroll the construction of Moroccan dams and massive irrigation systems for agribusiness. They also financed major industrial investment in Morocco's growing coastal cities.[9]

In the context of current debates about the relationship between migration and development, the role of Moroccan migrants as sponsors of national development seems improbable. Remittances are generally viewed as having a marginal impact on economic development despite the volume remitted. Some observers even argue that migrant transfers can depress economic growth.

This narrow assessment of remittances' impact on development stems from a set of assumptions about remittances and the migrants who send them. Although remittances can make up several percentage points of a nation's income when summed, they are, in effect, very small interpersonal payments. Precisely because the disbursements are small and shared among many people, they are generally viewed as having too diffuse an effect on an economy to catalyze structural change. For the same reasons, remittances are also viewed as difficult to aggregate. Grouping together tiny amounts of money that are dispersed throughout an economy, in order to transform them into capital for targeted investment, has been characterized as a herculean task. This is in part because of whose hands the money is in: the migrants who make up the vast majority of remittance senders worldwide, as well as the family members who receive their wages, are viewed as difficult to bring into the formal banking system, for reasons ranging from lack of financial literacy, to geographic mobility, to legal status. Daunted by the challenge of providing financial services to this population, governments, banks, and donor organizations have turned their attention instead to the mechanisms for money transfer, focusing, in particular, on reducing the cost and complexity of sending money across borders.

The role that Moroccan migrants played in financing their country's industrialization suggests that such assessment of remittances represents a lost opportunity. It reveals that the challenge of using remittances to fund development may rest neither with migrants nor with the small size and large volume of remittance transfers, but rather with the way financial intermediation for migrants has been conceived. Moroccan migrants became the kingdom's unlikely captains of industry, not because of the remittances they sent home, but because of the kind of financial institutions the Moroccan state set up to channel those funds to national development. From 1969 onward, the Moroccan government used its state-controlled bank, the Banque Centrale Populaire (BCP), to create a set of financial tools that allowed migrants to send money home, to save and invest, while simultaneously making funds available to the government for state-sponsored investment. The bank directed remittances it aggregated and transformed into capital toward large-scale projects that were considered centerpieces of the nation's development plan. The Moroccan state, through the BCP, devised a system of financial intermediation that allowed the government to borrow from migrants to pay for projects that promoted industrialization. That system still remains unparalleled today: Morocco, often considered a backwater kingdom with ossified governance structures, continues to deploy the world's most sophisticated and effective tools for bringing migrants into the formal banking system. And, through the BCP and increasingly through private banks that have emulated it, migrants continue to fund development projects and business investment via their deposits—deposits that amount to about one-fifth of the total money in the national banking system.

However, the process of creating the financial instruments that fueled the Moroccan development and investment was laborious. It required substantial investment in time, money, and manpower. This is because the bank had to engage intensively with Moroccan migrants, to design financial services that would appeal to migrant workers with little previous exposure to formal banking. It had to collaborate with migrants to identify what obstacles prevented them from accessing formal money transfer channels and to translate their financial aspirations into workable banking services. After a few false starts, the cooperation between migrants and the state bank produced a wide range of innovative transnational financial instruments. Those instruments, first launched in the late 1960s, have multiplied and become more nimble and sophisticated. They blend financial participation in Morocco with a sense of cultural belonging.

The Moroccan experience with the BCP challenges the current obsession with facilitating money transfers, and brings the process of institution-building to the fore of discussions about the relationship between migration and development. The effect of remittances on the Moroccan economy grew out of the institutions for financial intermediation that migrants and the state constructed together. It is a story of mutual engagement. Migrants did not *act on* a country of origin that served as a passive recipient of remittances. Neither did the state *act on* migrants to seize their remittances. Rather, migrants and state actors *acted with* one another to create institutions that allowed migrants to support the aspirations they had for themselves and their communities, even as they enabled the government to capitalize on the monies migrants sent home.

The engagement between migrants and the state—the process of *acting with*—not only allowed for the wholesale integration of migrants into Morocco's formal financial system. It also created an opening for the redefinition of what development was and where development, in Morocco, should occur. In a classic two-sector model, the Moroccan government defined development as a national project of rapid, urban industrialization and the promotion of large agribusiness to the deliberate and explicit exclusion of traditional agriculture systems that prevailed in the communities from which most migrants came. As Moroccan migrants became more invested in their home country's financial system, they began to challenge the national development schemes their wages were supporting. They used both the financial tools the bank provided and the political leverage the sum of their deposits afforded them to push for development in rural areas long neglected by their government. They advocated for the extension of basic infrastructure services, essential to support both small-scale agricultural production and microenterprises emerging in semiurban centers that they were building throughout the countryside. In time, they edged sustainable rural development and poverty alleviation in rural communities onto the government's list of principal economic development priorities. The shift was arguably the most transformative, if unintended, impact of the Moroccan government's aggressive efforts to capture migrant remittances. It had even greater influence on Morocco's development trajectory than the large industrial projects the government bankrolled with migrant wages.

Debating Remittances, Debating Development

In recent years, the money that migrants send home has risen to unprecedented levels, surpassing foreign direct investment by a large margin, and providing a quorum of countries with one of their most important sources of national income. Given the sums of cash at stake, it is no wonder that the debates about how migrant remittances foster development, if they do so at all, have been heated. Some have observed that remittances accelerate economic growth rates and reduce poverty levels, generally through standard Keynesian effects.[10] They have noted that remittances provide income support to families, act as insurance against income shocks, and allow households to make investments in housing and education.[11] Critics have countered that remittances have a modest impact on growth and that their positive effects are limited to specific sociogroups and regions.[12] Moreover, they add that remittances may dampen labor market participation, increase inequality, and create inflationary pressure.[13]

Despite the diversity of positions articulated in this debate, a set of shared assumptions broadly demarcate its contours. Most of the evaluations of remittances view them as categorically distinct from other monies flowing into and circulating within a given national economy. Remittances are seen as economic add-ons, as integrated into mainstream economic exchange only through the investment and consumption behavior of migrants themselves. Institutions have been noted to play a role in informing these behaviors: a favorable institutional environment, observers have noted, can attract increased remittance flows into an economy.[14] A stable macroeconomic environment that keeps currency values from ricocheting tends to do the same: migrants transfer more money when they enjoy some assurance that their earnings will not abruptly lose value. However, remittances themselves have little impact on the features of institutions that structure economic production and promote economic development. With few exceptions, remittances remain a supplemental resource, with minimal transformative effect on the economy.[15] To be sure, they may accelerate existing economic patterns, through the multiplier effect consumption and local spending can have. They may also accentuate economic differences, such as income inequality.[16] However, for the most part, they are not considered a factor that can alter the fundamental organization of production in an economy, either locally or nationally.[17] The predominant industries remain largely the same, and the economic institutions that govern them remain basically unaffected.

The analytic distinction of remittances from the rest of the money in an economy stems from attributes associated with them. Remittances are primarily defined as person-to-person payments of low monetary value. Furthermore, the small sums of money are characterized as being sent to individuals for uses already determined before the money is transferred. Thus, with remittances so tightly wedded to migrant and migrant-family expenditure practices, the assumption is that it is very difficult to aggregate the small transfers in the same manner as other money in the economy, to transform it into capital that can be reinvested for production.

Not only do these characteristics supposedly make remittances resistant to financial intermediation, but migrants themselves are portrayed as difficult to bring into the formal financial system. To use the vernacular of development organizations, migrants are viewed as "unbankable." The reasons are myriad. For one, the transaction costs to process large numbers of small transfers are too high to be profitable for traditional banking institutions, even given rapidly evolving information technology platforms. Two, migrants' lives, and their monetary transfers, often reflect their legal liminality, and the informal aspects of migrants' lives makes meeting security requirements on international finance more complex. Three, the mobility of migrants and the remoteness of many of their communities of origin creates challenges for banking systems that still rely mainly on the static physical infrastructure of bank branches. Furthermore, it is widely (but inaccurately) believed that because migrants have had limited exposure to banking systems, it would require significant resources to build financial literacy.[18] Migrants' tendency to have low savings amounts (as opposed to saving rates, which tend to be relatively high) or to use funds immediately for household expenditures compounds these perceptions and makes dedicating the resources to overcome those obstacles seem like a poor investment.[19]

Initiatives ostensibly geared toward providing migrants with greater financial access reflect this perspective. The emphasis has been on reducing the price associated with remittance transfers.[20] Significantly less attention has been paid to ensuring that migrants have easy and reliable access to mainstream financial institutions, especially traditional banking services in their countries of origin.[21] This is true even though recent surveys have demonstrated that migrants do in fact want greater access to formal financial services, and have a somewhat higher propensity to have bank accounts in the countries to which they migrate than in their home countries.[22]

Instead, governments, development organizations, and financial institutions have focused on altering migrants' behavior. Policy interventions designed to turn remittances into an economic input that can change the structure of an economy have focused on changing the preferences and practices of migrants, specifically on shifting migrant spending from expenditures viewed as consumption toward expenditures viewed as productive investment.[23] The line between spending and investment is a movable one, with some policymakers considering expenditures on housing, health, and education consumption, whereas others consider them investment. Regardless of where the distinction is drawn, the policies share a marked propensity to *act on* migrants. They endeavor to redirect a portion of migrant remittances toward development projects. They attempt to turn migrants into philanthropists or entrepreneurs. And they encourage migrants to invest in schemes for income generation in their communities of origin.

Financial experiments of such ilk have explored tactics ranging from marketing government bonds to migrants to pooling remittances into small funds for local development projects.[24] Remittance matching-funds programs in countries such as Mexico (described by David FitzGerald in his chapter of this book), have provided migrants with incentives—in the form of government grants that equal or exceed migrant donations —to pool a portion of the remittances they would otherwise have sent to their families for development projects. What qualifies as development projects has been tensely contested among migrants and their governments. Migrants elect projects that have symbolic and cultural value for them, churches and rodeo rings, for example, while governments vie for projects they consider productive, such as infrastructure investment and small business support.[25] Efforts by small community banks and credit unions to create banking services for migrants, in both countries of origin and destination, also reflect the tendency to *act on* migrants to change their spending practices. The local institutions often have a deep knowledge of their customer base and the specific linguistic, cultural, and financial challenges the migrants among them face, so that to create tailor-made services for migrants requires minimal additional investment.[26] Even so, they instead have concentrated on providing remittance transfer services that are competitively priced.[27] When they have offered additional financial products to migrants, such as current deposit, savings accounts, and microcredit, they have tended to pair the services with financial education, to alter the mix of migrant spending practices away from consumption and toward investment considered productive. This drive to reorient migrant expenditure occurs at both the individual and community level through, for example, campaigns that claim saving with credit unions will foster local business development, including migrant businesses. Although small community banks at times integrate some migrants into formal financial systems, they have had little influence on larger conversations about the direction national development policy should take.[28]

The Moroccan government's approach to remittances was not constrained by concerns about the feasibility or cost of integrating migrants into the country's formal financial systems. The Moroccan administration viewed Moroccan emigrants as an arm of the national economy and the wages they earned in Europe as a source of hard cash for its national investments, cash to which it was fully entitled. As a result, it viewed no transaction as too small and no aspect of migrants too socially complex to discourage it from bringing migrants into the national financial system. As a result, it also did not attempt to change migrant spending behavior, to direct more of their wages to expenditures considered investment. The Moroccan government had little interest in *acting on* migrants in this fashion, because it had no desire to involve migrants or their communities in development policy. Quite to the contrary, it was keen on using their wages to fund megaprojects in what it defined as the modern industrial sector—a sector in which migrant rural economies had no part. Ironically, the government's ambitious and determined approach to banking migrants integrated them into the financial system so deeply that migrants were ultimately able to amend the government's development strategy to include the rural areas it initially had deliberately sidelined.

Wages for Development

The Moroccan government had two goals when it launched its policy of exporting workers: to reduce the level of unemployment within its borders, and to use the wages of Moroccan emigrant workers as capital for national investment.[29] In all the accords it crafted with European labor-recruiting nations, it was careful to include language contractually protecting the flow of worker earnings to Morocco. "Moroccan workers shall be able to transfer their savings to Morocco in compliance with existing legislation and regulations," read the compact signed with France in 1963.[30] The kingdom's national development policy codified the function of migrant wages even more explicitly. The 1968–1972 National Development Plan predicted that labor emigration "would permit the increase of transfers of foreign currency which would finance internal investments." It stated that the government's goal was thus "to achieve the augmentation of workers abroad by the end of the five-year period [covered by the plan]," especially since labor export ensured "the employment of a portion of our population that cannot be absorbed within [Moroccan] frontiers."[31] The 1973–1977 National Development Plan continued in a similar vein, deeming emigration to be "the equivalent, in economic terms, of the export of a product produced in Morocco" that promoted cash flow into the country.[32]

Although unemployment remained high, migrant transfers quickly yielded a sizable addition to national income. In 1964, a year after the first labor-export agreements were signed, Moroccan migrants remitted an estimated 93 million dirhams (which was roughly equivalent to 9 million U.S. dollars, as they were valued in 1968). By 1967, that sum more than doubled, to 208 million dirhams, accounting for about 1.3 percent of the country's GDP.[33] Because the number of Moroccan workers that the Moroccan government formally sent abroad under the auspices of labor agreements was growing by about 20 percent annually, and because the number of "tourist" workers was increasing even more, remittances were expected to rise substantially.[34] However, much to the Moroccan government's consternation, migrants bypassed the formal transfer channels, the postal money orders the government had taken pains to protect in the 1960s. Migrants sent their money home informally. They brought back their earnings in cash when they returned, or sent money home through trusted couriers. These informal transfers, and the black market currency exchanges that went with them, entirely bypassed the formal banking system. Short on hard currency and running a deficit that stood at a third of its operating budget, the government had launched an all-out public relations campaign to promote savings and investment.[35] It pressed citizens to deposit their money in bank accounts, and required all banks to purchase treasury bonds equivalent to no less than 30 percent of their deposits. Although it doubled savings between 1968 and 1974, the initiative failed with migrants and their families. Migrant wages remained unavailable for national development use.[36]

In response, the minister of finance took the extraordinary step in 1968 of issuing an official missive to the BCP, directing it to bring migrant wages into the formal financial system. The state-owned bank, based on a network of credit unions, was already the main implementing institution of the government's private savings and investment initiative. It had embraced "bancarizing the masses" as both its mission and its slogan, and introduced banking services to wide swathes of Morocco's merchant class in cities and small towns.[37] The minister ordered the bank to complete "the elaboration of a very refined system such that the repatriation of savings by the workers abroad no longer escapes state control."[38] Had the "workers abroad" remained in Morocco, the bank would never have extended services to them. Before their departure, migrant workers belonged to an economic stratum in which the bank had been uninterested. Most of them were illiterate, rural laborers. According to a household survey, only 23 percent of migrants who left Morocco between 1965 and 1975 had any formal schooling, and only 7 percent were more than marginally literate.

Although the wages migrants earned abroad catapulted them into the Moroccan middle class, the BCP had little sense of how to approach a demographic group bank staff had viewed as inherently "unbankable." Moreover, the bank had no experience offering financial services to people whose everyday financial practices stretched across national borders, with wages earned in Europe and family expenditures in Morocco. Its lack of expertise in this area was unremarkable. Save for one bank in Portugal that was just beginning to experiment with offering financial services to migrants, no bank anywhere was providing banking access to emigrants in the 1960s. As one former BCP director recalled, "Everyone thought [the minister] was crazy. No one—no one!—at the bank or anywhere else—thought it could be done."[39] Under Morocco's authoritarian government, the BCP, nevertheless, was bound by the minister's stern dictate to ensure that remittances "no longer escaped state control." Unable, however, to design financial services for migrants on its own, the bank was compelled to *act with* migrant workers to discover how to bring them into the Moroccan banking system, and to direct their wages to the government's development priorities.

Tea and the Art of *Acting With*

Within months after receiving the ministry of finance's executive order, the BCP sent an exploratory delegation to Paris to come up with a prototype of financial tools that could capture remittances. Operating out of provisional offices set up in the Moroccan embassy in Paris, as well as out of suburban consulates, the BCP staff set out to "map the circuits" through which migrants moved their money from Europe to Morocco. To discover this information, staff attempted to conduct an informal survey of migrant workers about their remittance practices, but they were sharply rebuffed by migrants who were deeply suspicious of the Moroccan bureaucrats' sudden interest in their financial affairs. The staff thus abandoned their direct line of questioning, and instead tried to forge relationships with migrant workers that eventually enabled them to discuss money transfers. The bankers visited migrants at their worker dorms and factory trailers. They went to the barbers in the shantytowns Moroccan workers frequented, where they chatted with workers who had come in for a shave or a haircut. They also prayed with workers in basement prayer rooms, had lunch with them outside the factories where they worked, and relaxed with them over a glass of Moroccan tea when workers finished their shifts. Bank veterans recall running competitions over who had had the most glasses of tea during the course of a day.[40]

Over time, the relationships that the BCP staff forged with Moroccan emigrants in Paris opened up the space for discussions about the informal transfer systems the workers used. They explained that they relied on trusted representatives from their communities, from their Berber tribe, who traveled to Europe, to pick up their wages and hand carry them to their families in Morocco, for a fee. Moroccan emigrants called this arrangement, in a riff on the formal postal service, "playing post-men—*faire de la poste.*"[41] In addition to transporting money, "postmen" fulfilled a host of other quasi-social service functions for migrants and their families. They provided loans, using future remittances as collateral. They extended the equivalent of insurance against illness, crop failure, and migrant unemployment, deducting a fee from the remittances they carried for workers. They also organized collections among their clients for unfortunate expenses, such as for burials and the repatriation of bodies. Furthermore, they offered social and community support. They provided migrants with information about their families, their harvests, and home disputes, as well as about employment opportunities at other factories and in other cities in Europe.[42] "I take care of the business and family affairs of my relatives," explained a postman from a rural community in the north of Morocco. "The money repatriated varies by year, you know. There are illnesses, ups and downs. I take care of twenty-seven workers (eleven in Germany, seven in Holland, five in Belgium, four in France) and even if they are hardworking, sometimes there is nothing you can do about destiny."[43]

For emigrant workers, these informal arrangements were costly but invaluable. Postmen charged high fees for their service, taking a cut of the remittances when they picked them up from workers in Europe but also when they delivered them to families. Reported charges hovered around 10 percent of the money delivered.[44] Moreover, it took several weeks for migrant monies to be delivered to their families, and frequently funds were lost in transit, with couriers claiming that they had been robbed. Postmen, in addition, charged for currency exchange, typically transacted on the black market, because of the government's stringent currency exchange regulations at the time. Aside from carefully controlling prices, the government only authorized a limited number of institutions to change currency, and it imposed onerous reporting requirements.[45]

Eventually, conversations between migrants and the BCP turned to the obstacles that prevented migrants from using formal money transfer alternatives, and to how a suitable transnational banking system might be developed. The discussion brought to the surface barriers that prevented Moroccan workers from accessing formal transfer channels in France, and the disconnect in Morocco between the government services and the financial needs of Moroccan emigrants and their families.

In France, prevailing social attitudes toward North African immigrants made government offices, including post offices, inaccessible to Moroccan workers. Entering an official institution at a time when North African workers were often barred from grocery stores was daunting for many migrants. Even those who braved offices that they experienced as exceedingly inhospitable reported being treated dismissively. They described receiving poor service and little help filling out postal orders. Furthermore, Moroccan migrants, like all North African workers during this period, were subjected to policing and frequent identity checks in public spaces and government offices. Leaving worker barracks and Arab shantytowns meant risking police harassment, and possible deportation if a worker could not prove legal employment.

Even if Moroccan workers frequented post offices, they faced another barrier, rooted in their low literacy level, especially in French and the Latin alphabet. Sending a postal money order required filling out a basic form in French. For workers who were functionally illiterate, this was an impossible task. Even those who were able to fill out the forms made frequent errors in the address noted for the recipient. When an error made it impossible to deliver funds, the formal transfer agreements stipulated that the monies were to be returned to the postal office where the transfer order was submitted. However, the workers frequently failed to receive the money.

Meanwhile, in Morocco, the transfer services the government provided failed to meet the needs of Moroccan emigrants and their families. In the 1960s and 1970s, post offices in the rural mountains of the north and south, from where most migrants originated, were few in number and often at some distance from migrants' villages of origin. Further complicating matters, the post offices were often too far for a woman to travel to alone, given gender norms at the time, and migrants had to grant a male relative power of attorney to pick up the funds, a bureaucratic process that was prohibitively convoluted. Moreover, postal transfer services did little to address either the challenges of exchanging foreign currency at the time or the desires of migrants and their families to secure occasional loans and insurance.

Based on insights that emerged from the conversations between Moroccan workers and BCP staff, the bank addressed the obstacles that had kept migrants from using formal postal transfers, in a manner that brought migrants into the Moroccan banking system. The new services, packaged in an initiative that was formally launched in 1969, known as Operation Moroccan Workers Abroad, reflected a new way of conceptualizing banking. More than simply providing financial access, bringing migrants into the formal banking system involved *acting with* migrants in the context of a larger relationship, of which banking services were only one part.

To ensure that migrants had access to formal money transfer systems, bank staff engaged in what the BCP termed "a strategy of accompaniment." Bank staff literally went with Moroccan workers to French post offices, and filled out the money order for them. When accompanied by a Moroccan professional, fluent in French and able to advocate for migrants' rights, Moroccan workers received markedly better service than when they had gone alone. "Postal clerks became much more patient with Moroccan workers when they saw us with them," remembered one BCP veteran. Once the BCP staffer completed the transfer form, the migrant worker who was with him only had to sign his name. "In the early years [of the program], sometimes they just used a thumbprint," explained one BCP staffer. The BCP thereby resolved challenges that marginal literacy had posed. The migrant's money was then wired to a general BCP account in Casablanca, at no cost. (The BCP absorbed the nominal fee charged by the French postal service for transfer services.)

Thus, migrant wages were brought into the formal banking system as part of remittance transfers, not as an additional service offered alongside remittance delivery. Once migrants felt confident enough to use postal transfers on their own, the BCP supplied them with preprinted transfer forms with all the necessary information, save for the amount to be transmitted and the sender's signature.[46]

At the BCP headquarters in Morocco, each migrant's funds were rerouted to an individual personal account, which he or whoever else was a signatory to the account could access at will. The transfer from a Paris post office to a migrant account took only two or three days, which, in 1969 (when the technology available was telex and filing card accounting systems) was considered highly efficient, and much faster than when delivered by informal couriers, who often took weeks, if not months, to deliver funds. The families of migrants could withdraw funds at the bank's extensive and growing network of branches and regional centers or from mobile "van-branches," Volkswagen vans refurbished to serve as ambulatory bank branches, which ambled through

TABLE 8.1. Migration, Remittances, and BCP Results, 1969–1976

	1969	1970
Remittances (in millions of Dh)	302	316
% of GDP	1.6	1.6
Proportion of Transfers through BCP (%)	22.3	49
Number of BCP Migrant-held Accounts	16,550	35,000
Number of Moroccan Migrant Workers in Europe	143,397	170,835

Sources: BCP in Bossard (1979), World Bank (1966, 1981), BCP (1986).

small towns and villages in rural Morocco on market days.[47] While not delivering door-to-door service, the BCP restructured in a manner convenient for remittance recipients.

The BCP complemented these logistical solutions with the same social support that informal postmen had provided. In France, the bank's staff began to help migrants with various day-to-day tasks, such as going to the doctor, reading or writing letters, and filling out administrative forms relating to their employment. This engaged style of banking became core to the BCP's approach, so much so that three decades later, the BCP delegate general remarked that the functions that the BCP staff performed were "not exclusively commercial. They are often called upon to provide a whole menu of other services. They are called upon to write a letter or resolve an administrative problem."[48]

Concomitantly, in Morocco, the BCP, through its decentralized network of credit unions, offered migrants and their families many of the same financial services postmen had provided informally, including small loans and crop insurance. The bank very quickly developed a compendium of products designed specifically for their migrant clients, including insurance policies for the repatriation of bodies and for travel expenses incurred due to family emergencies. The mobile van-branches, and the hundreds of physical offices that the BCP later opened throughout the Moroccan countryside, became gathering places for migrant families, where information about migrants and employment opportunities in Europe were exchanged. Bank staffers were also on hand to extend financial advice, if requested. Other service providers important to migrant families, for example, village scribes, in turn gravitated to the bank branches. The BCP viewed this strategy as broader than just extending their banking network into rural areas. As Benaces Lahlou, director for emigrant services at the bank, would later remark, "We are not satisfied

1971	1972	1973	1974	1975	1976
480	640	1,020	1,557	2,159	2,417
2.2	2.8	4.0	4.6	6.1	4.7
72					
159,000					
194,296	218,146	269,680	302,294	322,067	347,984

with opening branches. We bring the bank to the emigrants. We follow them all the way to their homes."[49]

Money in the Bank

"Operation Moroccan Workers Abroad," with its engaged style of banking based on "accompaniment," showed remarkable results within a very short time. By the end of 1969, transfers through the BCP reached 13 million Moroccan dirhams a month, a sum equal to almost a quarter of all remittances to the kingdom that year. Moreover, an impressive 16,550 migrants had opened accounts at the BCP in the first year of the initiative, and their accounts represented 9 percent of all deposits in the bank. Over the next several years, the BCP's reach among Moroccan migrants continued to grow: by 1970, the number of migrants the institution counted among its clients had doubled to 35,000, and by 1975 the number had increased nearly another fivefold, to 159,000, at a time when the total population of Moroccan migrants in Europe was estimated at only slightly more than 300,000. By 1976, the BCP was handling 50 percent of all remittance transfers to Morocco, with all transfers held for some period of time as deposits in migrant current accounts (see table 8.1). With the remittances as a whole making up close to 5 percent of GDP by that time, the BCP was bringing in about 2 percent of national income by banking on those who by today's standards still are considered unbankable.[50]

The Moroccan government was keen on strengthening its financial intermediation so that it could access a larger portion of migrant funds for long-term investments. In late 1974, the government, through the BCP, offered a 3 percent interest rate on savings accounts. The government complemented these incentives for savings with compensation

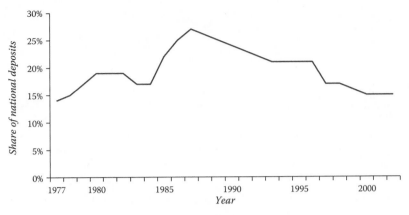

FIGURE 8.1. BCP Moroccan Emigrant Deposits as a Share of
Total National Deposits, 1977–2002

for variable gaps between European currencies and the Moroccan dirham. When the French franc began to slip in relation to the Moroccan
dirham in 1978, for example, the Moroccan treasury covered the difference and mandated that the BCP extend a 3 percent "fidelity bonus" on
all bank deposits. Although the government, struggling with its own
budget constraints, was not always able to offer bonuses on deposits, it
was careful to protect migrants from shifts in exchange rates, especially
at times when a drop in prices of phosphate (Morocco's main export), a
war (in the western Sahara), and a rise in petroleum costs increased the
government's need for foreign currency.[51]

Through the provision of these services, the BCP brought migrants
and their remittances into the formal banking system and kept them as
loyal clients who continued to increase their bank deposits and savings.
It continued to expand its migrant client base and the remittances it
channeled to Morocco, even after Europe fundamentally redefined its
immigration policy when its demand for labor contracted (in 1974).
Major firms that had hired Moroccan labor, especially in heavy industry, began to let workers go, invariably laying immigrants off first, and
European countries allowed for limited family reunification, just as Moroccan workers had begun to have their wives and children join them.
Nonetheless, during the 1980s remittances rose, and migrant deposits,
which averaged 20 percent of total BCP deposits in all Moroccan banks,
peaked at nearly 30 percent in 1987 (see figure 8.1).[52] By 1990, when the
number of Moroccan men, women, and children living in Europe was

estimated at 1 million, the BCP had an astounding 400,000 emigrant clients.[53]

Such a large emigrant contribution to the liquidity in the Moroccan financial sector would, by definition, have a significant impact on the Moroccan economy, but its impact was magnified by the BCP's position in the Moroccan banking system. As a state-controlled bank, the BCP also served as one of the state's main financiers.[54] Definitive data on exactly where and to whom the BCP tendered its funds is impossible to obtain. The boundary between the state's and the bank's accounting columns were porous, and laws against reporting the crown's income, investments, and expenditures made the BCP's funds especially fungible. Nevertheless, available evidence suggests that its involvement in national development investments was substantial. In addition to the 30 percent of its equity that the bank was required by law to invest in government bonds, which the state used to fund such major infrastructure projects as dams, in the 1960s and early 1970s, and transportation, beginning in the mid 1970s, the annual BCP reports indicate that it was a major creditor to the phosphate, energy, fishing, and food-processing industry.[55] Accounts in the Moroccan press also suggest that the BCP played a significant role in the kingdom's "Moroccanization" program, launched in 1973 but lasting throughout the 1970s, to buy majority ownership in the country's dominant firms, and that it underwrote the Moroccan government's war in the western Sahara, which began in 1975.[56] The BCP also supported capital investment in public, semi-public, and to a lesser extent, private enterprises in Morocco's coastal cities.[57] By banking with the BCP, migrants were bankrolling the development of heavy industry and agribusiness, and transforming the structure of the Moroccan economy. They were never directly responsible for the changes, via a shift in their outlays from consumption to productive investments. They continued to spend on themselves and their families. However, they recognized that they simultaneously helped fund a development strategy that bypassed the communities from which they came and where many of their families still lived.

How Close Is Too Close?

Although the migrants relied heavily on BCP financial transfer and banking services, they did so with some ambivalence. The mistrust many migrants felt when the BCP first approached them in the late

1960s never completely dissipated, and several migrants who would later become labor activists accused the BCP of trying to co-opt migrant workers' wages.[58] Moreover, migrants met up with Moroccan government representatives at European worksites whom they distrusted. The Moroccan government sent a number of shadowy "management consultants" to large firms that were especially heavy users of Moroccan labor. These consultants were dispatched to factories and mines to "protect the Moroccan brand name," as one migrant activist wryly put it.[59] They were sent to assist in the supervision of Moroccan workers and ensure that they remained "obedient and hardworking."[60] Bank staff occasionally resolved administrative issues for Moroccan workers that were related to their employment, but they tended to steer clear of labor disputes. Under the circumstances, many migrants suspected that the Moroccan consultants exercised a disciplinary function. "You saw the working conditions in the smeltering factories, you saw the Moroccan police, and you saw the Banque Chaabi [Banque Centrale Populaire] collecting the workers' money—it was enough to make your blood boil," recalled one migrant activist.[61]

Beginning in the early 1970s, the management consultants were largely replaced by a more informal but more brutal form of labor control. The Moroccan government organized a network of "Friendship Societies," ostensibly cultural associations, made up of migrants who were government loyalists and who collaborated closely with Moroccan consular offices in Europe. Their members functioned as agents of the Moroccan government in labor disputes involving Moroccan workers, and they informed on labor activists to the Moroccan and European authorities. As a result, labor leaders experienced difficulty renewing worker contracts and arrest upon return to Morocco, and workers experienced verbal and physical abuse.[62] As one worker employed in a mine in the north of France recounted, "The representative of the Friendship Society came to our mine and he told [us]: 'You are here to work, not to protest or to go on strike. Anyone who doesn't want to work, I'll send him back to Morocco, and his problems will start as soon as he clears customs.'"[63]

As production in European heavy industry began to slow down and then contract, starting in the mid 1970s, and as companies began laying off many workers, labor battles around work conditions and employment became more pitched. Much to the Moroccan government's consternation, Moroccan workers were at the vanguard of migrant protest movements, first against layoffs and then for parity with nonmigrant workers in severance benefits. This was especially the case in France, as well as in Belgium.[64] Following a massive and highly publicized strike over safety violations at the Pennaroya foundries in Lyon and Paris in 1971, Moroccan workers mobilized protests at automobile factories, steel mills, mines, and chemical processing plants throughout Europe.[65] Retaliation by the Moroccan government through their Friendship Societies turned thuggish. In labor disputes, striking workers were beaten up, their families in Morocco were threatened, and their cars and homes subjected to arson, until the end of the 1980s. Also, a number of workers were incarcerated when they traveled to Morocco.[66]

The Moroccan government viewed migrant employment as essential to maintaining remittance flows it had come to rely on, and deemed what it considered "labor agitation" as jeopardizing its revenue stream. In addition to cracking down on labor organizing, the government attempted to discourage Moroccans from mobilizing for greater civic rights in destination countries, such as for voting rights in local elections and for easier naturalization procedures. Hassan II, Morocco's authoritarian monarch, complemented the government's use of on-the-ground dissuasion by its Friendship Societies with stern public pronouncements in European media throughout the 1980s. He warned Moroccan migrants to refrain from seeking integration in destination countries.[67]

The Moroccan government's heavy-handed attempt to control migrants began to affect the delicate relationship that the BCP had established with Moroccan emigrants through its "strategy of accompaniment." Moroccan activists remembered the late 1980s as a time when they "grieved for [their] country and let it go—*on a fait le deuil de notre pays.*"[68] At a plenary organization of Moroccan labor and community organizations in Europe, held in Paris, one representative summed up the sentiments of Moroccan workers, activists, and laymen alike. He noted that "the maneuvers of the Moroccan authorities weigh heavily on us. They isolate us . . . By compelling us to work here and not return to Morocco, they oblige us to remain more than loyal; [they demand] a complete loyalty to the Moroccan regime. . . . It weighs heavily on us and we need to make an effort to free ourselves from it."[69] Moroccan activists pushed for a complete disengagement with the Moroccan government, and as a result, naturalization rates of Moroccan migrants surged. The annual acquisition of French nationality, for example, rose from

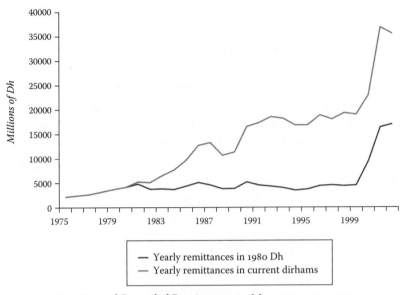

FIGURE 8.2. Annual Recorded Remittances to Morocco, 1975–2003

Source: Government of Morocco, Office de Changes. Yearly remittances–data series: 1975–2002; IMF Balance of Payments Statistics Yearbooks, 1975–2002

3,000 in 1988 to 12,000 in 1992.[70] More troubling to the Moroccan regime were the explicit calls for "remittance boycotts." While it is impossible to say whether these calls had an impact on remittance flows, transfer levels (adjusted for inflation) dropped by 20 percent between 1986 and 1988.[71] Furthermore, Moroccan emigrant deposits in the BCP, as a percentage of national deposits, fell steadily after 1987 and would never recover their previous levels (see figure 8.2).

In an effort to revive Moroccans' connection to their homeland, and more saliently, to boost flagging remittance receipts, the Moroccan government, and Hassan II personally, established a set of new institutions to reengage with migrants. In 1990, the king created a royal foundation, the Hassan II Foundation for Moroccans Living Abroad, a ministry for the Moroccan community abroad, and he opened a new bank, Bank al-Amal, to support migrant business investment. However, the government's attempt to broaden the BCP's style of engagement, with its "strategy of accompaniment," to cultural and political realms was clumsy, and it ultimately backfired. The foundation's board was stacked with presidents of Friendship Societies, while the foundation itself was funded through a diversion of the bonuses that had previously been offered to migrants for their deposits in BCP savings accounts, in what one emigrant activist called "the biggest hold-up in history." The ministry, in turn, was downgraded to a department in the Foreign Affairs Ministry just three years after its founding, and then shut down completely in 1995 because it had become disturbingly clear to the crown that it could not co-opt emigrant political organizers. Moreover, Bank al-Amal never got off the ground. The BCP, unwilling to broker any state-sanctioned competition in the emigrant market it considered its territory, starved the new initiative by delaying indefinitely the transfer of start-up funds the king had mandated.[72]

Calls for remittance boycotts continued throughout the 1990s and into the 2000s, occasionally spiking in stridency, depending on the political issues at stake. After the Ministry for the Moroccan Community Abroad was dismantled, the Hassan II Foundation positioned itself as the main intermediary between migrants and their government and excluded migrant groups it viewed as disloyal to the regime. It sidelined migrant labor and migrant rights groups, in particular. These organizations reminded their constituents that the BCP was a de-facto arm of the same Moroccan government that refused to acknowledge them and their concerns.

In 1998, when the ailing Hassan II allowed for a transitional government to midwife a limited political aperture, migrant issues were completely overlooked in the detailed review of government portfolios and the preparation of new strategic plans.[73] Migrant groups bristled at this political erasure and underscored an appeal, issued through the Forum for Immigrants in the European Union, that the Moroccan government "give the Moroccan diaspora its rightful place and role in Morocco," with a reminder of how important remittances were to the country's income.[74] Increasingly, statements that Moroccans were akin to the "goose that hatches golden eggs" were tied to complaints about the government's abject and long-standing neglect of Morocco's rural areas in its development policy.[75] Migrants widely derided "the state's complete abandonment—*la démission totale de l'état*" in rural Morocco. They criticized the low levels of service provisioning and government development investment in their communities of origin, and demanded a broader role in shaping development policy, in exchange for their contribution to national income and for the role their monies had played in financing the government's development initiatives.[76] "Moroccans living abroad want political compensation for their economic contribution . . . They want real participation in the management of the country; if not, they will shut off the [remittance] faucets," summed up the lead editorial in one of Morocco's best-selling economics magazines in the summer of 2003.[77]

Certainly, calls for remittance boycotts were politically powerful, and suggested an awareness among migrants generally, and migrant activists more pointedly, of the role their remittances had played in bankrolling national development, thanks to the government's determination to bring remittances into the formal banking system. However, migrants may have ultimately had a greater impact on the direction of Morocco's development strategy through their quiet, everyday use of the financial tools to which they had access, thanks to their integration into the financial system and into the BCP in particular.

The Formation of a Different Vision of Development

The Moroccan migrants that traveled to Europe during the 1960s and 1970s, and who made up the BCP's first emigrant client base, overwhelmingly came from the rural areas in the center-south region of Morocco called the Souss, or from the northern, mountainous regions of the Rif. Those areas have, since the 1970s, experienced accelerated processes of microurbanization and mesourbanization.[78] In other words, villages located in these regions have "urbanized," expanding into towns and experiencing internal migration from within their provinces. The growth and emergence of secondary cities, particularly in provinces that were overwhelmingly rural, have been significant throughout the country, with small and medium cities growing at twice the rate of Morocco's largest city, Casablanca.[79] Rates of growth have been highest among towns with 20,000 to 50,000 inhabitants.[80] However, growth has been greatest in areas with the highest historical numbers of out-migration.

Studies tracking the accelerated micro-urbanization in historical emigration areas of Morocco posit that migrant investment in housing drove the change. A national survey conducted in 1975, as well as a follow-up survey published in 2000, found that roughly 70 percent of Moroccans had invested in housing in Morocco.[81] However, they did not always construct houses in their communities of origin. Instead, migrants of rural origin gravitated toward the small but growing towns near their home villages and hamlets. As a result, such secondary cities as Agadir, Taroudant, Tetouan, and Ouarzazate experienced marked, if disorganized, growth over the last three decades, and several cities emerged as completely new urban settlements, such as Nador, in the Rif, and Zagora and Tinghir, in the south. In the isolated Todgha valley, in the south of Morocco, for example, only 5 percent of houses financed by migrants were built outside the region. However, 20 percent of the houses migrants built were not in their villages of origin, but in Tinghir, the valley's local boomtown.[82] Although migrant investment in sectors other than housing has been marginal, at less than 16 percent of total investment, even those ventures follow similar patterns.[83] For example, when migrants have invested in small businesses, they have chosen to locate them in the burgeoning secondary cities near their hometowns.[84]

Migrants' access to credit through their participation in Morocco's formal financial system may have accentuated this process of microurbanization. In the discussions that the BCP had with their migrant clients throughout the 1970s, migrants emphasized their concern with constructing homes in Morocco. In response, the BCP launched a program in 1978 to offer migrants subsidized loans to construct or purchase housing in Morocco. The bank used migrant deposits as collateral and their remittance transfer history as a proxy to predict their creditworthiness. The program was an instant hit. Within a couple of years, the bank extended nearly 8,000 migrant mortgages, 85 percent of its real estate investments at the time.[85] After 1982, the bank stopped disaggregating its mortgages by the migrant or nonmigrant status of its borrowers, but staff accounts suggest that the program continued to expand. Bank data on the location of the homes purchased or constructed with its loans is not available. However, a parallel but much smaller government subsidized housing program in the 1980s also shows that migrants preferred homes in secondary cities near their villages, over more established littoral cities.[86] In addition, the BCP became an important supplier of microcredit for small businesses in emerging secondary cities. Those loans have never been disaggregated by the migrant status of the borrower, but the BCP's evisceration of the bank Hassan II set up for migrant investment suggests that the proportion of migrant clientele was significant.[87]

As secondary cities grew in migrant sending areas, provisioning of basic infrastructure services became a political imperative for the government.[88] In the 1970s and 1980s rural infrastructure had been minimal. Among rural residents, barely more than 20 percent had electricity, less than 15 percent had access to potable water, and fewer than 40 percent had access to roads of any kind, paved or unpaved.[89] Once the government began to extend services to the burgeoning secondary towns it became politically untenable to continue to neglect nearby villages. Thus, the government improved its rural infrastructure delivery dramatically. By the end of the 1990s rural electrification came to exceed 90 percent, access to water topped 80 percent, and the rural roads network expanded by 11,000 kilometers, or 20 percent.[90]

The strides the government made in infrastructure provision were soon matched by an explicit policy shift in its approach to rural development. In 1999, shortly after Mohammed VI ascended to the throne, following his father's death, he issued a directive indicating that his top priority for the forthcoming National Development Plan was "the promotion of neglected regions and their integration into the dynamic of economic development, notably by reducing the delay that rural areas suffer in the matter of basic infrastructure and social service provision."[91] In subsequent official communications, Mohammed VI formally acknowledged the role of migrants in shifting the development paradigm that the country had relied on for so long. In a letter to the prime minister on development policy, he called migrants "dynamic agents" of development, and praised "the laudable efforts of our loyal subjects living outside the national territory in the matter of investment," encouraging them to "continue in this vein given the numerous and great benefits that they have generated for themselves and for Morocco."[92] He stressed, in particular, that their involvement with "the reduction of vast poverty and the improvement of basic service provision in rural areas [brought the crown] great satisfaction."[93]

With such royal pronouncements, migrants were recognized as more than purveyors of money for development, whose wages should "not escape state control." They were formally acknowledged as important agents of the social and economic transformation of their homeland.

And important agents migrants have remained. During the Arab Spring of 2011, the secondary cities in the heartland of the country were the sites of some of the most active protests against the political status-quo. Cities like Taounate, Ouezzane, Fikh Ben Salah, and Oued Zem that were largely tranquil during the protests of the 1980s and 1990s, if they could even be described as cities and not rural hamlets, saw significant unrest in 2011. Arguably, it was tumultuous unrest of these burgeoning cities, removed from the geographical center of power in Morocco's littoral strip that motivated the crown to offer a reformed constitution for a referendum vote in July of that year.

Lessons for Financial Intermediation and the Dangers of Losing Touch

The excuses proffered for not providing migrants with greater access to formal banking services are legion. They include the claims that the technological infrastructure to manage large volumes of small transfers and depository accounts in a cost-effective manner do not yet exist; that migrants are too dispersed and geographically mobile; that they have special cultural and linguistic needs; that their financial literacy, to say nothing of their actual functional literacy, is weak; and that the regulatory structure governing international transactions is rigid and complex.

The historical example of Morocco's Banque Centrale Populaire reveals that these excuses are, for the most part, hollow. The Moroccan government established a compendium of services that enabled it to integrate the vast majority of its citizens abroad into the kingdom's formal banking system. It did so beginning in 1968, when paper ledgers and the telex were the technology of the day. And it serviced a clientele made up of many who were only marginally literate, and who faced significant obstacles when attempting to use formal money-transfer channels. As a result of its initiative, Operation Moroccan Workers Abroad, the government annually brought an amount equal to several percentage points of Morocco's national GDP through the formal banking system, and a sizable portion of the funds were transformed, through traditional financial intermediation, into capital that funded major national development projects. However, its success hinged on its partnership with its migrant clients. Never did it attempt to alter migrant spending practices, to direct their expenditures toward investments considered productive. Instead, the bank, and the government that stood behind it, acted with migrants to create financial products that would allow them to meet the objectives that they had set for themselves and their families.

The BCP continues to enjoy success. Even though other Moroccan banks have entered the remittance market and have worked hard to attract migrant clientele, remittances held in BCP accounts still represent about 12 percent of total national deposits.[94] Its outreach to Moroccan migrants in newer destination countries, such as Spain and Italy, has been aggressive and effective. Through its tried and true strategy of accompaniment, it has drawn new migrants into the formal banking system, as well as into a system of financial intermediation that supports government development priorities, even since it became a public company in 2004 (albeit with majority state ownership). By continuing to work with migrants, the BCP has introduced new and innovative services, from cell phone banking to new payment and borrowing mechanisms, tailored to their concerns.

However, the BCP, and the other Moroccan banks following its lead, are struggling to appeal to more recent migrants. Migrants who came in the early waves of Moroccan emigration, in the 1960s, 1970s, and even 1980s, continue to be strong senders of remittances, both in terms of the amount they send home and the proportion of migrants who remit, even though most theories of migrant remittance behavior posit that transfers decline with length of stay abroad. The Moroccan exceptionalism can, arguably, be attributed to the BCP initiative. However, fewer of the more recent migrants in France send money home or invest in Morocco. On the whole, the newer migrants to France are more educated, and more tightly integrated into French professional networks. Although they maintain strong ties to Morocco, fewer of them plan to return permanently.[95] The BCP has been slow to connect with these migrants, a client base that is not only able to access a wider array of banking institutions both in Morocco and in the countries in which they have settled, but that has more sophisticated understandings of the services they need and that is more exacting in its standards. It has failed to invest in the practice of *acting with* this class of migrants and has thus fallen short of creating the full range of transnational banking services that could meet their needs both in Morocco and in France.

The BCP's mixed performance contrasts sharply with its success in providing banking services to Moroccan migrants in new destination countries like Italy and Spain. The demographic profile of Moroccans emigrating to these two countries, in particular, echoes that of early migrant waves: they are relatively less-educated migrants who leave Morocco with minimal exposure to formal banking services and who experience significant social exclusion in the destination country. In Italy and Spain, the BCP has engaged with new migrants with relative ease. Thus, the BCP seems caught in a model of engagement with migrants based on an understanding of who they are and what they need that is stuck in the past. To continue its remarkable success in drawing

Moroccan migrants into the national financial system, and using traditional financial intermediation to make remittances available as capital for a growing economy, the bank, and the government that stands behind it, needs to connect with Moroccan migrants in all their diversity. The bank needs to draw on its own historical memory of how it cultivated the art of *acting with* migrants, rather than simply limiting itself to a set of practices that it used to connect with earlier waves of migrants. This is critical because, thanks to its engagement with migrants, Moroccans abroad were not asked to choose between their household needs and development projects, as has been the case, for example, in Mexico, and they came to trust the bank that channeled its deposits to national development projects, unlike Cuban recipients of remittances, who, to date, lack confidence in how the official bank might use their deposits—as David FitzGerald and Susan Eckstein describe in their respective chapters. More importantly, the Moroccan government's engagement with Moroccans abroad about their remittances equipped migrants with the political leverage and access to the financial tools they needed to push for alternate approaches for development, to their own good as well as that of their home country.

Notes

1 This article draws on a multiyear, multimethod research project to evaluate Morocco's migration and development policies. To analyze the Moroccan government's provision of financial services to Moroccan emigrants specifically, I conducted significant documentary and archival research, including an archival press review and a careful analysis of the BCP's financial statements from 1974 to 2010, and of their marketing material over that same period. I also conducted numerous interviews with bank staff, bank users, and migrants who chose not to use the bank's services, both in Morocco and in France. I also interviewed Moroccan government officials, current and past, about Morocco's national development plans, and I reviewed both internal and external descriptions of Morocco's formal development plans. Finally, I interviewed staff at Morocco's numerous institutions that provide services to Moroccan migrants, services that were in some way related to the BCP's financial services, as well as migrants who used the services.

2 "Groupe d'Etudes et de Recherches Appliquées (GERA), Etude des mouvements migratoires du Maroc vers la communauté Européene" (Rabat: Université Mohammed V, 1992); Georges Tapinos, *L'immigration etrangère en France* (Paris: Presses Universitaires de France, 1975).

3 Quoted in Yamina Benguigui, *Mémoires d'immigrés: L'heritage Maghrébin* (Paris: Canal + editions, 1997), 37–38.

4 Brahim Benaïcha, quoted in Pascal Blanchard, Eric Deroo, Driss El Yazami, Pierre Fournié, and Gilles Manceron, *Le Paris Arabe* (Paris: La Découverte, 2003), 183.

5 Alexis Spire, *Étrangers à la carte: L'admistration de l'immigration en France* (Paris: Bernard Grasset, 2005).

6 Ibid., 189–205; Vincent Viet, *La France immigrée: Construction d'une politique, 1914–1997* (Paris: Fayard, 1998), 281–90.

7 Zakya Daoud, *Travailleurs Marocains en France: Mémoire restituée* (Casablanca: Tarik éditions, 2004), 12.

8 Anne Frennet-De Keyser, "La convention Belgo-Marocaine de main d'oeuvre: Un non-événement?" in *Trajectoires et dynamiques migratoires de l'immigration Marocaine de Belgique*, ed. Nouria Ouali (Louvain-La Neuve, Belgium: Bruylant-Academia, 2004). The Belgian consul-general in Casablanca, for example, lauded Moroccan labor as a source of manpower for employers, a source "appreciate[d] very much" for being just as capable but more malleable than workers from other North African countries (Frennet-De Keyser, "La convention Belgo-Marocaine de main d'oeuvre," 220).

9 Natasha Iskander, *Creative State: Forty Years of Migration and Development Policy in Morocco and Mexico* (Ithaca, NY: Cornell University Press, 2010).

10 Quentin Wodon, Diego Angel-Urdinola, Gabriel Gonzalez-Konig, Diana Ojeda Revah, and Corinne Siaens, *Migration and Poverty in Mexico's Southern States* (Washington, DC: Regional Studies Program, Office of the Chief Economist for Latin America and the Caribbean, World Bank, 2002); Devesh Kapur and John McHale, "Migration's New Payoff," *Foreign Policy* 139 (2003): 49–57; Dani Rodrik, "Feasible Globalizations" (Working Paper 9129, National Bureau of Economic Research, 2002); Germán Zarate-Hoyos, "Consumption and Remittances in Migrant Households: Toward a Productive Use of Remittances," *Contemporary Economic Policy* 22, no. 4 (2004): 555–65; Stuart Brown, "Can Remittances Spur Development? A Critical Survey," *International Studies Review* 8, no. 1 (2006): 55–76.

11 Alejandra Cox-Edwards and Eduardo Rodríguez-Oreggia, "Remittances and Labor Force Participation in Mexico: An Analysis Using Propensity Schore Matching," *World Development* 37, no. 5 (2008): 1004–14; Reena Argarwal and Andrew Horrowitz, "Are Remittances Altruism or Insurance? Evidence from Guyana Using Multiple-Migrant Households," *World Development* 30 (2002): 2033–44; Catalina Amuedo-Dorantes, Cynthia Bansak, and Susan Pozo, "On the Remitting Patterns of Immigrants: Evidence from Mexican Survey Data" (paper presented at the Payments in the Americas Conference, Federal Reserve Bank of Atlanta, October 7–8, 2008); Fernando Borraz, "Assessing the

Impact of Remittances on Schooling: The Mexican Experience," *Global Economy Journal* 5 (2005): 9.

12 Ralph Chami, Connel Fullenkamp, and Samir Jahjah, "Are Immigrant Remittance Flows a Source of Capital for Development?" *IMF Staff Papers* 52, no. 1 (2005): 55–81; Barry McCormick and Jackline Wahba, "Overseas Employment and Remittances to a Dual Economy," *Economic Journal* 110, no. 463 (2000): 509–34.

13 Jorge Durand, Emilio Parrado, and Douglas Massey, "Migradollars and Development: A Reconsideration of the Mexican Case," *International Migration Review* (1996): 423–44; Raul Hinojosa-Ojeda, *Transnational Migration, Remittances, and Development in North America: Globalization Lessons from Oaxaca California Transnational Village/Community Modeling Project* (report prepared for IMF-IADB on behalf of the North American Integration Department Center, UCLA, 2003); Susan Eckstein, "Dollarization and Its Discontents: Remittances and the Remaking of Cuba in the Post-Soviet Era," *Comparative Politics* 36, no. 3 (2004): 313–30.

14 Natalia Catrinescu, Miguel Leon-Ledesma, Matloob Piracha, and Bryce Quillin, "Remittances, Institutions, and Economic Growth," *World Development* 37 (2009): 81–92.

15 Eckstein, "Dollarization and Its Discontents."

16 Douglas Massey and Emilio Parrado, "Migradollars: The Remittances and Savings of Mexican Migrants in the United States," *Population Research and Policy Review* 13, no. 1 (1994): 423–41.

17 Raúl Delgado Wise and Héctor Rodríguez, "The Emergence of Collective Migrants and Their Role in Mexico's Local and Regional Development," *Canadian Journal of Development Studies* (2000): 747–64.

18 Anna Paulson, Audrey Singer, Robin Newberger, and Jeremy Smith, "Financial Access for Immigrants: Lessons from Diverse Perspectives" (Washington, DC: Brookings Institution, 2006).

19 Sheila Blair, "Improving the Access of Recent Latin American Migrants to the U.S. Banking System," in *Beyond Small Change: Making Migrant Remittances Count*, ed. Donald Terry (Washington, DC: IADB, 2005): 95–132.

20 Inter-American Development Bank—Multilateral Investment Fund, *Sending Money Home: Remittance to Latin America and the Caribbean* (Washington, DC: IADB, 2004); Donald Terry and Steven R. Wilson, eds., *Beyond Small Change.*

21 Brown, "Can Remittances Spur Development?" 69.

22 Manuel Orozco and Rachel Radewa, "Leveraging Efforts of Remittances and Financial Intermediation" (Working Paper 4, Inter-American Development Bank—Integration and Regional Programs Department Working Paper Series, Washington, DC, 2006).

23 Natasha Iskander, "Social Learning as a Productive Project: The Tres Por Uno (Three for One) Experience at Zacatecas, Mexico," in *The Development Dimension: Migration, Remittances and Development*, ed. Organisation for Economic Co-operation and Development (OECD) (Paris: OECD, 2005).

24 Suhas Ketkar and Dilip Ratha, "Development Financing during a Crisis: Securitization of Future Receivables" (World Bank Policy Research Working Paper 2582, 2001); Suhas Ketkar and Dilip Ratha, "Development Finance via Diaspora Bonds," in *Innovative Financing for Development*, ed. Suhas Ketkar and Dilip Ratha (Washington, DC: World Bank, 2009).

25 Iskander, "Social Learning as a Productive Project"; Rafael Fernández de Castro, Rodolfo García Zamora, and Ana Vila Freyer, *El Programa 3<{x}>1 Para Migrantes: Primera Política Transnational En México?* (Mexico City: Instituto Technológico de México and Universidad Autónoma de Zacatecas, 2006).

26 Paulson et al., "Financial Access for Immigrants."

27 A few large banks in the United States and Europe have started to follow suit with modest initiatives targeted at migrants, and have begun offering bilingual services, training courses in financial literacy that expose the client to a full range of products, from current accounts to mortgages, and products that are low cost, such as accounts with no minimum balance and overdraft protection. Still, these initiatives are extensions of their community banking services (Blair, Orzoco, and Radewa, "Leveraging Efforts of Remittances and Financial Intermediation").

28 David Grace, "Exploring the Credit Union Experience with Remittances in the Latin American Market," in *Remittances and Development: Development Impact and Future Prospects*, ed. Samuel Maimbo and Dilip Ratha (Washington, DC: World Bank, 2005).

29 Iskander, *Creative State*.

30 Government of Morocco, "Convention de main d'oeuvre entre le Maroc et la France" (Rabat: Ministry of Labor, 1963), article 13.

31 Abdelkrim Belguendouz, *Les Marocains à l'etranger: Citoyens et partenaires* (Kénitra, Morocco: Boukili Impression, 1999), 34–35.

32 Ibid., 39.

33 World Bank, *The Economic Development of Morocco* (Baltimore: Johns Hopkins University Press, 1966).

34 Abdelkrim Belguendouz, "L'émigration des travailleurs marocains," in *La grande encyclopédie du Maroc*, 37–64 (Rabat: GEM, 1987).

35 World Bank, *The Economic Development of Morocco*; World Bank, *Morocco—Economic and Social Development Report* (Baltimore: Johns Hopkins University Press, 1981).

36 World Bank, *Morocco—Economic and Social Development Report*.

37 Banque Centrale Populaire, *25 ans d'expansion: 1961–1986* (Casablanca: Banque Centrale Populaire, 1986).

38 Boujemaa Laftasse, Abderrahim Haoudi, and Meryem Fhal, "Les transferts d'epargne des R. M. E" (Rabat: Université Mohammed V, 1992).

39 Iskander, *Creative State*, 93.

40 Ibid., 94.

41 Daniel Bossard, "Un espace de migration: Les travailleurs du Rif oriental (Province De Nador) et l'Europe" (Montpellier, France: Université Paul Valery, 1979), 172.

42 Ibid.; Iskander, *Creative State*; Mohammed Charef, "Les transfers d'épargne des émigrés Marocains en France: Évaluation de leur importance et de leurs effets," in *Maghrébins en France: Émigrés ou immigrés?* ed. Larbi Talha (Aix-en-Provence, France: University of Aix-en-Provence, 1981), 217–28.

43 Charef, "Les transfers d'épargne des émigrés Marocains en France," 220–21.

44 Ibid., 221.

45 Bossard, "Un espace de migration"; Iskander, *Creative State*; Charef, "Les transfers d'épargne des émigrés Marocains en France."

46 The BCP was able to provide these preprinted forms after 1972, thanks to an agreement it concluded with the French postal service (Iskander, *Creative State*, 101).

47 Banque Centrale Populaire, *30 ans: 1961–1991* (Casablanca: Banque Centrale Populaire, 1991).

48 C. Monnard, "L'éternel retour: La population Marocaine dans le monde," *Jeune Afrique* (1998).

49 Rafik Ikram and Malika El Jouhari, "Essoufflement des transfers financiers," *L'Economiste*, May 17, 1997.

50 Banque Centrale Populaire, *25 ans d'expansion*; 1986 Banque Centrale Populaire, *30 ans*; Office des Changes, "Data on Remittances—Sources and Types," data series (Rabat: Government of Morocco, 1963–2006).

51 Jean-Pierre Garson and Mohamed Bennabou, "Les Marocains," in *L'argent des immigrés: Revenues*, in *Épargne et transferts de huit nationalités immigrées en France*, ed. Jean-Pierre Garson and Georges Tapinos (Paris: Presses Univer-sitaires de France, 1981); Groupe d'Etudes et de Recherches Appliquées, "Etude des mouvements migratoires du Maroc vers la communauté Européene."

52 Office des Changes, 1975–1990; Banque Centrale Populaire, *Rapport Annuel* (Casablanca: Banque Centrale Populaire, 1980–1990); International Monetary Fund, *Balance of Payments Statistics Yearbook* (Washington, DC: Interna-tional Monetary Fund, data series, 1977–2002).

53 Groupe d'Etudes et de Recherches Appliquées, "Etude des mouvements mi-gratoires du Maroc vers la communauté Européene." Banque Centrale Popu-laire, *Rapport Annuel* (Casablanca: Banque Centrale Populaire, 1991).

54 Banque Centrale Populaire, Annual Reports, 1977–2000.

55 Ibid.

56 Jean Francois Clément and James Paul, "Morocco's Bourgeoisie: Monarchy, State and Owning Class," *MERIP Reports* 142 (1986): 13–17.

57 A. Claisse, "Makhzen Traditions," in *The Political Economy of Morocco*, ed. I. W. Zartman (New York: Praeger, 1987); A. D. N., "Resultats Bancaires Pour 1992: BCP—Les RME Constituent 65% des Dépots," *L'Economiste* (September 18, 1993); Iskander, *Creative State*, 141.

58 Daoud, *Travailleurs Marocains en France*, 25–27. Iskander, *Creative State*.

59 Interview, Paris, 2004.

60 Daoud, *Travailleurs Marocains en France*; Spire, *Étrangers à la carte*.

61 Interview, Paris, 2004.

62 Iskander, *Creative State*; Daoud, *Travailleurs Marocains en France*.

63 Benguigui, *Mémoires d'immigrés*, 40.

64 A. Zancarini-Fournel, "La question immigrée après 68," *Plein droit* (2002): 53–54; Antoine Dumont, "Polarisation et fragmentation identitaires au sein du mouvement associatif des migrants Marocains en France (1956–2006)." Paper presented at Colloquium: Classe, ethnicité, genre . . . : Les mobilisations au piège de la fragmentation identitaire?, Université de Poitiers, Poitiers, March 8–9, 2007.

65 Daoud, *Travailleurs Marocains en France*.

66 Ibid.; Association des Travailleurs Marocains en France (ATMF), *Ils ont écrit . . . dignité*. (Gennevilliers, France: ATMF, 1984).

67 Iskander, *Creative State*, 159–60.

68 Ibid., 158.

69 Association des Travailleurs Marocains en France, "La communaute Marocaine en France: Quelles evolutions? Quelles perspectives?" in *Recontre Nationale ATMF 28/29 January 1989*, ed. ATMF (Paris: ATMF, 1989), 68.

70 Zoubir Chattou and Mustapha Belbah, *La double nationalité en question: Enjeux et motivations de la double appartenance* (Paris: Editions Karthala, 2002), 137.

71 Office des Changes, 1986–88.

72 Iskander, *Creative State*; Laurie Brand, "States and Their Expatriates: Explaining the Development of Tunisian and Moroccan Emigration-Related Institutions" (Working Paper 52, Center for Comparative Immigration Studies, University of California, San Diego, 2002).

73 Chattou and Belbah, *La double nationalité en question*.

74 Ibid., 145.

75 Nizar Al-Aly, "Morocco: Emigrants Press for True Citizenship Back Home." *Africa News*, August 20, 1999.

76 Iskander, *Creative State*; Zakya Daoud, *Marocains de l'autre rive* (Casablanca: Editions Maghrébines, 2005).

77 *Economie & entreprise, Hors série, MRE* (Casablanca: July–August 2003), 5.

78 Khachani, Mohammed, "The Impact of Migration on the Moroccan Econ-

omy," *Journal of Ethnic and Migration Studies* 35, no. 10 (2009): 1609–21; Hein de Haas, "Morocco's Migration Transition: Trends, Determinants, and Future Scenarious" (Working Paper 3, Migration and Development Revisited [MDR], 2005); Hein de Haas, "The Impact of International Migration on Social and Economic Development in Moroccan Sending Regions: A Review of the Empirical Literature" (Working Paper 3, International Migration Institute, University of Oxford, Oxford, 2007).

79 United Nations Human Settlements Programme, *The State of African Cities 2008.* (New York: United Nations, 2009), 41.

80 Haas, "Morocco's Migration Transition," 24.

81 B. Hamdouch, A. Berrada, W. Heinmeyer, P. de Mas, and H. van der Wusten, *Migration de développement, migration de sous-développement?: Une etude sur l'impact de la migration dans le milieu rural du Maroc, série etudes et recherches* (Rabat: INSEA, 1979); INSEA, *Les Marocains résidant à l'étranger : Une enquête socio-économique* (Rabat: INSEA, 2000).

82 Haas, 22–24.

83 INSEA, *Les Marocains résidant à l'étranger.*

84 Mohamed Berriane, "La ville, le développement sectoriel et la relance des provinces du nord," in *Le développement du Maroc septiregional: Points de vues de géographes,* ed. Mohamed Berriane and Abdellah Laouina (Neustadt an der Aisch, Germany: Justus Perthes Verlag Gotha, 1998).

85 Banque Centrale Populaire, 1979–1982.

86 GERA, "Etude des mouvements migratoires du Maroc vers la communauté Européene," 94–100.

87 Iskander, *Creative State.*

88 Mohammed Berriane, "Fonctionnement du système migratoire et naissance d'un petit centre urbain (Taouima) dans la banlieue de Nador (Maroc)," in *Les nouvelles formes de la mobilité spatiale dans le monde Arabe,* ed. Robert Signoles Escalier and Pierre Signoles Escalier (Tours: URBAMA, 1995).

89 Daoud, *Marocains de l'autre rive*; Iskander, *Creative State.*

90 World Bank, *Implementation Completion Report: Morocco, Second Rural Electrification Project* (Washington: World Bank, 1998); World Bank, *Morocco: A Watershed for Education and Health* (Washington: World Bank, 2003); World Bank, *Rural Roads Project for Morocco: Project Appraisal Document. Project ID P082754* (Washington, DC: World Bank, 2004).

91 Mohammed VI, "Lettre de S. M. Le Roi Mohammed VI au premier ministre, M. Abderrahmane El Youssoufi définissant le cadre et les orientations du plan quinquennal," December 1999.

92 Mohammed VI, "Discours de trône de Sa Majesté Le Roi Mohammed VI," December 1999.

93 Mohammed VI, "Allocution se S. M. Le Roi Mohammed VI devant les membres de la communauté Marocaine en France," September 2000.

94 Banque Centrale Populaire, *Rapport Annuel* (Casablanca: BCP, 2009).

95 Luis Miotti, El Mouhoub Mouhoud, and Joel Oudinet, "Migrants and Determinants of Remittances to Southern Mediterranean Countries: When History
Matters!" Paper presented at the Second International Conference on Migration and Development, Washington, DC, September 10–11, 2009.

9

The Gender Revolution in the Philippines
Migrant Mothering and Social Transformations

RHACEL SALAZAR PARREÑAS

[When I was seven years old,] my mom went to Malaysia, first for one to two years. Then she went to Saudi Arabia and then from Saudi Arabia, she went straight to the U.S. When she went to the United States, that was the longest—10 years—that we did not see each other at all. She came back and when we saw each other, I was already 21 years old.
—ISABELLE TIRADOR, Philippines

Isabelle is a child of a migrant domestic worker who first worked in Malaysia, then Saudi Arabia, and lastly the United States.[1] Left in the Philippines under the care of her aunt, Isabelle has what we could call a typical childhood. In the Philippines, nongovernmental organizations claim that there are approximately 9 million children growing up with at least one migrant parent. This figure represents approximately 27 percent of the youth population in the Philippines. Many, but not all, are children of migrant domestic workers.

More than 3 million Filipinos are believed to have emigrated and resettled elsewhere permanently. Another 4 million reportedly work abroad on temporary contracts. Migration has become so much a part of the Filipino experience that, in recent years, about 1 million Filipinos reportedly go abroad annually, to set up roots in another country. Another 4 million work abroad on temporary contracts, and 900,000 are irregular or undocumented migrants.[2]

Due to the demand for migrant domestic workers in the richer countries throughout the world, we are witnessing tremendous social transformations in countries such as the Philippines. The migration of women ruptures the traditional gender division of labor in the family. Migration makes women into breadwinners, not only in their families but also for the nation. Next to electronics manufacturing that are exported, labor migration generates the second largest amount of foreign currency in the Philippines.[3] Migrant remittances to the Philippines have escalated just since the turn of the century, from about $6 billion in 2000 to $12.7 billion in 2006.[4] After India, China, and Mexico, the Philippines receive the most migrant remittances.[5]

Not even the president of the Philippines ignores the economic dependence of the country on migrant labor. On July 23, 2001, a headline in the *Philippine Daily Inquirer* read, "OFWs [Overseas Filipino Workers] told: Stay abroad."[6] The article recaps an open forum with then-president Gloria Macapagal-Arroyo, in which she conceded that the Philippine economy depends heavily on the remittances of overseas Filipino workers for foreign currency. As she stated, "Jobs here [in the Philippines] are difficult to find and we are depending on the people outside the country. If you can find work there, and send money to your relatives here, then perhaps you should stay there." The president continued, "For now, sad to say, that's about it. The reality is that for now and many years to come, OFWs will still be a major part of the economy."

Addressing the country's economic dependence on migrant remittances even before the turn of this century, the journalist Gina Mission noted, "In the past decade, the number of overseas workers has risen beyond everyone's expectations to become an essential part of the economy. Between 22 to 35 million Filipinos—34 to 53 percent of the total population—have come to be directly dependent on remittances from migrant workers."[7]

Yet, it is not just overseas workers per se, but women overseas workers in particular, whom the nation has come to rely on for foreign currency. Beginning in 1995, women accounted for most migrants.[8] The percentage of migrants who were women rose from 54 percent in 1997 to 75 percent in 2006. Some 69 percent of these women were employed as care and domestic workers in private households, in more than 160 countries, in Asia, Europe, and the Americas.[9] However, with the global recession and concomitant decline in demand for domestic workers, the percentage of migrants that were women dropped to 44 percent in 2008.[10]

Even with the global recession, remittances sent in 2008, from both men and women, accounted for approximately 9 percent of the nation's GDP.[11] About one-third of remittances come from the Middle East, another third from Asia, 9 percent from North America, and 16 percent from Europe.[12] Many analysts, according to Alejandro Portes (in this volume) consider out-migration to have a positive impact on the home country, ensuring family survival and enhancing macro financial stability. Yet, Portes also recognizes that some development experts in the Global South consider out-migration a symptom of underdevelopment. Despite the emergence of competing views, the burgeoning discussion on migration and development still ignores the gender perspective, and rarely addresses the impact migration has on families. World Bank reports on remittances, for instance, do not disaggregate migrant remittances by gender, despite acknowledging the spike in women's labor migration globally.[13]

From the perspective of gender relations in the sending country, there are three ways we could think about women's labor migration. First, we could see it as indicative of a remarkable gender transformation. It leads not only to the greater earning power of women and their greater contribution to household income, but also to a redefinition of mothering. In this vein, biological mothers are shown to not necessarily be the primary caretakers of children, a victory for feminism. Feminists have long described the family as an oppressive institution for women, designating women as caretakers and burdening them with housework that limits their labor market options.[14] According to a second perspective, we could view women's migration as a tragedy, one that results in the forcible separation of children, such as Isabelle, from their mothers. This view is the dominant perspective in the Philippines, where the public looks at children's suffering when women migrate. From this perspective, women's migration also reflects a national economic tragedy. It is assumed that women would not migrate and leave their children behind if they had better labor market options in the Philippines. The solution would be the return migration of mothers, realistic only if job opportunities expand in the local labor market. From a third vantage point, transnational families formed by migrant mothers are seen as transforming gender relations, but by force, not choice, owing to the limited economic options available for both men and women in the Philippines. Indeed, poor economic conditions in the Philippines mainly account for the formation of transnational households and the concomitant reconstitution of gender in migrant families.

In public discourse in the Philippines, the rise of transnational mothering is seen as a reflection of the disintegration of the family as well as the failure of the economy. For many, including members of local advocacy groups for migrant families, the separation of children from their biological mothers signifies the economic woes of the Philippines. Many reason that mothers would not migrate if they had better labor market options in the Philippines. Seeing the separation of children from migrant mothers as a social problem, a logical solution would be to create jobs in the local economy. The concern with transnational mothering calls attention not merely to the economic problems of the Philippines but to rescuing the Filipino family from collapse. This conception rests on the time-worn assumption that biological mothers naturally provide the best care for children.

Without question, less economic dependence on labor migration would signify domestic economic development. The advocacy of economic growth, without a conscious rejection of its social implications, could inadvertently uphold romantic notions of biological mothering and call for a return to the patriarchal nuclear family. That is, a misguided call for the preservation of traditional culture would underlie desires for economic growth and less dependence on labor migration. Indeed, this seems to be the puzzling case in the Philippines.

The stunning example of Isabelle calls attention to her plight, which is what those who lament the migration of mothers would do, but also to society's compulsion to view her as a victim. The experience of Isabelle is a window through which to view social lives of Filipino migrant mothers in their home country.

It is important to recognize that migrant workers inhabit transnational spheres.[15] Thus, their labor migration involves not only their incorporation in the host society, but also their renegotiation of the social relations they maintain back home. Their migration also triggers social transformations back home. Women's migration forces reconstitution of the traditional gender division of labor in the household.

Sending societies are not passive recipients of the changes migration forces on them. Unfortunately, the literature on migration to date has constructed sending societies as such. For instance, Peggy Levitt's formulation of "social remittances," namely the ideas, practices, identities, and social capital that flow from receiving-country communities to sending-country communities, shows a one-way flow that is assumed to be smoothly accepted by sending societies.[16] Yet, the global flow of ideas and information is a more dynamic process, one described by Arjun Appadurai not as a unidirectional flow but as an exchange that occupies various "scapes," such as the "ethnoscape," the "ideoscape," and the "mediascape." The boundaries of scapes are constantly shifting. Moreover, the ideas disseminated in scapes have different meanings that would change according to the spectator as well as the context of reception.[17] For instance, the cultural interpretation of a Hollywood film would differ depending on the cultural tools used by the audience to make meaning of the images in the film. Consistent with Appadurai's thesis, José Miguel Cruz (in this volume) describes the flow of social and cultural practices in migrant communities not as one-way but circular and dynamic. The "social remittances," of gang culture from the United States to Central America shape everyday life because of a preexisting gang culture. In other words, a cultural collusion between the migrant's destination and community of origin underlies the processes of "social remittance." Moreover, according to Cruz, the cultural values of gang life do not remain static but instead transform upon incorporation, resulting in a transnational gang community that extends back to the United States.

In the case of the Philippines, migration imposes tremendous cultural transformations, including a redefinition of mothering prompted by the feminization of migration. Yet, we cannot simply assume that society passively accepts the cultural transformations that migration engenders in the country of origin. Unfortunately, existing literature inadvertently suggests so. While discussions of transnational mothering have called attention to migrant women's efforts to redefine mothering to encompass breadwinning, the literature has failed to consider how other members of the family respond to, and perhaps even reject, the new household arrangement.[18] So as not to flatten the experiences of those in the homeland, we need to analyze not only "how immigrants impact their homelands" but how people in the homeland respond to the changes migration unleashes.

I am especially concerned with the response of the homeland to the growing phenomenon of "transnational mothering."[19] Sociologists Pierrette Hondagneu-Sotelo and Ernestine Avila define transnational mothering as the organizational reconstitution and rearrangement of motherhood to accommodate the temporal and spatial separations forced by migration.[20] They found that this arrangement redefines motherhood, to include breadwinning. Societal rejection of "transnational mothering," results in the vilification of migrant mothers in public discourse, the rejection of care work by fathers, and the refusal of children to recognize the efforts of mothers. The moral economy of the

Philippines, and national identity, is deeply tied to the ideology of female domesticity. This ideology places migrant mothers in a no-win situation, in that it pushes them to pursue labor migration at the expense of their fulfillment of the "proper" duties relegated to women in the family.

The Backlash against Migrant Mothers

In the Philippines, the public views such children as Isabelle as victims who have been abandoned by their mothers. It considers women's migration as bad both for the welfare of children and for the sanctity of the family. It does not disdain migrant fathers, only migrant mothers. The prevailing view is if one parent must migrate, best it be the father.

The negative view associated with women's migration seems to haunt migrant mothers, not only in the Philippines, but in many other domestic-worker sending countries, including Poland, Sri Lanka, and Romania.[21] In Poland, public discourse labels the children of migrant women as "Euro-orphans," meaning children who have been orphaned by the outflow of migrant mothers to Western Europe. A Minister of Education in Poland, blaming failing test scores and growing truancy on parental migration, noted, "Kids get into trouble with the law, have social problems, behavior and attitude problems in school, and absences."[22] Similarly, in Romania the out-migration of women has been perceived as a "national tragedy," triggering social upheaval involving not only the collapse of the family, but also increased child delinquency and child psychological problems, including, occasionally, suicide.[23] And in Sri Lanka, as in the Philippines, the government has called for the return migration of mothers as the solution to problems that children of transnational families incur. As recently as 2007, for instance, the cabinet of Sri Lanka, in acknowledging the emotional difficulties that children of migrant mothers confront, passed legislation prohibiting mothers with children below five years of age from working overseas.[24] While the government in Sri Lanka never implemented the law, it never renounced it.

How does one explain the vilification of migrant mothers? Why is there a moral compulsion to equate women's migration with the abandonment of children? After all, migrant mothers provide children they "leave behind" with monthly remittances and see that other kin tend to the daily care of their children. While women attempt to reconstitute mothering when they migrate for work, society resists their efforts and insists on holding them accountable to the ideology of women's domesticity.[25] The outcome is to naturalize mothering at the expense of the social transformations women's migration induces.

By questioning the societal lament about the separation of children from their migrant mothers, I do not deny the struggles that individuals confront when mothers migrate. Rather, I call attention to the fact that the problems children confront are not so much caused by their mother's migration as by the resistance to migrant mothers' efforts to redefine mothering. It is the romanticization of biological mothering and the refusal of sending societies to recognize the reconstitution of the gender division of labor that fuels the emotional difficulties of children.

Illustrating the ideological belief that women's rightful place is in the home, headlines on May 26, 1995, from two of the largest circulating newspapers in the Philippines read, "Overseas employment a threat to Filipino families" and "Ramos [then president] says Pinay OCWs [Overseas Contract Workers] threaten Filipino families." In a speech delivered to the Department of Social Welfare the day prior to the release of these newspaper reports, President Ramos had called for initiatives to keep migrant mothers at home. In his words, "We are not against overseas employment of Filipino women. We are against overseas employment at the cost of family solidarity."[26] By calling for the return migration of mothers, President Ramos did not necessarily disregard the increasing economic dependence of the Philippines on the foreign remittances of its female migrant workers. However, he did make clear that only single and childless women are morally acceptable migrant workers.

Consistent with the president's views, public discourse vilifies migrant mothers. The media has reinforced the pathological view about the effects on women's migration on families.[27] It instills in public consciousness the view that migration facilitates a child-care crisis in transnational families. The crisis purportedly causes family instability, and, consequently, the use of drugs, gambling, and drinking among the children of migrant workers.[28] Without doubt, sensationalist reports fuel the vilification of migrant mothers. Their migration is equated with the abandonment of children and the source of their emotional and psychological difficulties. Yet, in the course of vilifying migrant mothers, news media reports leave fathers free of any responsibility for the care of children. The media presumes men to be naturally incompetent family caregivers.

Mainstream views at the community level concur. During my field research, I met with members of various community support groups in the region of my study. I traveled to places far from and near to the city center, where I was based, often not in the most comfortable conditions. I rode on top of passenger jeepneys, hitchhiked in delivery trucks, and hired private vehicles to reach areas not so accessible from the city center. I visited remote places, in order to gather interviews with support groups of migrant workers and their families, which the regional office of the Overseas Worker's Welfare Administration (OWWA) had identified to me. In my area of study, there had been fourteen local community organizations catering to transnational families, nine of which remained quite active during the time of my research. My research assistant and I met with members of all nine of these organizations.[29]

Based on our discussions, it was quite clear that community groups did not look favorably on the gender transformations engendered by migration. They frowned upon the limited time migrants spent with their families and upon how women's migration impacted the family. I also found that many individuals felt that fathers, not mothers, should migrate to support their family economically. A focus-group discussion I conducted with members of migrant families, for instance, left me stunned by the litany of depressing responses that participants gave concerning the effects of women's migration on the family. The participants said:

1   They are neglected.
2   Abandoned.
3   No one is there to watch over the children.
4   The attitudes of children change.
5   They swim in vices.
6   The values you like disappear.
7   They take on vices.
8   Men take on mistresses.
9   When you leave, they are still small, and when you come back, they are much older. But they do not recognize you as their real parents. And what they want, you have to follow. They get used to having a parent abroad and they are used to always having money.
10 That's true. That's true.

These negative sentiments were shared with me by members of the families of migrant fathers, who believed that transnational households with migrant men are more conducive than households with migrant women to healthy family life.

In general, the opinions of members of community groups reiterated mainstream views of the family. They frequently described the transnational families of migrant mothers as worse off than those of migrant fathers, as the remarks of a wife of a male migrant worker conveyed:

> Well, I think it's much better if the fathers leave, because mothers can do it better, to play the role of both the mother and the father. But if the mother leaves, what's likely to happen is that the father cannot play the role of the mother, for the children. Not unless the father does not have any vice, does not smoke, does not drink or gamble. And men have this tendency to [pause], because in the marital relationship, if the mother is absent, the father might look for another one [pauses, then laughs]. It's just natural, right? It's just natural, their natural needs, and if that happens, for sure the children will not be taken care of very well [pause]. If the husband drinks, for sure, every afternoon, he will be found in a drinking session [pause]. It's always better for children to come home in the afternoon with a parent in the home. What if the father who is left behind is not there and is spending his time drinking? It's an advantage if the father is the one to leave and work, [pause] because the mother can take the role of being the mother and the father, but the father, most likely he cannot play both roles. Men who do not have vices? You can only count them [and gestures with their hands to count them off on their fingers].

Other participants did not disagree.[30] Many naturalized both the ineptitude of men to do care work and their tendency to stray in marriages.

While community representatives convey strict gender boundaries of mothering and fathering, they do give greater flexibility to concepts of mothering than they do to concepts of fathering. For instance, mothers can "mother and father," but fathers can only be breadwinners and cannot take on mothering roles, such as nurturing and caring for children. One respondent, a wife of a seafarer working in a cargo ship, said, "It is really the mother who takes care of the children, prepares for their needs. Unlike the father, he is only the breadwinner of the family. All he does is give his earnings to the mother and it is really the mother who manages everything in the house. So most of the time the children really run to the mother. Even if the father is abroad, as long as the mother is in the home, it is better."

Often, concepts of fathering are narrowly restricted to breadwinning. Communities do not question, but accept, the notion that men are incompetent care providers. This conventional view of the family resonates in all of the interviews and group discussions I conducted with community representatives.

Absentee Fathers: Men Reject Child Care

The accepted view that men are naturally incompetent caregivers gives fathers free rein to refuse to do the reproductive labor that migrant mothers leave behind when migrating. Without doubt, this view hurts the welfare of children, because it facilitates the rejection of care work by the fathers left behind in the Philippines. I found that in spite of the greater economic contributions of migrant women to the family, fathers did not increase the amount of their household responsibilities. Instead they left it to other women—daughters, domestic workers, aunts, and grandmothers—to do the care work left behind by their wives upon migration. This situation is reminiscent of the "stalled revolution" identified by Arlie Hochschild in the 1980s among dual-income-earning couples in the United States.[31] Men back then, likewise, did not increase their housework when women's economic contributions to the household increased.

We should look at the rejection of housework by men back then and today as not only a stall but a form of protest. By rejecting women's work, fathers left behind in the Philippines do their share of gender boundary work in the family: they resist the redistribution of labor forced by women's greater economic contributions to household income, and in so doing help keep the conventional gender division of labor intact. However, fathers left behind do not completely turn their back on the needs of their children. Some men do care. For instance, some working-class men have found themselves having to do housework, for they lack the resources to hire other women. In contrast, middle-class men often hire domestic workers. Yet, regardless of class, if men do housework, they do not do much. The women left behind— eldest daughters, aunts, grandmothers, and domestic workers—do more care work than fathers.

Men's rejection of housework hurts the women in the family. Female extended kin resent the burden of care they feel obligated to perform as women. Meanwhile, the education of eldest daughters often suffers due to their greater responsibilities for housework. This, for instance, was the case with Isabelle. She complained that her studies suffered since the migration of her mother. Notably, the absence of fathers is not always invisible to children, including Isabelle, who complained, "It's annoying. I cannot help but feel resentful . . . It's because my father is here but he does not care. He does not support us, especially when it comes to school." Isabelle even noted that her mother did a great deal more care work than her father. As she described: "My mother is the one far away but she is the one who is close. It's because I think that my father is there physically but he does not care. He does not get involved with us. My mother, even if she is outside the country minds our business."

However, not all children recognize the care work of migrant mothers. More often than not they still blame the inadequacy of their care on their mothers, rather than on their physically present but emotionally absent fathers.

Yet, the institutional rearrangement of the household has forced some men to take on certain aspects of women's work. For example, one father left behind in the Philippines by his wife, a migrant domestic worker in the Middle East, Lurenzo Lacuesta, had to quit his job as a security guard. He found himself the stay at home father of his eleven-year-old son upon the sudden death of his mother. The situation of Lurenzo suggests that women's migration makes the reconstitution of the gender division of labor in the family unavoidable. Yet, Lurenzo did not view the care he provided his son as women's work. Instead, he considered it an extension of his previous duties in the military. Describing the cooking and cleaning he had to do, Lurenzo stated: "This is just the skills I learned during my military training as a soldier. I was trained to do this work as a soldier." We can imagine that Lurenzo, as a soldier, performed domestic chores without the emotional labor of affection. This surely limits the extent of care work that his eleven-year-old son receives in the absence of his migrant mother. It also reflects men's resistance to gender transformation in the family.

In my study, a sizeable group of fathers deliberately avoided caregiving responsibilities. They did this by relocating to another area of the Philippines. In so doing, they were freed from assuming women's work and addressing the daily routines of family. For instance, nine of thirty children in my sample told me that their fathers work elsewhere in the

Philippines. These men include a stockbroker, a fabric-machine operator, a security guard in Manila, a college professor in Cebu, a fruit grower in the other island of Mindoro, and a business proprietor on another island, Romblon.

By disappearing, men seem to resist the reconstitution of gender in the family when women migrate. This is perhaps because they still insist upon essentialist notions of gender. According to one father I interviewed, men discipline and women care. Carmelo Ledesma, a military officer and father of two whose wife works as a nurse in Saudi Arabia, explained:

> The role of the father is to discipline the child. Right? . . . While
> the father also is the one who will provide for the financial needs
> of the family, the mother takes care of their emotional needs.
> That is why it is good that their mother always calls them. She
> gives them guidance, and she does this even if it is very expensive
> to talk on the telephone. But it is very important for my sons to
> hear from their mother, to get advice from her, or just even hear
> her voice. This is necessary to uplift them.

In the Ledesma household, as in most mother-away households, the migrant mother still bears most of the caring work assigned to women. She is expected to "uplift" the emotions of her children, even cross-nationally by telephone. This is despite the fact that Carmelo resides with his children.

When I asked Carmelo about his feelings regarding the extension of his wife's responsibilities to include those traditionally defined to be his, he responded without hesitation that he did not mind her greater earnings as long as they did not contest the gender hierarchy in their household. He stated, "I am fine with that matter. This is because my wife is submissive. . . . I mean, it is not always me who makes decisions. We often reach an agreement. But if we do not agree, then . . . it is my decision." The Ledesma household, it seems, had yet to witness a gender revolution inspired by the greater earnings of his wife outside the country.

However, Carmelo Ledesma was one of the few men in my study who did housework. Unlike most fathers, he cooked, and he cleaned his comfortable three-bedroom home in the city center. He provided more care than other fathers in my sample, but he, like the three other fathers who provided care, did not expand the definition of fathering to include acts of nurturing. As his son told me, he ran his household as if it were a "barrack," with his sons as "soldiers" in boot camp. As a military officer, he acted with authority, and his sons knew that they must obey him with one command. He made "intensive disciplining" part of the daily routine of his household, so as to instill his masculinity against the threat posed by the earning power of his wife.

As suggested by the cases of Carmelo and Lurenzo, men cannot always avoid female-gendered care work, such as grocery shopping, attending meetings at school, and doing various activities in public with their children, such as walking them to school. These activities underscore and make visible the absence of mothers from the country. Although men seem to resist the changes forced by the institutional rearrangement of their households, they have sometimes found themselves with no other choice but to adjust accordingly to their new household arrangement. This fact leaves us with a glimmer of hope that transformations in gender ideologies could eventually follow suit in the transnational families of migrant mothers.

The Discourse of Abandonment

The negative view of migrant mothers in public and the rejection of child care by fathers left behind adversely affect the experiences of children such as Isabelle. It not only absolves fathers of the responsibility to care for their children, but it makes it difficult for children to recognize the unorthodox care they receive when their mothers migrate. When talking to children of migrant mothers, one gets the impression that they receive no care. They often describe their situation as one of "abandonment." One must, however, read between the lines. A closer look shows that children are not abandoned and left without adequate care when their mothers migrate. What they often mean by abandonment is not the absence of day-to-day maternal care, but the lack of physical intimacy from their biological mothers. Generally, children uphold biologically based views about mothering. In so doing, they believe it impossible for mothers to provide care from a distance. Moreover, they assume that the work of extended kin, even including those they call "mom," cannot adequately substitute for the nurturing acts of a biological mother.

Recognizing the tremendous care work provided by their female kin, the children of migrant mothers often refer to their aunts or grandmothers as *mother*. They consider one *mommy* and the other *mama*, or sometimes *nanay*, which means *mother* in Tagalog. Indeed, children do not overlook the extensive care work provided by female relatives. They acknowledge and credit their efforts by name and title. As one child told me, "I do not refer to my auntie as auntie, but instead I call her *mama* and my mother *mamang*."[32] Many children do the same, including Roan Leyritana, who kept on clarifying himself when he spoke about his mother and aunt during the course of our interview.[33] As Roan said, "I am much closer to my mommy, oh, I mean to my auntie, than to my mother." Indeed, the aunt does more than her fair share of mothering work for Roan. Not daunted by the distance, she travels by bus for over ten hours, from her home in a remote province, to visit Roan in the city center twice a month. She does this to keep track of his performance in school.

While Roan recognizes the care work performed by his aunt, he still assumes that his mother would have provided greater care. Children often describe the care that their migrant mothers provide from a distance as "not enough." Likewise, they insist that the care extended by other relatives never could match what their mothers would have provided if they had not migrated. We see this situation in the case of Roan. He describes the care that he received from his aunt as "not enough," even though his mother also visited him quite frequently in the Philippines. This is because Roan believes that the care work of his mother would have naturally exceeded the quality of care that his aunt provided him. Although he has yet to experience the same intensive caring by his mother as he has received from his aunt, Roan assumes that the act of walking him to school, helping him with his homework, cooking him breakfast, and so on would have naturally been better performed by his mother. Roan exclaims: "What is right is for [my mother] to be by my side . . . The love that I received from my father and mother was not enough. I received a lot of love from my aunts and my grandmother, but that was it."

Similarly, the affection of fathers is believed not to be interchangeable with that of mothers. For instance, Phoebe Latorre, the daughter of a domestic worker in Hong Kong, states:

I do not know if I could identify the love of my parents when I was growing up. We should have grown up with her [the mother]. Then, she would have been the one taking care of us, of our needs.

And your father? Doesn't he live with you? Did he take care of
your needs?

Sort of, but surely the way a mom takes care of you is different
from the way a father does. Isn't that right?

Children often assume that the gender division of labor between
mothers and fathers is natural. Fathers discipline and mothers nurture.
Fathers provide financial stability and mothers ensure emotional stability. Not surprisingly, Phoebe thinks she would have had a more stable
upbringing if her mother had stayed at home. Her mother left behind an
alcoholic and jobless husband to work as a domestic worker in Hong
Kong. Yet, she calls sufficiently frequent to know the weekly routine of
her children, and she financially supports all of her children's education.

Children do not always recognize the efforts of migrant mothers to
redefine mothering, to include breadwinning responsibilities, and to
provide care from a distance. In this respect, Isabelle's recognition of
her mother's care work is exceptional. The attitude of Rosette Cabel-
lero, a nineteen-year-old whose single mother works in Qatar, reflects
the views of most children I met in the Philippines. Rosette recognizes
that she has benefited materially from her mother's migration, but she
does not feel the economic contribution frees her mother of caregiving
responsibilities. Rosette noted, "We were able to have a house built.
Then, we were able to buy appliances." Rosette lives in a modest home
three hours from the city center, with her blind grandmother who has
been her primary guardian since her mother departed for the Gulf
region. According to Rosette, the home still lacks flooring, but it is a far
cry from the bamboo hut they used to live in. Although Rosette appreci-
ates the material gains that she has incurred from her mother's migration, she still thinks that her mother has failed in her maternal duties. As
she poignantly told me, good mothering requires constant nurturing.
When I asked her to elaborate on what she meant, Rosette proceeded to
tell me: "What I want is, for example, what I see with other children. I
see their mothers get frantic whenever they get hurt. They rush to their
child's side, apply ointment on the wound. On my own, I do not get that
attention. Then your mother should also brush your hair. You do that
on your own without her."

Children expect mothers to demonstrate their love via what the sociologist Sharon Hays calls "intensive mothering," meaning the work of
expending a "tremendous amount of time, energy, and money in raising

[one's] children."[34] In the process, children often lose sight of the fact that other individuals, not only their biological mothers, may demonstrate these acts of care. Children of migrant mothers are not necessarily denied daily acts of nurturing. Rather, they are denied what they think is proper care, the proximate care provided by biological mothers. In so doing, they downplay the extent of care they receive from other kin.

The care expectations of such children as Rosette undeniably follow a grid of gender conventions. Children generally expect to be nurtured by their mothers more than their fathers, and assume that only the intimacy achieved in the daily routine of family life—one denied transnational families—can provide such reassurances of love. Without doubt, physical intimacy, as a measure of the quality of life in the family, places migrant mothers and their children in a no-win situation. I found that a great number of children defined the quality of their family on the basis of how well it fit the traditional gender conventions of fathers' providing and mothers' nurturing in proximity.

Remarkably high care expectations haunt the families of migrant mothers and burden women as they toil in other countries. Mothers may economically provide for their children, but it does not free them, even partially, from the responsibility of nurturing their family. Expressing the shortfalls of distance mothering, Marinel Clemente, the daughter of a domestic worker in Libya, asserts this "lack" in her mother's love, when she stated: "My mother did not give me enough love. I would have wanted her next to me, so that I could feel her love. I feel it, but only a little bit. I know she loves me because she is working hard over there. She is working hard so that we could have everything we want and everything we need. Even when she is sick, she continues to work. . . . But still, I want her to be with me here every day . . . Since I was small it was only my grandparents showing me love. She was not here."

Weekly phone calls, daily text messages, and letters are considered insufficient expressions of maternal care. This suggests that for children money is not enough. Their disgruntlement over their transnational family arrangements speak to the limits to their satisfaction with the material gains from their mother's migration.

In contrast, children are more accepting of transnational fathering. The twenty-six children of migrant fathers I interviewed in the Philippines consistently valorized their fathers as "heroes" who made sacrifices for the collective good and economic mobility of the family. Children can accept transnational fathering because this practice agrees with traditional notions of parenting in the Philippines. Transnational fathers maximize their ability to provide financially for the family through migration.

Children of migrant women are not likely to accept a reconstituted form of mothering, one that redefines mothering to involve being a good provider and a distance nurturer, because they, like their migrant fathers, tend to hold on to staunch moral beliefs regarding the family, based on the conventional nuclear family. Theresa Bascara, a daughter of a domestic worker in Hong Kong, for example, said: "You cannot say it is a family if your mother and father are not there with you. It's like it's not a whole family if your father and mother are not here, if they are far. A family, I can say, is only whole if your father is the one working and your mother is staying at home. It is OK if your mother is working too, but somewhere close to you, not somewhere far away."

Such sentiments illustrate the ideological stronghold of the conventional nuclear family among children of migrant mothers. This ideology is inculcated in them not only by the media and the state, reflected in President Ramos's previously cited commentary, but also by religious institutions. In religious services and schools in the community where I did research the plight of transnational migrant families was rarely addressed. The state mandated family values course does not acknowledge the presence of transnational migrant families. Consequently, many children of migrant mothers grow up believing they are being raised in the wrong kind of family. They tend to describe their families as "broken," which is a term often used in Philippine public discourse to refer to the "deficiencies" in nonnuclear households. Yet, the families tend to be broken not because children have been abandoned when their mothers migrate, but because the migration of mothers threatens the organization of gender in society.

CURRENTLY, THERE IS A gender revolt in the Philippines, involving a resistance against the reconstitution of the gender division of labor in the family, a reconstitution rooted in the migration of women. This resistance adversely affects the welfare of children. It results in feelings of neglect among children, simply because they do not receive care conventionally. The care provided by mothers from a distance and by extended female kin up close are constructed as "not enough." Moreover, men's resistance to take on care work aggravates, in turn, the difficulties children face when their mothers migrate.

We should recognize that the family is not a static institution. As Judith Stacey notes, we are now in the age of the postmodern family, an age in which economic realities can no longer sustain a dominant household structure but, rather, multiple household forms, including single-parent and dual-wage-earning households.[35] To the diversity of household forms noted by Stacey, I would add transnational migrant households.

Children do not necessarily receive optimal care in conventional nuclear households. However, the notion that biological mothers should nurture their children somehow retains its ideological stronghold. Holding on to the ideological belief that biological mothers are the most suitable caregivers of children aggravates the problems children of migrant mothers experience. Without question, it makes it more difficult for children to adjust to their new family form—the transnational family—grounded in economic globalization.

How, then, can we help ease the emotional difficulties confronting children of migrant mothers? Going back to the three ways we could perceive transnational mothering, those who see this form of mothering as a victory for feminism would insist on reconstituting traditional gender ideologies in the Philippines. Perhaps richer nations should earmark development aid for the welfare of children such as Isabelle. Programs that would promote the recognition of transnational families in schools, churches, and the community would, without doubt, normalize the experience of children. Dismantling the ideology of women's domesticity would, likewise, encourage acceptance of unconventional ways of receiving care.

Moving to the second way society perceives transnational mothering, as a tragedy that forces the separation of mothers and children, the solution would be for family reunification and the assurance of the close proximity of family members. We could demand the return migration of women. However, a call for the return migration of mothers for the sake of family reunification could send the wrong message to women to stay at home. This would undoubtedly threaten the gender advancements they have made in the process of migration and hurt families economically.

We should remain mindful that the choice for Isabelle to live in close proximity of her mother is a human right that is denied to her and most other children of migrant workers. Many countries do not grant migrant caretakers the right to sponsor the migration of their dependents. This is true, for example, of Taiwan and the Netherlands.[36] We should perhaps consider family reunification in the host society, to allow migrant mothers better balance between their work and family life. This solution would draw attention to the third way we could perceive transnational families, as a gender transformative institution imposed by the limited labor-market options for workers in the Philippines. This third option would not close or deter the option of labor migration. Instead, it would recognize the labor of migrant workers as benefiting both the sending and receiving societies. Hence, it would call for the recognition of such labor by not only the sending but also the receiving state. Granting family reunification in the host society would recognize the contributions of migrant labor and allow migrant women the human right to a family life. It would make transnational mothering a choice that women make instead of an option forced upon them by the legal restrictions that deny migrant workers a family life throughout the world. Only then could the transnational families of migrant mothers be a gender-transformative institution that we could celebrate and not mourn for challenging the conventional division of labor in the family.

Notes

1 This chapter draws from my book *Children of Global Migration: Transnational Families and Gendered Woes* (Stanford, CA: Stanford University Press, 2005). I use pseudonyms in this chapter. Between January 2000 and April 2002, I spent eighteen nonconsecutive months in the central region of the Philippines, to do research on the experiences of children left behind by migrant parents. Altogether, I interviewed sixty-nine young adults raised in transnational migrant families: thirty children of migrant mothers, twenty-six of migrant fathers, and thirteen of two migrant parents. Their parents were scattered throughout the world, working in East and West Asia, the Americas, and Europe, as well as in cargo ships. My interviews with young adult children focused on their family lives, relationships with their parents and other relatives, feelings about parental migration, and finally their goals and aspirations in life.

2 Kanlungan Center Foundation, *Fast Facts on Filipino Labor Migration* (Quezon City, Philippines: Kanlungan, 2009), 12, 1, 4.

3 Steve McKay, *Satanic Mills or Silicon Islands? The Politics of High-Tech Production in the Philippines* (Ithaca, NY: Cornell University Press, 2006).

4 Bangko Sentral ng Pilipinas, "'Overseas Filipinos' Remittances by Country, by Source."

5 Robert Burgess and Vikram Haksar, "Migration and Foreign Remittances in the Philippines" (International Monetary Fund Working Paper WP/05/11, International Monetary Fund, Washington, DC, 2005), 4.

6 "OFWs Told: Stay Abroad," *Philippine Daily Inquirer*, July 23, 2001.

7 Gina Mission, "The Breadwinners: Female Migrant Workers," *WIN: Women's International Net Issue* 15A (November 1998).

8 Kanlungan Center Foundation, *Fast Facts on Filipino Labor Migration* (Quezon City, Philippines: Kanlungan, 2000); Kanlungan Center Foundation, *Fast Facts on Filipino Labor Migration* (2009).

9 Deployed New Hire Landbased Workers, by Sex," Philippine Overseas Employment Administration, accessed on June 26, 2009, http://www.poea.gov.ph/html/statistics.html.

10 Kanlungan Center Foundation, *Fast Facts on Filipino Labor Migration* (2009).

11 Ibid.

12 Burgess and Haksar, "Migration and Foreign Remittances in the Philippines," 5.

13 World Bank, *Migration and Remittances Factbook 2008* (Washington, DC: World Bank, 2008).

14 Heidi Hartmann, "The Unhappy Marriage of Marxism and Feminism: Towards a More Progressive Union," in *Women and Revolution: A Discussion of the Unhappy Marriage of Marxism and Feminism*, ed. Lydia Sargent (Boston: South End, 1981), 1–41.

15 Peggy Levitt, *The Transnational Villagers* (Berkeley: University of California Press, 2001).

16 Ibid.

17 Arjun Appadurai, *Modernity at Large: Cultural Dimensions of Globalization* (Minneapolis: University of Minnesota Press, 1996).

18 Pierrette Hondagneu-Sotelo and Ernestine Avila, "'I'm Here but I'm There': The Meanings of Latina Transnational Motherhood," *Gender and Society* 11 (1997): 548–71.

19 Ibid.

20 Ibid.

21 Sylwai Urbanksa, "Mothers of the Nation as a Target of Public Therapy— Transnational Parenting and Moral Panic in Poland" (paper presented at Mosaics of Transnational Spaces Workshop, Krakow, May 9, 2009).

22 "Poland Sees Host of Problems among 'Euro-Orphans,'" *Chicago Tribune*, September 21, 2008.

23 Dan Bifelski, "In Romania, Children Left Behind Suffer the Strains of Migration," *New York Times*, February 14, 2009.

24 Additionally, mothers with children who are five years of age or above can only migrate if they can prove they have secured alternative arrangements for

childcare. "Welfare System for Migrant Women Workers' Young Children Favoured," *Daily News*, March 15, 2007.

25 Hondagneu-Sotelo and Avila, "'I'm Here but I'm There.'"

26 "Ramos: Overseas Employment Threat to Filipino Families," *Philippine Daily Inquirer*, May 26, 1995.

27 Various captions reveal this propensity in the media. While the caption "Overseas Job vs. Family Stability" equates transnational family life with instability, other captions reveal the supposed causes of this instability. See Lorie Toledo, "Overseas Job vs. Family Stability," *People's Journal*, December 15, 1993. For instance, the caption "Sleeping Beauty gets raped while her mom works as a (domestic helper) in Hong Kong" points to the inadequate protection of children in these families. See Philippine Tonight Staff, "Sleeping Beauty gets raped . . . while her mom works as a DH in Hong Kong," *Philippine Tonight*, July 16, 1993. The insufficient guidance of children was established four years later with the caption "Education of OFW's [Overseas Filipino Workers] children suffer." See Mac Cabreros, "Edukasyon ng mga anak ng OFWs nassaskipisyo" [Education of children of OFWs suffers], *Abante*, June 23, 1997. Finally, the absence of emotional security is reported a year later, in Lynette L. Corporal's "OFW's kids emotionally troubled," *Manila Standard*, August 18, 1998.

28 Susan Fernandez, "Pamilya ng OFWs maraming hirap" [Many hardships in the families of OFWs], *Abante*, January 27, 1997.

29 With a research assistant, I gathered interviews with the officers of each of these organizations and conducted focus-group discussions with members of five organizations. I arranged the focus-group discussions weeks ahead of time and, with the cooperation of officers, arranged to hold discussions with the most active members of each organization. Focus-group discussions ranged from four to fifteen individuals in size. They were approximately one hour in length. The discussions addressed problems and issues family members regularly confront in running a transnational household, for instance, issues concerning the reintegration of the migrant parent and the struggles of raising children single-handedly or from a distance.

30 The families of migrant mothers could not share their own perspectives, as they were conspicuously absent in the discussion group. I also could not observe whether these claims rang true for the children of migrant women growing up under the care of their fathers or other relatives in this specific town.

31 Arlie Hochschild, *Second Shift* (New York: Avon Books, 1989).

32 *Mamang* means "mother" in the local dialect.

33 Roan Leyitana is a seventeen-year-old college student whose never-married mother has worked outside the Philippines for eleven years, first as a domestic worker for eight years in Kuwait, then as a bookkeeper in the United Kingdom

for the last three years. On average, she visits her son every two years and stays in the Philippines for no more than one month.

34 Sharon Hays, *The Cultural Contradictions of Motherhood* (New Haven, CT: Yale University Press, 1996), x.

35 Judith Stacey, *Brave New Families: Stories of Domestic Upheaval in Late-Twentieth-Century America* (New York: Basic Books, 1991).

36 Pei Chia-Lan, *Global Cinderellas: Migrant Domestics and Newly Rich Employers in Taiwan* (Durham, NC: Duke University Press, 2006); Rhacel Salazar Parreñas, *The Force of Domesticity* (New York: NYU Press, 2008).

10

Beyond Social Remittances
Migration and Transnational Gangs in Central America

JOSÉ MIGUEL CRUZ

The Mara Salvatrucha 13 (also known as MS-13) and the Eighteenth Street Gang (also known as 18th Street or Barrio 18) are the names of the largest street gangs in Central America.[1] They have become powerful in El Salvador, Guatemala, and Honduras. First formed in the United States, they have spread across northern Central America. Migrants who returned from the United States to their home countries brought the U.S. gangs with them, where the gangs contributed to a surge in crime and public insecurity.[2]

Young Salvadoran immigrants who returned to El Salvador in the early 1990s, after the civil war in their home country ended, initially brought the U.S. gang model to the region. However, some years later, young return-migrants brought the gangs to Guatemala and Honduras, and reinforced internal Central American migration that involved Salvadoran gang members. The combination of the early Salvadoran return migration and the internal flows in Central America contributed to gang expansion in the region. The transnationalization of the U.S. gangs has rested, however, not merely on return migration, but also on returnees' integration into preexisting gangs and the appeal of their gang culture and lifestyle to socially and economically marginal nonmigrants.

The transnationalization of U.S. gangs has entailed what the sociologist Peggy Levitt calls social remittances, namely "ideas, behaviors, identities, and social capital that flow from host-to-sending-country communities."[3] Return-migrants brought U.S. gang identities and norms to their home countries. These social remittances transformed how gangs in Central America form, operate, and battle with rival groups, law enforcement institutions, and the society at large.

Yet, the flow of social remittances is not necessarily unidirectional, from host to home country, and social remittances may change in the contexts in which they become embedded. Gangs' social remittances were reshaped in El Salvador. Norms of gang-life and warfare were transformed and disseminated across the region, after which new transnational identities were then exported back to the United States. Salvadorans redefined the gangs in the transnational space they created and sustained, thus showing that social remittances are not fixed.[4] In essence, the transnationalization of U.S. gangs has involved far more than a simple one-way translocation of ideas and practices across country borders.

The transnationalization of gangs depends on local conditions. Not all return, or cyclical, migrants have transplanted U.S. gangs, and only a minority of gang members ever lived abroad. U.S.-style gangs took hold only in countries where return-migrants established close ties with preexisting local gangs, where communities did not offer alternative reference groups, and where state security officials oversaw harsh crackdowns on marginalized youth.[5] Because Central American countries and Mexico differ in these dimensions, they differ in the pervasiveness of U.S. gang life.[6]

Salvadoran Migration

Emigration from El Salvador has a long history. In the twentieth century there were four different waves of migration.[7] First, there was an economically driven migration between 1920 and 1969, largely to other Central American countries. The second wave occurred between 1970 and 1979. It followed the expulsion in the late 1960s of more than 100,000 Salvadorans from Honduras. Immigration to the United States began during this period.

The Salvadoran civil war of the 1980s unleashed the third period of out-migration. This wave played an important role in the development of Salvadoran youth gangs in the United States. Political violence led more than 400,000 Salvadorans to emigrate between 1980 and 1987, mainly to the United States.[8] In a seminal work on migration and repression, Segundo Montes argued that the rate of migration to the United States served as an indicator of the intensification of the political crisis in El Salvador.[9] Many fled to the United States in desperation, without legal entry rights.[10] Passage of the U.S. Immigration Reform and Control Act (IRCA), in 1986, had the unintended effect of spurring further emigration. The new law allowed undocumented immigrants to legalize their status and legal immigrants to sponsor the move to the United States of family who until then remained in their homeland.[11] By the time the civil war ended, in 1992, many immigrants had built an important transnational web of community and organizational infrastructure that induced subsequent emigration.

The fourth wave occurred in the mid-1990s. Migration had slowed down after 1992, when the civil war ended and the economy improved, and Salvadorans became optimistic about the future of their country.[12] However, migration resumed when the economy stagnated and the society polarized anew a few years later.[13] Against the backdrop of a century of migration, Salvadorans came to consider migration their best solution to domestic problems. In the course of the 1990s, the economy suffered from a deep fall in world coffee prices, natural disasters (especially Hurricane Mitch in 1998), and an escalation of crime.[14] Under the circumstances, the Salvadoran population in the United States rose from approximately 584,000 in 1990 to 1,118,000 in 2000, a 92 percent population increase.[15] Salvadorans became so pessimistic that a survey conducted by the Vanderbilt University 2008 Americas Barometer found that 25 percent of the population planned to move to another country within three years.[16]

According to the U.S. Census, 1.7 million Salvadorans lived in the United States as of 2010.[17] They made up 88 percent of all Salvadoran migrants abroad.[18] Salvadorans live throughout the United States, but mainly in Los Angeles and Washington, D.C. Other important communities are found in Houston, New York, and San Francisco. Within Greater Los Angeles, Salvadorans are clustered in Long Beach, Riverside-San Bernardino, and Orange County.

The impact of migration on El Salvador changed in the 1990s. For

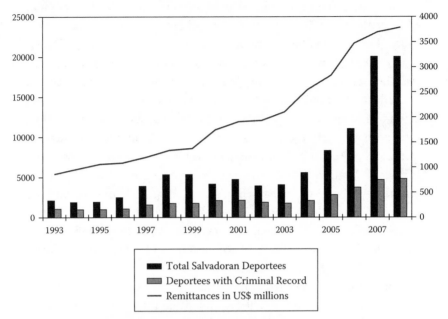

FIGURE 10.1. Salvadoran Deportees and Remittances, 1993–2008

Sources: Banco Central de Reserva de El Salvador, Boletines Estadísticos Mensuales, Enero 1995–Enero 2009, available at http://www.bcr.gob.sv/?cat=1130&lang=es; Department of Homeland Security, Yearbooks of Immigration Statistics, 2006–8 available at http://www.dhs.gov/files/statistics/publications/yearbook.shtm.

one, Salvadorans abroad, especially those who had moved to the United States, began to send remittances to family left behind. Remittances rose from $1 billion in the early 1990s to $3.7 billion in 2008 (see figure 10.1). Remittances came to account for 18 percent of GDP, and for 70 percent of the country's hard-currency revenue.[19] Thus, remittances came to play a central role in the economy, while helping thousands of relatives of migrants in El Salvador improve their material level of well-being, their housing, their health welfare, and the education of their children, and reducing the portion of the population living in extreme poverty.[20] Also, once the civil war ended, return-migration increased and contact between Salvadorans, who had come to live across borders, strengthened.

During the war, the U.S. government had deported about 3,000 Salvadorans yearly.[21] Then, additional expulsion of Salvadorans occurred after U.S. passage of the Illegal Immigration Reform and Immigrant Responsibility Act (IIRIRA) in 1996. The act both expedited procedures for deportation and restricted conditions for suspending certain deportations.[22] In addition, IIRIRA established that any "alien" who served a sentence longer than three years would be subject to removal from the United States after completion of their prison term.[23] As a result, the number of Salvadoran deportees doubled between 1996 and 1998 (see figure 10.1). While the number of deportees leveled off during the following few years, partly because El Salvador qualified for Temporary Protected Status/Deferred Enforced Departure (TPS/DED), the number of forced returns increased again, beginning in 2004.[24] In 2007 and 2008 they reached nearly 20,000 per year.

Despite the new law, the number of deportees with criminal records barely rose (until 2006), and their percentage of all deportees decreased (see figure 10.1). A crackdown in U.S. immigration enforcement, not increased immigrant Salvadoran criminal activity, accounted for the increase in deportations. Furthermore, as soon as deportees arrived in their country, they made their way back to the United States. They contributed to cyclical migration between El Salvador and the United States.

Voluntary return migration also increased after the civil war ended. The Salvadoran government estimated that nearly 375,000 Salvadorans returned during the first fourteen months following the signing of the peace accords.[25] Return migration probably continued for two more years, until the economy deteriorated and crime spurred the most recent wave of out-migration.

Meanwhile, homeland visits by Salvadorans, who settled abroad, increased. Air-traffic between the United States and El Salvador rose tenfold between 1990 and 2004, and the number of homeland visits nearly doubled between 2000 and 2004, from 161,000 to 301,000.[26] While it is impossible to know how many of the visitors were Salvadoran, the figures point to increased immigrant homeland visits and increased circular migrant flows between the United States and El Salvador.

In sum, large-scale Salvadoran migration to the United States created a transnational space in which Salvadorans and dollars flowed. It also created an area in which ideas, norms, values, and identities circulated, including those that fueled transnational gang formation and the expansion and transformation of gang identities. With the new transnational networks and cultural practices appealing to impoverished youth, U.S. gangs gained a footing in El Salvador.

Gangs and Social Remittances

Salvadoran gangs, known in El Salvador as *maras*, involve a vast network of groups of people associated with franchises of two street gangs that had their origins in the city of Los Angeles, but that took on their own dynamics in Central America, independent of American directives: the Mara Salvatrucha 13 and the Eighteenth Street gang. In Central America, they went on to form transnational networks involving powerful crime rackets.

According to the police, in 2010 an estimated 21,000 young Salvadorans belonged to these transnational gangs—and 30,000 in Guatemala and Honduras.[27] The Salvadoran gangs are responsible for much of the surge in criminal violence in the country since the mid-1990s. Police records, for example, indicate that street gangs are responsible for slightly more than half of the nearly 1,600 homicides that were recorded in El Salvador between January and June 2008, and for about 70 percent of Salvadoran extortions.[28] Contemporary maras include extortion rings that operate from local prisons.

Youth gangs are not new to El Salvador, although they were transformed with their transnationalization.[29] Salvadoran youth gangs first received public attention in the late 1980s, during the civil war.[30] At the time, they involved young males from poor outlying areas. They were turf-based groups or cliques that controlled well-defined neighborhoods and streets. Already, then, they were known as maras, even though they had no ties to any U.S. gang. Typically, their names denoted the neighborhoods where their members lived, such as Mara Fosa, Mara Quiñónez, and Mara Florencia.[31] However, some adopted names associated with U.S. gangs, such as Mara Salvatrucha, MS, Locos 13, Mara 18, and names inspired by American mass culture, such as Mara AC/DC, Mara Black Sabbath, and Mara Thriller.[32] While engaging in some criminal activity, they mainly hung out together and consumed "soft" drugs.

During this period many of the Salvadoran migrants and refugees in the United States struggled economically, with hundreds of the younger generation growing up on the streets of U.S. cities, especially in Los Angeles, where the largest concentration of Salvadorans lived. They joined the gangs there. A Salvadoran who joined the Eighteenth Street gang in California explained:

> The (Salvadoran) government is to blame for our suffering, initially for the war that devastated the country . . . What did the war cause? It led many families to flee to the United States. Our distressed mothers had to go. Then, terrified of the war, they brought their sons, including many of us . . . We went there to work night and day. Then . . . what? Zero communication [between parents and] their children. Then we got mad and had to find some shelter—among . . . mad people, the homeboys (gang members).[33]

Living socially and economically marginal lives, young Salvadoran migrants found that the gangs offered them a sense of identity, respect, and support.[34] Initially they joined gangs that Mexican-origin and Chicano teenagers had formed, the Eighteenth Street Gang in particular. However, when imprisoned, they formed their own Salvador-based gangs, which the growing number of immigrants from other Central American countries later joined. These gangs tended to be less entrepreneurial and more violent than other gangs (such as the African American and Vietnamese gangs).[35]

Alex Sánchez, a former member of MS-13, who went on to serve as the director of the Los Angeles chapter of Homies Unidos, an NGO devoted to rehabilitating gang members, described how MS-13 evolved: "MS was not formed in the streets but in the Juvenile Detention Centers of California. We were all kids hanging out with some gangs. . . . While locked up . . . we recognized that many of us were Salvadoran and we could form our own barrio [gang] to protect ourselves. We decided to form Mara Salvatrucha. Then, word reached the streets."[36]

Sánchez reveals that the U.S. criminal system had the unintended effect of spawning new gangs among Salvadorans and other Central Americans. The return-migration to El Salvador that began in the 1990s, especially following passage of the IIRIRA, included gang members and felons deported upon release from U.S. jails.[37] In other words, they went from U.S. jails to their home country, El Salvador.

The deportees transformed gang life and gang culture where U.S. authorities forced them to resettle. They did not form new gangs or engage in territorial wars with preexisting street gangs.[38] Rather, they joined preexisting gangs that they then transformed. They diffused identities and sociocultural styles of U.S. gangs, particularly those of the southern California Chicano gangs.[39] The gangs they joined took on U.S. gang names, such as MS-13 and Eighteenth Street Gang, and adopted cultural practices of the U.S. gangs, such as body-tattooing, hand "language," means to distinguish friend from foe, and, most important, their norms, values, and conceptions of "appropriate" gang behavior.[40] The adoption of practices of U.S. gangs were host-to-home-country social remittances.

Salvadorans who had belonged to U.S. gangs, been imprisoned in the United States, and then been deported played a key role in introducing the U.S. gang lifestyle and behavior to El Salvador. A Salvadoran gang member spoke to the point: "Remember that most of us were deported and we come from prisons. And in California, when you are imprisoned, you go with your race: Latino, whatever. We learned to be united there. And the principles and values that we've learned in a gang are never forgotten. That's the school we bring here."[41]

However, it would be a mistake to ascribe the expansion of gang memberships in the 1990s merely to the growth of gang deportees and returnees, to a sort of "flooding effect." Salvadoran youth gangs mainly involved local teenagers without firsthand U.S. experience. A 1996 survey of gang members in San Salvador, the country's capital, found only 16 percent of all gang members had been to the United States. The others had never left the country. More recent surveys concur. One in 2001 found that just 12 percent of gang members had been to the United States, while interviews conducted in 2006 with imprisoned gang members found only 7 percent to have been to the U.S.[42] Furthermore, the surveys done in 1996 and 2006 found, respectively, that only 11 and 4 percent of the interviewed gang members had been deported from the United States.[43]

These figures highlight the low participation of actual American-affiliated gang members in the Salvadoran cliques. But, at the same time, they highlight the enormous impact returnees have had on Salvadoran gang culture and dynamics. Although the number of immigrants deported to El Salvador increased in the last two decades, they never constituted the majority in the local cliques. A researcher of Salvadoran gangs noted some time ago that "the influence of U.S. urban and marginal cultures is not essential to the existence of Salvadoran gangs, but it affects and shapes those gangs."[44]

The essential features of American gang culture were transmitted by Salvadoran gang members who had affiliated with gangs in the United

States, who were imprisoned there, and who were later deported to their home country. But, representing only a tiny fraction of gang members in El Salvador, they could not impose American standards.

But why did only two U.S. gangs take hold? To understand why only the two gangs took hold in El Salvador, and why their specific social remittances were transmitted, it is important to understand the relational character of social remittances. Social remittances transpire when many people assign meanings to practices and relationships.

This relational character underscores the fluid and unsettled nature of social remittances, which allows them to be reinterpreted in the initial sending country (El Salvador) and to be utilized again in the expansion of the transnational space generated by cyclical migration. Gang social remittances sent by Southern California maras were received in El Salvador, but repacked there and sent back to the United States and to other Central American countries. They helped make sense of the behavior and relationships of other migrant youth and gang members in different places and countries. Once in El Salvador, gang social remittances gave rise to transnational gang identities.

Three aspects highlight the relational character of gang social remittances and explain their diffusion in El Salvador and to some other Central American countries. First, the graphic nature of Latino gang culture in the United States meant that the symbols, dress codes, tattoos, and graffiti could easily be adopted by people who found it attractive. Teenagers looking for an identity noticed the newcomers to their neighborhoods who dressed and acted in riveting ways. Testimony by a MS-13 gang member, immediately upon his return from Los Angeles, spoke to the point:

> Something that attracted folks here was the machismo [virility]. I used to threaten everybody. The dollars that I brought also attracted them. They saw that chicks preferred me because of my money. And when I took my shirt off, and the folks could see my tattoos . . . it seemed like a privilege to have the tattoos. Me . . . talking to them . . . ? It was like an honor to them. They respected me. I invited them to a soda, a beer, a spliff [marijuana cigarette]. These folks felt they were us. And so the gang ideology was introduced.[45]

Nonmigrants were also attracted to the U.S. gang culture because it built on U.S. popular culture, already familiar to them. Before the arrival of deportees who had been involved in U.S. gangs, Central Americans knew Chicano and Latino gang culture through music, films, and television. Against this backdrop, return-migrants embodied in situ American symbols and identities nonmigrant youth found appealing. The returnees integrated the U.S. acquired culture into their daily lives in ways local youth understood and liked.

Second, gang social remittances were effortlessly spread because young returnees also sought a group to belong to in their home country. Having grown up abroad, many of the deportees had few local friends and family to whom they could turn. Some of them only spoke English, no Spanish. The only groups to welcome them were preexisting street gangs. As a former U.S. gang member, interviewed in a focus group, noted: "We're family. . . . When I first came here, the next day I met the homies [the members of the gang], I saw the opportunity they gave us, because being with them is like being in the [U.S.] gang. Nothing changed. We are from nine different gangs here [in this focus group]. We're from different cliques. Most of us don't have any family left here [in El Salvador]. Even if we had family here, they wouldn't support us."[46]

The local gangs served as family. They provided the deported U.S. gang members with support and protection that helped them cope with the traumatic shock of relocation. And in return, the deportees provided their nonmigrant peers with new identities, values, and norms that helped them make sense of their lived experiences. This seems to explain why the same remittances did not similarly take hold in certain countries, namely in Mexico and Nicaragua. Research in the two countries found that maras did not put down roots there, because local gangs had deep social networks of protection at the community level. Strong Mexican and Nicaraguan social and cultural identities and community networks limited the permeation of imported gang identities.[47]

Finally, U.S. gang social remittances took hold in El Salvador because they helped adherents cope with local social life. Local gang members adopted the cultural ways of Southern California because the norms, identities, and values helped them to make sense of their own life experiences and their relationships with others in El Salvador, especially with the state. They lived in a society shattered by poverty, social inequality, and political violence. The 1990s peace accords left the structural problems that fueled the civil war, unresolved. Sixty-five percent of the population lived below the poverty line, and the poorest 20 percent received only 3 percent of the national income. The civil war also left a fragmented and traumatized civil society, with problems subsequently compounded by a surge in crime.[48] In addition, violence persisted, perpetrated by state institutions, by former state agents, and by civilians who formed social cleansing groups and death squads.[49] Some youth joined the gangs as a way to deal with the violence affecting their communities. As Mo Hume has argued, the cases of police brutality, summary justice, and revenge killings in postwar El Salvador "should be contextualized as an endpoint in a broader continuity of exclusion and polarization, not outside normal social relations."[50]

In general, youth gangs thrive in environments of economic marginalization, social exclusion, and violence, and Salvadoran gangs are no exception.[51] Accordingly, these gangs used U.S. gang norms and values to make sense of the exclusion and violence they routinely faced, as a former U.S. gang member who returned to El Salvador explained: "Many of us had calmed down, then we came to this country [El Salvador] and we encountered the same situation: crime, unemployment, the economy . . . So we didn't have any choice but to go back to the same."[52] Thus, sharing a life of social exclusion and marginality, deportees and nonmigrants found meaning in the same gangs that deportees infused with U.S. gang culture. The nonmigrant and return-migrant youth came to identify with one another. An MS-13 gang member spoke to the point: "Thank God. What has kept us together, those who came deported and those of us who have been here always, is that we have the same objectives, the same goals to help our *raza* [people]. They [the deported] lived a part of their lives there, with other language, with other lifestyles, but they lived the life of their "barrio" there and we have lived it in our own ways here."[53]

The Transformation of Salvadoran Gangs

Following the infusion of U.S. gang culture, Salvadoran gangs changed. They consolidated and adopted American gang identities, but concomitantly took on a life of their own, grounded in local conditions. Within approximately five years, they assimilated to the U.S. identity. They imitated returnees' style, and then changed their group names to one or the other of the most representative southern California gangs: Mara Salvatrucha or Pandilla de la Calle 18. During this process, a constellation of small gang groups evolved. The groups shared the same name and gradually copied the norms and values that made them part of a gang franchise. Former territorial groups evolved into a federation of gangs who identified themselves with a virtual "neighborhood," either the Eighteenth or the MS-13.[54]

With their new identities, gang warfare surged. This has been, arguably, the most devastating aspect of the social remittances. Southern California gang culture reconfigured the Salvadoran gang world. Youth gangs in El Salvador started to fight over their identities. Instead of generating different gangs, U.S. gang social remittances solidified and consolidated existing gangs. To be a *Salvatrucho* or an Eighteenth became more important than controlling specific turf, which induced gang warfare. The process is nicely described by a Salvadoran Eighteenth gang member in the early 1990s:

> I hung out with the *Mara Gruesa* from here several years ago. In fact, I've been hanging out a long time. I've been in these groups since 1983. In those days, there were no Eighteenth in *Soyapango*, or MS-13. Nothing. We defended neighborhoods. There were fights between the barrios. They tried to eliminate us but they couldn't. The story about the Eighteenth is new. They came here two years ago. I am an Eighteenth now because some MS-13s came to the barrio and they wanted to beat us. They even stabbed some of us. They wanted us to be MS, but we didn't let them because we had been hanging out since long ago. It occurred to me to rule Eighteenth, so they wouldn't beat us again. We had to rule the opposing gang.[55]

The cultural significance of U.S. gangs sometimes got lost in translation. Violence became an important factor in the evolution of gangs. Nonetheless, the U.S. association was enough to appeal to youth in El Salvador. In the words of a deported gang member:

> "Whoever brought my neighborhood back here in the '90s, they fucked up, really fucked up my country. Because, man, you really see the writing on the walls in the streets. That came in the '90s . . . It's like you're seeing the freeways from L.A., and they don't even know how to write on the walls. They write real stupid, you know. They put "Westside 18th Street" or "Northside MS," and we're not really on the Northside or Westside here. We're in South Central. Or they put area 213. Man, that's a telephone call from downtown California, or they put 818. That's El Monte, you know. They get me real mad because they don't even know about

the Southside thing, or the Northside thing. They just know enemy Eighteenth Street, or enemy MS.[56]

Youth joined Mara Salvatrucha or the Eighteenth Street Gang because a particular clique happened to control the community where the aspiring gang member hung out. Upon affiliating with a particular gang, members were to show loyalty by fighting the rival gang. Gang members and wannabes attacked and killed rival franchise gang members, even if they imposed no threat. "I wanna go on with this [in gangs] cuz I'm not gonna put up with what they did to my homeboy, cuz there have to be more skulls [I have to kill more] . . . If death finds me, welcome, I tell the homeboys. I'll die in my hood I tell them. What's the problem. . . . they kill me or I kill them."[57]

Gang wars came to dominate gang life. The violence had the effect of increasing social cohesion among members of the same franchise, even when they barely knew each other.[58] Also, when wishing vengeance against murderers of their friends, they turned to gangs.[59]

The violence, in turn, redefined the struggle for urban space and cultural practices.[60] Instead of controlling specific turfs, gangs began to rule sections of large cities and entire small cities. And members came to spend more time tattooing their bodies to show allegiance to the gang franchise than marking their territories with wall graffiti. Identity became more important than turf. In the process, normative constraints that existed among gangs in the United States broke down in El Salvador. The breakdown reflects how Salvadoran gangs reinterpreted U.S.-to-El Salvador social remittances, as a former gang member conveyed: "There [in the United States], if one runs into an enemy *vato* [boy] with his family, say, his mother, one cannot do anything. I couldn't do anything myself once, when I wanted to shoot. Here it is different. They do not respect the rules. One can be with one's entire family and yet be targeted."[61]

The Transnationalization of Salvadoran Gangs

Renewed identities and distorted norms were sufficient to facilitate further exchanges between Southern California and Central America. They created a large transnational space where information, practices, and rules circulated, gang social capital expanded, and mara-like organizations were transmitted to other countries.

However, the decisive push for the transnationalization of gangs came from the Salvadoran government. The state's repressive policies, designed to crack down on gangs, had the unintended effect of spreading their reach. In 2003, the government implemented a series of policies known as *mano dura* (hard hand) and *súper mano dura* (super hard hand). It reformed penal laws to ban groupings of young people and to permit imprisonment of suspicious-looking youth.[62] More than 30,000 gang members were arrested in a two-year span, which served to transform prisons into new nodes of gang life, and from 2002 to 2005 murders attributed to youth gangs in El Salvador jumped from 4 to 13 percent nationally.[63]

Some gangs, in response, prepared an all-out war against the state and agents of the state. But violence drove many of the gang members out of the country.[64] In their journey to the United States, to Mexico, and to some Central American countries, Salvadoran-enrolled gang members spread the now American-Salvadoran gang identities and created a transnational space through which other gang members navigated and related.

The transformed Salvadoran gangs and their gang warfare spanned to other countries in the region, and even influenced gangs in the United States. Recent news reports indicate that members of MS-13 cliques in Washington, D.C., had migrated from El Salvador, not from California. Hence, they had contacts and responded to directives from gang members imprisoned in Salvadoran penitentiaries.[65] Following the same processes that took place in El Salvador during the 1990s, Salvadoran gangs contributed to the dissemination of American gang culture in Guatemala, Honduras, and southern Mexico while en route to the United States. In doing so, they forged bonds and transformed gang culture in the countries they passed through. Indicative of the cross-border ties Salvadoran gangs developed, the previously noted survey with imprisoned gang members in El Salvador, conducted in 2006, found 28 percent to have contacts or relationships with gang members in other countries. Forty-three percent of those with contacts said they exchanged information, 23 percent said they exchanged orders and rules, and 18 percent spoke of business dealings, which involved the shipment of money, drugs, and weapons.[66] Salvadoran gangs came to have vested economic interests in their transnationalization. By the late 2000s, the MS-13 and Eighteenth Street Gang were powerful groups operating in Guatemala and Honduras, while in the United States the Salvadoran-tied MS-13 took hold in Maryland and Virginia.

Salvadoran gang members thereby transmitted gang identities, norms, and values across the hemisphere. While U.S.-to-El Salvador social remittances initially influenced how gangs evolved in the Central American country, draconian Salvadoran state policies had many unintended effects. Hard-hand policies turned gangs more violent, and induced them to develop criminal economies, to earn more money than possible in the legally sanctioned labor market. In the process, gangs developed strong ties across the region and advanced their own ways of gang membership.

Maras in Comparative Perspective

The social remittances of gang life in southern California played a key role in the development of Central American maras. They did not create street gangs either in El Salvador or in other countries in the region, but they provided the tools to refashion earlier formed gangs, in a manner that appealed to marginalized local youth, and, in so doing, expanded the social base of gangs. Gang social remittances became a commodity young migrants brought with them when they returned to their homeland. They were adopted, remade, and even exported, in turn, abroad. They provided new identities for some of the urban underclass that dramatically expanded in the last decades of the twentieth century, and contributed to the build-up of a distinctive type of social capital that spawned new patterns of youth behavior across Central America.

Maras have spread to Guatemala, Honduras, and some towns in southern Mexico, where they universalized gang warfare and provided channels for illicit activity rooted in shared codes, identities, and patterns of behavior. However, maras have been unable to establish strongholds in Nicaragua and in most of Mexico, even in areas long transformed by international migration. The Nicaraguan and most-of-Mexico examples reinforce my argument that the key variable in the development of southern California gangs across the region is not merely return migration and deportation, but the transmission of cultural norms and identities in some but not all places.

In Nicaragua and most of Mexico, maras did not put down roots because local gangs met up with protective community-level social networks that limited the penetration of imported gang identities.[67] Even the Eighteenth Street Gang, originally formed by Mexican migrants in East Los Angeles, did not establish significant roots in Mexico.[68]

Migration may generate social remittances that perversely impact the homeland. The homeland may reshape the remittances, and export them anew. Specifically, gang related social remittances may create and transform the transnational "spaces" where the migrant gangs circulate. The extent of the violence and havoc generated by the cultural diffusion of alternative identities of street power depend on local conditions, and on whether extant institutions are capable of dealing with the identities migration creates.

The implications of the Salvadoran, as well as Honduran and Guate-malan, experience for the future impact of migration in countries ridden with violence and youth marginalization do not bode well. Circular migration contributes to an expansion of gangs and youth violence in the home country, where youth social exclusion and violence prevail. As Alejandro Portes argued in his illuminating chapter in this volume, governments must create suitable conditions if migrants, including returnees, are to make migration a positive force for development.

Notes

1 I would like to thank Susan Eckstein, Jonathan Hiskey, and Cinzia Solari for helpful comments on previous versions of this chapter.
2 Ana Arana, "How the Street Gangs Took Central America," *Foreign Affairs* 84 (2005): 98–110; Thomas C. Bruneau, "The Maras and National Security in Central America," *Strategic Insights* (2005); Sam Logan, Ben Bain, and Kate Kairies, "Deportation Feeds a Cycle of Violence in Central America," in *The Americas Program* (Washington, DC: International Relations Center, 2006), 1–6.
3 Peggy Levitt, "Social Remittances: Migration Driven Local-Level Forms of Cultural Diffusion," *International Migration Review* 32 (1998): 926–48.
4 For a similar point regarding transnational identities, see Keumjae Park, "Constructing Transnational Identities without Leaving Home: Korean Immigrant Women's Cognitive Border-Crossing," *Sociological Forum* 22, no. 2 (2007): 200–218.
5 Researching gangs and *maras* in Mexico, Carlos Mario Perea, for instance, argues that Mexican social and cultural identity and community networks prevented Central American gangs from expanding into the country, despite extensive circular migration in Mexico and the United States. See Carlos

Mario Perea, *Con el diablo adentro. Pandillas, tiempo paralelo y poder* (Mexico City: Editorial Siglo XXI, 2007).

6 Elana Zilberg, "Fools Banished from the Kingdom: Remapping Geographies of Violence between the Americas (Los Angeles and San Salvador)," *American Quarterly* 56 (2004): 759–79.

7 Programa de las Naciones Unidas para el Desarrollo (PNUD), *Informe sobre el desarrollo humano 2005: Una mirada al nuevo nosotros, el impacto de las Migraciones* (San Salvador: PNUD, 2005), 450.

8 Adrian Bailey and Joshua Hane, "Population in Motion: Salvadorean Refugees and Circulation Migration," *Bulletin of Latin American Research* 14 (1995): 171–200.

9 Segundo Montes, "Migration to the United States as an Index of the Intensifying Social and Political Crises in El Salvador," *Journal of Refugee Studies* 1 (1988): 107–20.

10 Carlos B. Cordova, *The Salvadoran Americans* (Westport, CT: Greenwood, 2005).

11 Ibid., 45.

12 José Miguel Cruz, "The Peace Accords Ten Years Later: A Citizens' Perspective," in *El Salvador's Democratic Transition Ten Years after the Peace Accords*, ed. Cynthia Arnson (Washington, DC: Woodrow Wilson International Center for Scholars, Latin American Program, 2003), 5–13.

13 Elisabeth Jean Wood, "Challenges to Political Democracy in El Salvador," in *The Third Wave of Democratization in Latin America: Advances and Setbacks*, ed. Frances Hagopian and Scott Mainwaring (New York: Cambridge University Press, 2005), 179–201.

14 PNUD, *Informe sobre el desarrollo humano 2005*, 33.

15 John R. Logan, *The New Latinos, Who They Are, Where They Are* (Lewis Mumford Center for Comparative Urban and Regional Research, September 2010), http://mumford.albany.edu/census/HispanicPop/HspReport/MumfordReport.pdf.

16 Ricardo Córdova Macías and José Miguel Cruz, *The Political Culture of Democracy in El Salvador, 2008: The Impact of Governance* (San Salvador: LAPOP, 2008).

17 United States Census Bureau, "The Hispanic Population: 2010," in *2010 Census Briefs* (May 2011), 3.

18 Taking into account undocumented migrants, some sources estimate over 2.5 million Salvadorans living in the United Stated in 2008. See "Salvadoreños en el mundo," in *Briefing Paper on Voting Rights for 3.3 Million Disenfranchised Salvadoran Migrants Living Overseas* (Geneva: Salvadorans in the World, 2008), 6.

19 Banco Central de Reserva de El Salvador, "Boletin Estadístico Mensual" (San Salvador: Banco Central de Reserva de El Salvador, 2009), http://www.bcr.gob.sv/bcrsite/uploaded/content/category/1151448933.pdf.

20 PNUD, *Informe sobre el desarrollo humano 2005*, 13.

21 Cordova, *The Salvadoran Americans*, 37.

22 Some deportations were suspended when, according to the authorities, immigrants were able to "demonstrate good moral character." The new regulations reduced these cases (ibid.).

23 Geoff Thale and Elsa Falkenburger, "Youth Gangs in Central America: Issues on Human Rights, Effective Policing, and Prevention," in *WOLA Special Report* (Washington, DC: Washington Office on Latin America, 2006).

24 Salvadorans had received Temporary Protective Status between 1990 and 1995.

25 Tracy Wilkinson, "Returning to Reclaim a Dream—More Salvadorans Are Going Home to a Land Transformed by War—and Peace. They Seek a Quality of Life They Could Not Find in the U.S.," *Los Angeles Times*, May 19, 1993.

26 PNUD, *Informe sobre el desarrollo humano 2005*, 170; Bureau of Transportation Statistics, *U.S.-International Travel and Transportation Trends: 2006 Update* (Washington, DC: U.S. Department of Transportation, 2006), 23.

27 Carlos Martínez and Roberto Valencia, "'Hay pandilleros que dan hasta tumbes de droga en altamar a narcotraficantes locales': Entrevista con Douglas Omar García Funes," *El Faro*, April 24, 2011; United Nations Office on Drugs and Crime (UNODC), *Crime and Development in Central America: Caught in the Crossfire* (New York: United Nations Publications, 2007); USAID, *Central America and Mexico Assessment* (Washington, DC: USAID, Bureau for Latin American and Caribbean Affairs, 2006), 45.

28 Salvador Martínez, "Vuelven a nueve los homicidios por día," *La Prensa Gráfica*, July 4, 2008; Oscar Iraheta, "El setenta por ciento de las extorsiones son cometidas por maras," *El Diario de Hoy*, August 19, 2009.

29 Wim Savenije and Katherine Andrade-Eekhoff, *Conviviendo en la orilla: Violencia y exclusión social en el área metropolitana de San Salvador* (San Salvador: FLASCO Programa El Salvador, 2003); Marcela Smutt and Lissette Miranda, *El fenómeno de las pandillas en El Salvador* (San Salvador: UNICEF/FLASCO Programa El Salvador, 1998).

30 "Denuncian el grave daño causado por mara gallo," *La Prensa Gráfica*, March 2, 1990, 56.

31 Sandra Argueta, Suyapa Caminos, Margarita Mancía, and María de los Ángeles Salgado, "Diagnóstico de los grupos llamados 'Maras' en San Salvador: Factores psicosociales en los jóvenes que los integran," *Revista de Psicología de El Salvador* 11 (1992): 53–84.

32 Smutt and Miranda, *El fenómeno de las pandillas en El Salvador*, 28.

33 María Santacruz and José Miguel Cruz, "Las maras en El Salvador," in *Maras y pandillas en Centroamérica*, ed. IDESO, ERIC, IDIES, IUDOP (Managua: UCA, 2001), 44–45 (quote translated by the author).

34 James Diego Vigil, *A Rainbow of Gangs: Street Culture in the Mega-City* (Austin: University of Texas Press, 2002).

35 Malcolm W. Klein, *The American Street Gang: Its Nature, Prevalence, and Control* (New York: Oxford University Press, 1995).

36 Alex Sánchez, interviewed by the author, Miami, FL, January 18, 2008.

37 "U.S. Ousting More Gang Members," *San Francisco Chronicle*, April 12, 1989.

38 Scott Wallace, "You Must Go Home Again: Deported L.A. Gangbangers Take Over El Salvador," *Harper's*, August 2000, 47–56; Max Manwaring, "Gangs and Coups D'Streets in the New World Disorder: Protean Insurgents in Postmodern War," *Global Crime* 7 (2006): 505–43.

39 José Miguel Cruz and Nelson Portillo Peña, *Solidaridad y violencia en las pandillas del Gran San Salvador: Más allá de la vida loca* (San Salvador: UCA Editores, 1998).

40 José Miguel Cruz, "El barrio transnacional: Las maras centroamericanas como red," in *Redes transnacionales en la cuenca de los huracanes*, ed. Francis Pisan, Natalia Saltalamacchia, Arlene B. Tickner, and Nielan Barnes (Mexico City: Miguel Ángel Porrúa, 2007), 357–81; María Santacruz and Alberto Concha-Eastman, *Barrio adentro: La solidaridad violenta de las pandillas* (San Salvador: IUDOP-UCA/OPS-OMS, 2001).

41 Santacruz and Cruz, "Las maras en El Salvador," 96 (translated by the author).

42 Jeannette Aguilar, "Pandillas juveniles transnacionales en Centroamérica, México y Estados Unidos: Diagnóstico de El Salvador" (San Salvador: IUDOP, 2007).

43 Cruz and Portillo Peña, *Solidaridad y violencia en las pandillas del Gran San Salvador*, 203.

44 Elvio Sisti, quoted in ibid., 56.

45 Smutt and Miranda, *El fenómeno de las pandillas en El Salvador*, 37.

46 Santacruz and Cruz, "Las maras en El Salvador," 92 (translated by the author).

47 Nielan Barnes, "Maras trasnacionales y pandillas locales: Capítulo comparativo," in "Maras transnacionales en Centroamérica y México," ed. Rafael Fernández de Castro (forthcoming); Carlos Mario Perea Restrepo, "El frío del miedo: Violencia y cultura en México," *Revista CIDOB d'Afers Internacionals* 81 (2008): 17–43.

48 PNUD, *Informe Sobre Desarrollo Humano, El Salvador 2003: Desafíos y opciones en tiempos de globalización* (San Salvador: Programa de las Naciones Unidas para el Desarrollo, 2003); Wood, "Challenges to Political Democracy in El Salvador," 185.

49 Joint Group, *Report of the Joint Group for the Investigation of Illegal Armed Groups with Political Motivation in El Salvador* (Washington, DC: National Security Archives, 1994); International Human Rights Clinic, *No Place to Hide: Gang, State, and Clandestine Violence in El Salvador* (Cambridge, MA: Human Rights Program, Harvard Law School, 2007).

50 Mo Hume, *The Politics of Violence: Gender, Conflict, and Community in El Salvador* (Oxford: Wiley-Blackwell and the Society for Latin American Studies, 2009), 9.

51 Argueta et al., "Diagnóstico de los grupos llamados 'Maras' en San Salvador"; Marlon Carranza, "Detención o muerte: Hacia dónde van los niños pandilleros en El Salvador," in *Ni guerra ni paz: Comparaciones internacionales de niños y jóvenes en violencia armada organizada*, ed. Luke Dowdney (Río de Janeiro: Viveiros de Castro Editora Ltda., 2005), 242–66.

52 Smutt and Miranda, *El fenómeno de las pandillas en El Salvador*, 36 (translated by the author).

53 Santacruz and Cruz, "Las maras en El Salvador," 97 (translated by the author).

54 José Miguel Cruz, "Central American Maras: From Youth Gangs to Transnational Protection Rackets," *Global Crime* 11 (2010): 379–98.

55 Smutt and Miranda, *El fenómeno de las pandillas en El Salvador* (translated by the author).

56 Zilberg, "Fools Banished from the Kingdom," 764.

57 Cruz, "Factors Associated with Juvenile Gangs in Central America," in *Street Gangs in Central America* (San Salvador: UCA Editores, 2007), 13–65.

58 Santacruz and Concha-Eastman, *Barrio adentro.*

59 Santacruz and Cruz, "Las maras en El Salvador."

60 Cruz, "El barrio transnacional."

61 Cruz and Portillo Peña, *Solidaridad y violencia en las pandillas del Gran San Salvador*, 54.

62 Mo Hume, "Mano Dura: El Salvador Responds to Gangs," *Development in Practice* 17 (2007): 739–51.

63 José Miguel Cruz and Marlon Carranza, "Pandillas y políticas públicas: El caso de El Salvador," in *Juventudes, violencia y exclusión: Desafíos para las políticas públicas*, ed. Javier Moro (Guatemala: MagnaTerra Editores, S.A., 2006), 133–76; United Nations Development Programme, *Informe sobre desarrollo humano para América Central 2009–2010* (New York: United Nations, 2009), 69.

64 Carmen Gentile, "The Gangs of El Salvador: A Growing Industry." *Time*, September 6, 2009.

65 Rubén Castaneda, "MS-13 Case Adds Salvadoran Inmates; International Calls Triggered Md. Killings, Indictment Says," *Washington Post*, June 7, 2007.

66 Aguilar, "Pandillas juveniles transnacionales en Centroamérica, México y Estados Unidos."

67 Perea, *Con el diablo adentro.*

68 It is important to note that drug-related violence in Mexico is very different from gang violence in Central America. While violence in Mexico is concentrated in the U.S. border region and has only slightly increased the overall

national homicide rates, in Central America gang violence reaches most of the cities and has a significant impact on the national rates. For a detailed account of the differences between Mexico and Central America, see José Miguel Cruz, Rafael Fernández de Castro, and Gema Santamaría, "Political Transition, Social Violence and Gangs: Cases in Central America and Mexico," in *In the Wake of War: Democratization and Internal Armed Conflict in Latin America*, ed. Cynthia Arnson (Washington, DC: Woodrow Wilson Center Press, 2011).

11

Economic Uncertainties, Social Strains, and HIV Risks

The Effects of Male Labor Migration on
Rural Women in Mozambique[1]

VICTOR AGADJANIAN, CECILIA MENJÍVAR, AND

BOAVENTURA CAU

In southern Mozambique, men's labor migration to neighboring South Africa generates fears and misgivings about HIV/AIDS risks among their nonmigrant wives. Women perceive these risks, and employ strategies and resources to navigate them, within a broader context of male migration's influence on their economic, social, and emotional well-being. Women's perceptions of and responses to the risks are embedded in ever-evolving contingencies and contradictions associated with men's labor migration to South Africa.

The Mozambican case is therefore far from straightforward. Poverty, the lack of local employment, and food insecurity push men to migrate to South Africa. Economic and political changes in that country, however, have diminished migrant men's earning power while exposing them to the HIV/AIDS epidemic, which, in turn, has introduced new tensions in their marriages and has induced their nonmigrant wives to take on new roles, involvements, and normative practices. Nonetheless, unlike in other parts of the world, the social and economic opportunities for women left behind do not necessarily improve when men from Mozambique migrate—even as the women take on new roles and obligations, and assume new decision-making authority in men's absence. Men's migration may even reinforce or exacerbate long-standing differences in gender power and women's insecurities.[2] In the Mozambican case, women's economic and social gains from their husbands' migration are counterbalanced by feelings of insecurity and misgivings generated by worries that their husbands, who engage in temporary, labor migration return from South Africa with HIV / AIDS.

The Setting

Mozambique, a country of some 23 million people in southeast Africa, gained independence from Portugal in 1975, and soon thereafter plunged into a prolonged, devastating civil war. Since the war ended, in 1992, the country has experienced impressive economic growth, an average of 8 percent annually.[3] International aid and economic restructuring contributed to the growth. In the process, the poverty level in the country fell from 69 to 54 percent between 1996 and 2003.[4]

Despite the macroeconomic improvements, Mozambique remains one of the world's poorest and least developed countries. The country ranks 172 of 177 countries on the UNDP Human Development Index.[5] It has an infant (under-age-one) mortality rate of 135 per thousand in rural areas and 95 per thousand in urban areas, and an under-age-five mortality rate of 192 per thousand in rural areas and 143 per thousand in urban areas.[6] About one-quarter of Mozambican children have low weight at birth, and only one-third of the population has access to adequate water sources.[7] Furthermore, Mozambican women are greatly disadvantaged compared to men. On the UN Gender Development Index (GDI), which summarizes key aspects of women's conditions and opportunities, Mozambique ranked 150th out of 157 countries in the middle of the first decade of this century (its GDI in 2005 was 0.373).[8] The adult literacy rate among men was nearly twice that among women.[9] And the country's maternal mortality rate, of over 500 per 100,000 live births, is one of the highest in the world.[10]

Male migration to South Africa has long been a key aspect of economic and social life in Mozambique, especially in its southern region. It is illustrative of the extensive "South-to-South" migration that Susan Eckstein describes in the introductory chapter of this book. In Mozambique migration dates back to agreements signed by colonial governments to provide labor for the mining industry. For most of the twentieth century, countries of the SADC, including Mozambique, have provided labor for South African mines. In the postcolonial era, thousands of rural Mozambican men have continued to be recruited for work in the mines, and their remittances have been a critical source of income for their households in Mozambique. In the first half of the 1990s, before the full dismantling of the apartheid system, labor migration flows to South Africa were highly controlled and included stipulations regulating length of stay, place of residence, and type of work. However, undocumented migrants also helped ensure an abundant supply of cheap labor for the mines.[11]

After the end of the civil war and the dismantlement of the South African apartheid system labor migration patterns in Mozambique changed. Most importantly, the recruitment of men to work in the mines of Witwatersrand tapered off, while the number of those who went to work in low-paying, often informal, jobs in commercial agriculture, construction, and other economic sectors increased. As the postapartheid South African governments sought to increase employment opportunities for that country's native population, it passed laws to limit the number of foreigners companies could employ. The new laws notwithstanding, South Africa continues to attract migrants from neighboring countries, especially from Mozambique, and from non-SADC African countries.[12]

The labor migration from Mozambique continues to involve mainly men (except in short-distance cross-border trade). Earnings generated by the new forms of male migrant employment are less predictable and generally much lower than in the mines. As a result, men send less remittances to their families in Mozambique than they had when working in the mines. Also, whereas mine workers in the past had part of their salaries automatically transferred to their families in Mozambique, ensuring their wives' access to at least a share of their husbands' earnings, men employed in informal sector work are not subject to comparable regulations.[13] Hence, the potential economic benefits of migration for the migrants and their families have diminished as men have shifted from mining to informal sector work.

Nonetheless, the diminished economic opportunities and returns, as well as growing anti-immigrant sentiment in South Africa, have not discouraged Mozambican migration.[14] Because Mozambique's macroeconomic growth has done little to improve rural employment, more and more men from rural areas have looked to more affluent neighboring South Africa for work, if only on a temporary basis. As a result,

Mozambicans remain one of the largest migrant groups in South Africa.[15] Between the mid-1990s and the middle of the first decade of the twenty-first century, Mozambique's share of all foreign workers in the mining industry rose from 10 to 25 percent.[16] Even though the absolute number of Mozambicans working in South African mines has diminished, more remain employed there than in Mozambique's own manufacturing sector.[17] Southern Mozambique's long history of migration to South Africa has created a sociocultural environment in which male labor migration is deeply entrenched and normative (similar to Mexican migration to the United States, as detailed in David FitzGerald's chapter in this book).[18] Despite the decline in economic returns to migration, men in southern Mozambique consider migration to South Africa their natural and most promising form of employment, and a vital source of income for their nonmigrant families.

Of the fifteen SADC member countries, Mozambique, along with Lesotho, receive the most foreign remittances, 98 percent from South Africa.[19] According to a UN estimate, in 2007 Mozambique received around $320 million in remittances.[20] Estimates by the International Fund for Agricultural Development are even higher, $565 million, the equivalent of 7.4 percent of the country's GDP.[21] Families have become dependent on such remittances. A survey of households with international migrants in southern Mozambique conducted in 2004 found that 76 percent of them received cash remittances and only 34 percent of them relied exclusively on domestic work for income.[22] However, remittances fuel inequality in that migrants differ in the amount of money they remit and not all families in the country received remittances. For example, the survey found annual income in households receiving monthly remittances to average about $825, compared to $123 in households that received remittances only once a year.[23]

While households that receive remittances frequently fare better than other households, cross-border economic transfers do not offer an automatic panacea to rural poverty. The above-mentioned UN survey found that 93 percent of remittance-receiving Mozambican households used the money mainly for purchases of food and other basic goods, but also that 40 percent of the remittance-receiving households had debts.[24] Families needed to borrow money primarily to purchase food but also to cover health-related expenses and funerals.

Most analyses of Mozambican migration have focused on its economic outcomes. In contrast, few studies have addressed how migration affects the social fabric and health welfare of Mozambican communities. Migrants have been known to be very vulnerable to infections, but AIDS probably has a closer relationship to migration than does any other infectious disease.[25] Labor migration channels the spread of HIV/AIDS from areas with higher rates of infection to areas with lower rates of infection. Separated from their marital partners, detached from traditional forms of social control, and with money to spend on commercial sex, labor migrants tend to have higher STD and HIV infection levels than nonmigrants. As a consequence, the HIV/AIDS-migration nexus has come to shape life in home communities.[26]

Spatial patterns of HIV prevalence support the notion that migration catalyzes the spread of HIV infection in Mozambique. Men's labor migration appears largely responsible for the rapid rise of HIV prevalence in the southern part of the country, the region from which most migrants to South Africa originate. For example, in Gaza province, where we conducted fieldwork for this study, the HIV prevalence among adults aged 15 to 49, as estimated from HIV surveillance data, rose from 16 to 27 percent between 2001 and 2007. It has the highest incidence of all Mozambican provinces and well above the national average rate estimated at 16 percent.[27]

Against the backdrop of these economic and epidemiological developments, this chapter examines women's social representations of HIV/AIDS risks. Specifically, it focuses on how women perceive and articulate their risks of getting infected by their migrant husbands, and by extramarital relations they have in their husbands' absence, and how their views and worries are influenced by their perceptions of economic security and insecurity, the stability of their marriages, and their social relationships. We base our analysis on semistructured, in-depth interviews conducted in 2006 in the rural Gaza province, with seventy-two women married to migrants.[28] All interviews and fieldwork were conducted in Changana, the main language in Gaza, and subsequently translated into Portuguese for analysis.[29]

Women's Perceptions of Risks Associated with the Migration of Husbands

In Gaza province the local rural economy consists of little more than subsistence agriculture and petty commerce. Therefore, migrant men's remittances are the most important, if not the only, source of income and goods for their families, as women, and probably everyone in the villages, recognize.[30] Remittances typically include money, but also oil, sugar, and other foodstuffs, and such household goods as soap and clothing. When migrants return home for holidays, they often bring with them bigger and more expensive items, for example, cookware, furniture, small electronics, bicycles, window frames, and other construction materials.

While valuing the remittances in cash and in-kind, women also realize that the longer their husbands spend in South Africa, the more likely are they to find other partners there. They concede that such sexual relations are nearly inevitable, and worry that they will receive less remittances, and possibly none, if their husbands prioritize their South African partners. Even when they continue to receive remittances, women worry that the situation may change. Thus, while wishing to continue to receive remittances, the fear of losing their husbands leads them also to wish their permanent return.

Yet, it is well known in the community that men often return home infected with HIV. For example, when asked about what she thought about her husband's eventual return from South Africa, Judite, a thirty-nine-year-old woman with three children, shared her fears: "He could be the one to bring the disease [AIDS]. I don't have the disease, so I am afraid that when he comes back for good while he is sick, he will infect me . . . and I will get sick as he is." Isabel, a twenty-nine-year-old mother of one child, also recognized "that the disease comes from South Africa." She added, "They say it often comes with men [who work there] who then infect their wives."

The connection between migration and HIV/AIDS is confirmed by stories about migrants who returned home sick and later died. "We conclude that a man has AIDS because he comes back sick from South Africa," explained Joana, a thirty-one-year-old mother of two. "I've seen those men who come home sick . . . They are skinny, covered in blisters. They have constant diarrhea, don't eat anything. If they eat something, they throw up, [food] doesn't stay in their stomachs."

Not surprisingly, migrants' wives are worried about the risks of contracting HIV from their husbands and the consequences for their families. Amélia, a twenty-nine-year-old mother of three, painted the following dark scenario: "We have to take care of ourselves because there is a lot of disease [of AIDS]. We all will die and leave our children to suffer, because this disease is no good news. If it comes into your house, it will finish your entire family [that is, the adults] and the children will be suffering."

Spousal physical separation compounds the social distance that the patrilineal kinship and marriage system imposes on them. Even when migrant men are home, communication between spouses is relatively limited and typically initiated by the husband. It is especially difficult for women to raise the issue of HIV / AIDS with their husbands, because the husbands and in-laws may interpret it as a sign of the women's own infidelity. Although patriarchal gender ideologies give men much greater freedom in sexual partnerships, they also tend to equate a man's extramarital sex to a woman's infidelity. Hence, women who initiate any discussion of sexual and related matters are automatically suspected of adulterous relations.

Nonetheless, several informants said they had conversed with their migrant husbands about HIV / AIDS risks and prevention. Their husbands' own awareness and fear of HIV / AIDS may facilitate such conversations. Thus, in the words of Laurinda, an eighteen-year-old with two children, her husband "also is afraid of AIDS and he also talks about it." In a similar vein, Benedita, a twenty-two-year-old mother of two children, recounted a conversation she once had with her husband.

> BENEDITA: I asked him one day if he had a woman in *Joni* [the colloquial Changana term for Johannesburg or South Africa in general] . . . and he said he did not. So, I told him if he will have one, he should use condom with her . . . I told him you should protect yourself from this AIDS disease because if it gets into you, it never comes out and there are no medicines [to cure it].
> INTERVIEWER: And what did he answer?
> BENEDITA: He said he will use condom when with a woman, but I don't know if he has used it or not.

Conversations about HIV / AIDS risks and prevention among spouses sometimes flow from conversations about the AIDS-caused deaths of people they know. The subject can also emerge in the context of HIV testing. De facto mandatory (even if officially voluntary) HIV testing of pregnant women at prenatal consultations is on the rise. Thus, in most couples the wives are tested first. The women can share their experiences of testing and their results with their husbands.

Nonetheless, discussing HIV / AIDS with husbands is not easy. Amélia noted her reluctance to raise the subject of HIV / AIDS risks and prevention with her husband because women's and men's "hearts" are so different, and she was not sure how he would react as "one day he would get angry at [her for raising the subject] but another day he would like it." Joana, who managed to overcome the fear of her husband's negative reaction, still observed that her conversations with her husband do not go very far. "We talk [about AIDS]," she said, "but he doesn't like it . . . He doesn't like talking about it because it is as if I told him that he likes women a lot [laughs] . . . He says he is not a womanizer . . . , [that] he doesn't need women there where he works."

Talking about condoms with husbands is particularly difficult. Most women do not feel comfortable even suggesting condom use to their husbands. A rare exception, Benedita insisted that she would not have unprotected sex with her migrant husband if she knew that he had the virus, even if it meant being physically abused by him and even thrown out of the house. However, few men know their serostatus and still fewer share their knowledge with their wives. Uncertainty about their husbands' status makes women less assertive about steps to take to protect themselves from infection.

Risks Stemming from Women's Own Sexual Ties

The literature on the relationship between migration and HIV and STDs typically focuses on male sexual ties formed where they migrate, the elevated vulnerability of migrants to infection from casual and commercial sexual partners, and the subsequent transmission of the infection acquired through such temporary partnerships to permanent partners back home. However, the erratic and limited remittances migrant Mozambican men send leads some women to seek other sexual partners for economic support. Women's economic needs are compounded by their emotional needs when their husbands are away for a long time. The disease can therefore be transmitted not only from migrants to their left-behind partners, but also the other way around—from non-migrating partners to migrants.[31]

The theme of women's own extramarital ties came up regularly during interviews and fieldwork in Mozambique. While the women were understandably reluctant to share their own experiences, they were generally more willing to talk about and evaluate other women's sexual behavior.[32] It was through references to others that women spoke about extramarital relations in the context of their husbands' migration.

In their accounts, women's decisions to engage in extramarital relations seem driven primarily by loneliness but also by emotional and sexual needs. "We all need a man when [our husbands] are not with us," said Amélia. Similarly, Lúcia, a twenty-five-year-old with two children, explained why some women look for partners outside their marriages: "Oh, one can follow her heart and say 'I will not be faithful because where he is now he is not faithful either.' A woman doesn't want to stay without being conquered [by a man]. A person cannot stay without being conquered. She knows that she has a home [that is, she is married], but if she has it in her heart that she can't calm down if he doesn't calm down [having extramarital partners], that is how it will happen."

Lúcia's explanation of why some migrants' wives engage in extramarital relations was shared by thirty-one-year-old Generosa: "[A migrant's wife] says she does it because her husband is in Joni and she can't just stay [alone] like that either. And her blood is running and she also goes around wishing to let her blood out, that blood that gives her a hard time."

Marta, a thirty-four-year-old mother of four children, admitted that she herself had sex with another man, which she also explained by her husband's long absence. "It happened because my husband stayed in South Africa, so I fell in love with another man because really I was very young then."

When husbands are not only physically absent but send no remittances, women sometimes seek partners for instrumental economic reasons. Inês, a mother of three, told a brief story of one such woman: "She ended up prostituting herself [engaging in an adulterous relationship] ... because her husband doesn't send her anything and she doesn't get any help from him. So, then she became a prostitute [got an extramarital partner]."

Even though adultery is looked down upon (and described in accordingly negative terms), the economic pressures that push some women to engage in it are recognized, a perspective that adds complexity to how gender roles and expectations are modified in the context of massive migration. In the words of thirty-one-year-old Glória, with one child, women look for extramarital partners to "diminish their suffering." The suffering "could force [Glória] to like [another man] so that he may give [her] 20 thousand meticals [about 80 US cents] because even this 20 thousand will be a great help."

Navigating the Risks through Informal Communication with Other Women

Informal peer communication plays a crucial role in navigating HIV/AIDS risks.[33] The narratives of the left-behind women in Mozambique illustrate how informal communication among migrant wives helps them articulate their fears of infection, and, in turn, convey their fears to their husbands and negotiate safer sex with them.

The HIV/AIDS-focused peer communication is embedded within a larger web of informal interactions among women, especially among those with migrant husbands. In general, women's economic, social, and emotional suffering in their husbands' absence brings migrant wives together.[34] Indicative of nonmigrant women's solidarity, they lend each other foodstuffs, soap, and money when remittances are late. Rosa, who did not know her year of birth but believed she was thirty-two years old, gave the following example: "It happens that my husband sends me something while my friend's husband hasn't sent her anything yet. So, she comes to me and says 'Hey, girlfriend, I have nothing. My husband hasn't sent me anything. So, I take out [money] and give her . . . Sometimes I [also] give her soap. Yeah . . . and when she has [money or other goods] she also gives me." Amélia also spoke to the point: "Yeah, we do have relationships [among migrants' wives]. Some of us are doing well, while others are down on their luck. So, the one whose life is good, does not come to you. So I talk with those whose life is down, like mine."

The sharing of anxieties about migrant husbands, remittances, the strength of their marriages, and the well-being of their children, help build trust among migrant wives. Once trust is established, informal communication may allow discussion about such sensitive matters as HIV/AIDS. Migrant wives share their worries about contracting HIV with each other. These worries may be raised in casual conversations on the way to and from the fields and during water-fetching, and at church events. Often the theme of the risks of getting HIV from husbands emerges from more general conversations about their husbands' absence, work, and support for their families. When asked how women come to talk about the disease, Judite said that it happens "because [husbands] are away and don't send anything. If they came back, [the wives] would work together in the field and would have something to eat, but there where they work, they only work for themselves. From that conversation [the wives] begin exchanging ideas." And, as Argentina, a twenty-three-year-old mother of one, described: "We talk. Ah, girlfriend, you know I think about my husband because in Joni there is a lot of disease, and here I am unhappy because he's in Joni and I don't want him to come back with disease. . . . many already came back sick, came back to die here. So, when we are together we pray for them not to come with disease."

Joana's words echoed Argentina's account: "A conversation can get to a point [when one of us says] 'Ah, girlfriend, I am worried because, to be frank, men are not to be trusted where they go.' They don't take care. You don't know . . . maybe sometimes he does take precautions, but your heart is never at peace because he is not to be trusted."

Similarly, Maria, a thirty-nine-year-old mother of five, spoke of the fears women shared concerning their men returning from South Africa with HIV/AIDS: "We talk about it [AIDS]. We live with fear. We have fear in our hearts. We want this disease to end. This disease . . . [cannot be treated] by witch-doctor, has no *Zione* [a local type of Pentecostal churches that practices miracle healing], even if [you] pray till dawn . . . that medicine is nowhere to be found."

The mysterious nature of AIDS, its prolonged latent period, and a variety of symptoms in which it manifests itself make women particularly anxious. They talk about their ailments, wondering if they are caused by HIV. As Maria commented, "We don't know how [HIV] gets into the body and after getting in how it moves around the body. We only see that a person is finished and with time her life is lost." Similarly, Sandra, a thirty-seven-year-old mother of four, noted: "We talk about illnesses—and there are many of them—we don't know whether or not we'll escape, because once one gets sick [with AIDS] he always dies . . . If it is AIDS or not we don't know, because when someone comes home from Joni sick, he only comes to get worse and then die. He's never cured and never gets well to go back to Joni, and we get together to talk and wonder about it. We all will end up dead."

The deaths occurring in the community often trigger conversations about whether they were caused by the disease. Benedita described a case in her village: "Some people were saying that it was AIDS when [the person who died] was coughing a lot. We didn't get to know what disease it was because some say it was AIDS, others say it was the coughing disease [tuberculosis]. We don't know the truth."

Such sharing of facts and rumors help heighten women's awareness of HIV/AIDS, and make them think about their own risks and the need to reduce them. "We say to each other," explained Isabel, "that if we aren't careful, we are going to pay." "Women talk that it is important that we, women, take care [to protect ourselves]," echoed Amélia. However, women acknowledge that they only have a limited repertoire of protective means at their disposal. In most cases they can only hope and pray that their husbands do not bring the infection home. When Maria was asked about what results come from conversations with other migrant wives, she said: "We don't come up with anything, because the men don't want protection, don't want *Jeito* [the most popular brand of condom]. They say that they cannot eat banana with the peel on. . . . Do you see the problem? . . . This prevention thing, with *Jeito* or what have you, I can take it [from the health center] but I'm not going to use it. We aren't going to use it if he doesn't want to."

Even though nonmigrant women share their concerns and build a sense of solidarity, their fears that their husbands or in-laws find out through gossip of their anxiety about contracting HIV undermines mutual trust. It discourages them from sharing their concerns. "We don't trust each other. I am afraid of getting into problems [with her husband]" said Inês, adding that her husband could even beat her up if he found out that she had such conversations with other women.

The very absence of husbands at times makes women reluctant to talk with other women about their marital relations, beyond a general mentioning of where he is, what he is doing, and what he sent lately. Here is how Hortência, a thirty-five-year-old mother of five children, described the barrier to communication: "I don't know about their [other left-behind women's] lives because they each mind their own life. They don't tell anything because they have their lives . . . I only see that there's someone who's suffering, which means that life is not going well in that home. I can help [such a woman] with certain things, but when her husband is not around. I can't try to find out about this or that in their lives, because we are not accustomed to talk about lives of others."

Conversations about HIV/AIDS are also limited and infrequent because women's lives are filled with other challenges, many of which are more immediate and subjectively more threatening to them than the disease, especially for women who receive little or no remittances and who have no alternative income sources. Food security is, by far, their main preoccupation. "We talk about how things are on *machambas* [fields]," said Sandra, "about lack of rain and how we will all die of hunger because of it, because now we plant but it doesn't rain and the plants are dying . . . rain is what would help us a lot." In the face of such daunting challenges of daily survival, concerns about HIV/AIDS inevitably lose prominence and even relevance for many a rural woman.

Policy Implications

Consistent with scholarship that points to a complex mix of gains and losses for nonmigrant women when their husbands migrate, our study of rural Mozambique shows that women's gains in material well-being come with costs of uncertainty and misgivings about the future of their marital unions and heightened concerns about contracting HIV infection from either their marital or extramarital partners, and about its potentially devastating consequences. At the same time, non-migrant women's increased vulnerability to and fears of HIV have the potential to create opportunities for new gendered forms of agency and female solidarity, as women come together to share their fears and strategies, and also to exchange material aid and information.

Our analysis, thus, deepens the understanding of the relationship between gender and the unintended social consequences that migration induces in the homeland. It also complements with Rhacel Parreñas's analysis in this book. She addresses the impact women's migration has on families, gender relations, and children, while we focus on the impact male migration has on marital relations in the context of the diffusion of a deadly health epidemic.

Our analysis also offers clues for more effective policies aimed at reducing the negative consequences of migration for the spread of HIV/AIDS. Confronted with the rapid rise of HIV levels that threaten to erase the country's post-civil war economic and social achievements, Mozambique has built a strong national response to the HIV/AIDS epidemic. The National Strategic Plan to Fight STD/HIV/AIDS, first adopted in 1999 and subsequently revised and updated, specifically addresses the role migration plays in the spread of the infection in the country.[35] The Mozambican government has worked in close partnership with national and international nongovernmental organizations (NGOs), UN agencies, and bilateral cooperation agencies, to raise the population's awareness of the epidemic and to foster HIV prevention.[36] Some of these efforts have focused on migrant men, such as preventive activities directed to miners.[37] Marketing campaigns that target prevention among migrants and long-haul truck drivers have been carried out in southern Mozambique.[38] Various NGOs have been actively working in the places most frequented by labor migrants and truck drivers, as well as by traders—organizing discussions about safer sex practices and distributing HIV prevention pamphlets, brochures, and condoms.[39] Access to HIV testing and antiretroviral treatment, in turn, has been rapidly expanding throughout Mozambique, including in rural areas such as the one examined in our study. Yet we argue that for all these efforts to be fully effective they must address specific needs and anxieties of migrants' left-behind partners.

Migration to South Africa from neighboring SADC countries, like many South-to-South migration flows, is fueled by differences in economic opportunities between sending and receiving countries. Migration from southern Mozambique therefore will continue despite attempts by South Africa's government to institute legal obstacles to immigration and despite increased anti-immigrant sentiment in that country. The HIV risks that this migration creates are therefore likely to persist.

The case we examined provides a window into the multidimensional consequences migration may have on the families, communities, and countries involved, and speaks to contradictory consequences migration may set in motion. A country and government may benefit at the macro level from migrant remittances that generate revenue and help alleviate poverty, while migrants, especially in southern Africa, may spread a deadly epidemic. Scholars and policymakers alike must take these complex consequences of migration into consideration.

Notes

1 We gratefully acknowledge the support of the Eunice Kennedy Shriver National Institute of Child Health and Human Development, grant # R21HD048257 for data collection.
2 María Aysa and Douglas S. Massey, "Wives Left Behind: The Labor Market Behavior of Women in Migrant Communities," in *Crossing the Border: Research from the Mexican Migration Project*, ed. Jorge Durand and Douglas S. Massey (New York: Russell Sage Foundation, 2004), 131–44; V. Neily Salgado De Snyder, "Family Life across the Border: Mexican Wives Left Behind," *Hispanic Journal of Behavioral Sciences* 15 (August 1993): 391–401; Cecilia Menjívar and Victor Agadjanian, "Men's Migration and Women's Lives: Views

from Rural Armenia and Guatemala," *Social Science Quarterly* 88 (December 2007): 1243–62.

3 United Nations Development Programme (UNDP), *Mozambique National Human Development Report 2005: Human Development to 2015, Reaching for the Millennium Development Goals* (Maputo: United Nations Development Programme, 2006), 6.

4 Ibid., 5.

5 UNDP, *Mozambique Human Development Report 2007: Challenges and Opportunities, the Response to HIV and AIDS* (Maputo: United Nations Development Programme, 2007).

6 Instituto Nacional de Estatística and Macro International, *Moçambique inquérito demográfico e de Saúde 2003* [Mozambique demographic and health survey, 2003] (Maputo: Instituto Nacional de Estatística and Macro International, 2005), 121.

7 "Mozambique Key Development Indicators." UN Mozambique, accessed November, 2009, http://www.unmozambique.org/por/About-Mozambique/Mozambique-Key-Development-Indicators.

8 Ibid.

9 UNDP, "*Mozambique Human Development Report 2007*," 10.

10 "WHO/UNICEF/UNFPA/The World Bank Estimates of Maternal Mortality, 2005," UNICEF, accessed November 2009, http://www.childinfo.org/maternal_mortality_countrydata.php.

11 Ramos Cardoso Muanamoha, Brij Maharaj, and Eleanor Preston-Whyte, "Social Networks and Undocumented Mozambican Migration to South Africa," *Geoforum* 41 (November 2010): 885–96; Brij Maharaj, *Immigration to Post-Apartheid South Africa* (Geneva: GCIM Global Migration Perspectives, 2004).

12 Ramos Cardoso Muanamoha, Brij Maharaj, and Eleanor Preston-Whyte, "Social Networks and Undocumented Mozambican Migration to South Africa." "Briefing Note on HIV and Labour Migration in South Africa," International Organization for Migration, 2009, accessed November 2009, http://www.iom.org.za/site/.

13 United Nations International Research and Training Institute for the Advancement of Women (UN INSTRAW), *Gender, Remittances and Development: Preliminary Findings from Selected SADC Countries* (Braamfontein, South Africa: South African Institute of International Affairs [SAIIA], 2007).

14 Jonathan Crush, *Covert Operations: Clandestine Migration, Temporary Work, and Immigration Policy in South Africa* (Cape Town: South African Migration Project, 1997); Fion De Vletter, "Migration and Development in Mozambique: Poverty, Inequality and Survival," *Development Southern Africa* 24 (March 2007): 137–53.

15 Aderanti Adepoju, "Continuity and Changing Configurations of Migration to

and from the Republic of South Africa," *International Migration* 41 (March 2003): 3–28.

16 Jonathan Crush, Vincent Williams, and Sally Peberdy, "Migration in Southern Africa" (paper for the Policy Analysis and Research Programme of the Global Commission on International Migration, 2005), 7.

17 Carlos Nuno Castel-Branco, "Economic Linkages between South Africa and Mozambique" (paper produced for the Department for International Development of the British Government, revised, 2002), 6.

18 See also William Kandel and Douglas S. Massey, "The Culture of Mexican Migration: A Theoretical and Empirical Analysis," *Social Forces* 80 (March 2002): 981–1004.

19 UN INSTRAW, *Gender, Remittances and Development.*

20 Ibid.

21 "Remittances in Africa," IFAD, accessed November 2009, http://www.ifad .org/remittances/maps/africa.htm.

22 De Vletter, "Migration and Development in Mozambique," 144.

23 Ibid.

24 UN INSTRAW, *Gender, Remittances and Development.*

25 R. Mansell Prothero, "Disease and Human Mobility: A Neglected Factor in Epidemiology," *International Journal of Epidemiology* 6 (September 1977): 259–67; John C. Caldwell, John K. Anarfi, and Pat Caldwell, "Mobility, Migration, Sex, STDs, and AIDS: An Essay on Sub-Saharan Africa with Other Parallels," in *Sexual Cultures and Migration in the Era of AIDS: Anthropological and Demographic Perspectives*, ed. Gilbert H. Herdt (Oxford: Clarendon, 1997), 51.

26 Victor Agadjanian, "Research on International Migration in Sub-Saharan Africa: Foci, Approaches, and Challenges," *Sociological Quarterly* 49 (July 2008): 407–21; J. Decosas, F. Kane, J. K. Anarfi, K. D. Sodji, and H. U. Wagner, "Migration and AIDS," *Lancet* 346 (September 1995), 826–28; Mark N. Lurie, "The Epidemiology of Migration and HIV/AIDS in South Africa," *Journal of Ethnic and Migration Studies* 32 (May 2006): 649–66.

27 Ministry of Health of Mozambique, *Relatório sobre a revisão dos dados de vigilância epidemiológica do HIV—ronda 2004* (Maputo: Ministry of Health of Mozambique, 2005); Ministry of Health of Mozambique, *Relatório sobre a revisão dos dados de vigilância epidemiológica do HIV—ronda 2007* (Maputo: Ministry of Health of Mozambique, 2008). The National HIV Prevalence Survey of 2009 produced a lower national estimate, 12 percent among adults aged fifteen to forty-nine, but the estimated seroprevalence in Gaza province, at 25 percent (30 percent among women), was comparable to the surveillance-based figures. See: Ministry of Health of Mozambique, *Inquérito nacional de prevalência, riscos comportamentais e informação sobre o HIV e SIDA (INSIDA), 2009. Relatório final* (Maputo: Ministry of Health of Mozambique, 2010).

28 The study presented in this chapter is part of a larger project that has examined the consequences for HIV/AIDS risks in the context of migration in general. The larger project also included the wives of men who migrate to Mozambique's capital, Maputo, and other urban areas.

29 All names we use are pseudonyms.

30 A survey conducted between 1999 and 2001 found that 55 percent of the rural households of the south of Mozambique had members engaged in wage employment. The figures were 18 percent in the center and 7 percent in the north of the country. The same survey also found that about 68 percent of the households in the south had workers earning the equivalent of more than $60 per month, compared to only 13.7 percent in the center. This difference has been attributed to higher wages in South Africa and Maputo-city (De Vletter, "Migration and Development in Mozambique," 139).

31 Mark N. Lurie, Brian G. Williams, Khangelani Zuma, David Mkaya-Mwamburi, Geoff P. Garnett, Adriaan W. Sturm, Michael D. Sweat, Joel Gittelsohn, and Salim S. Karim, "The Impact of Migration on HIV-1 Transmission in South Africa: A Study of Migrant and Non-Migrant Men and Their Partners," *Sexually Transmitted Diseases* 30 (February 2003a): 149–56; Mark N. Lurie, Brian G. Williams, Khangelani Zuma, David Mkaya-Mwamburi, Geoff P. Garnett, Michael D. Sweat, Joel Gittelsohn, and Salim S. Karim, "Who Infects Whom? HIV-1 Concordance and Discordance among Migrant and Non-Migrant Couples in South Africa," *AIDS* 17 (October 2003b): 2245–52.

32 A. N. Dlala, C. A. Hiner, E. Qwana, M. Lurie, "Speaking to Rural Women: The Sexual Partnerships of Rural South African Women Whose Partners Are Migrants," *Society in Transition* 32 (March 2001): 79–82.

33 Victor Agadjanian, "Informal Social Networks and Epidemic Prevention in a Third World Context: Cholera and HIV/AIDS Compared," in *Advances in Medical Sociology*, ed. Judith A. Levy and Bernice A. Pescosolido (JAI-Elsevier Science, Social Networks and Health, 2002), 201–21; Victor Agadjanian and Cecilia Menjívar, "Talking about the 'Epidemic of the Millennium': Religion, Informal Communication, and HIV/AIDS in sub-Saharan Africa," *Social Problems* 55 (August 2008): 301–21; Hans-Peter Kohler, Jere R. Behrman, and Susan C. Watkins, "Social Networks and HIV/AIDS Perceptions," *Demography* 44 (February 2007): 1–33.

34 Agadjanian and Menjívar, "Talking about the 'Epidemic of the Millennium.'"

35 The Strategic Plan also references the presence of immigrants in Mozambique as a threat to the spread of the disease, as some immigrants are from countries with high HIV prevalence rates, and they may be involved in HIV-risky behavior (for example, immigrants in the sex trade) (Conselho Nacional de Combate ao HIV/SIDA [CNCS], 55); CNCS, *Plano estratégico nacional de combate ao HIV/SIDA: Part I, componente estratégica—análise de situação* (Maputo: CNCS, 2004), 55.

36 UNDP, *"Mozambique Human Development Report 2007,"* 36.

37 CNCS, *Plano estratégico nacional de combate ao HIV/SIDA*, 72.

38 Cristiano Matsinhe, *"Tábula Rasa": Dinâmica da Resposta Moçambicana Contra o HIV/SIDA* (Maputo: Texto Editores, 2006).

39 United States Agency for International Development (USAID), *Corridors of Hope: Regional HIV/AIDS Cross-border Prevention Program: Secondary Analysis and Document Review* (Washington, DC: USAID, Office of HIV/AIDS, 2004), 22.

CONTRIBUTORS

VICTOR AGADJANIAN is Ellen Elizabeth Guillot International Distinguished Professor of Sociology at the School of Social and Family Dynamics at Arizona State University. His research has dealt primarily with gender, family, reproduction, and migration in sub-Saharan Africa and Central Eurasia.

BOAVENTURA CAU, PH.D., is a social demographer specializing in migration, HIV, fertility, and mortality. He is Head of the Department of Geography of Eduardo Mondlane University, in Maputo, Mozambique.

JOSÉ MIGUEL CRUZ is visiting assistant professor of Politics and International Relations and fellow at the Center for the Administration of Justice at Florida International University. He was the director of the Institute of Public Opinion at the University of Central America, in El Salvador. His most recent book, *Street Gangs in Central America*, summarizes an eight-year-long research project.

SUSAN ECKSTEIN is professor of International Relations and Sociology at Boston University. Her publications include *The Immigrant Divide: How Cuban Americans Changed the U.S. and Their Homeland* (2009), *Back from the Future: Cuba under Castro* (1994, 2003), *The Poverty of Revolution: The State and Urban Poor in Mexico* (1977, 1988), *Power and Popular Protest: Latin American Social Movements* (editor) (1989, 2001), *What Justice? Whose Justice? Fighting for Fairness in Latin America* (2003) (coeditor), and *Struggles for Social Rights in Latin America* (coeditor) (2003). She is a former president of the Latin American Studies Association. The books she has authored alone have won several prizes.

KYLE EISCHEN, MPIA, PH.D. research fellow, Center for Global, International and Regional Studies, and assistant dean for Academic Planning and Research, Division of Social Sciences, the University of California, Santa Cruz.

DAVID SCOTT FITZGERALD is the Gildred Chair in U.S.-Mexican Relations, associate professor of Sociology, and associate director of the Center for Comparative Immigration Studies at the University of California, San Diego. He is the author of *A Nation of Emigrants: How Mexico Manages Its Migration* (2009), coeditor of five books on Mexican migration, and author of articles on transnationalism, ethnographic methods, and the politics of emigration and immigration.

NATASHA ISKANDER is assistant professor of Public Policy at New York University's Wagner School of Public Service. Her most recent book is *Creative State: Forty Years of Migration and Development Policy in Morocco and Mexico* (2010).

RIVA KASTORYANO is a research director at the National Center for Scientific Research, and professor at Sciences Po, Paris. Her work focuses on identity and minority issues and more specifically on their relations to states in France, Germany, and the United States. She was a lecturer at Harvard University from 1984 to 1987 and has been teaching at the Institute for Political Studies in Paris since 1988, and at the New School for Social Research since 2005. Her most recent books are *Negotiating Identities: States and Immigrants in France and Germany* (2002). She also edited *Quelle identité pour l'Europe? Le multiculturalisme à l'épreuve* (1998, 2005); *Nationalismes en mutation en Méditerranée orientale* [Changing concept of nationalism] (with A. Dieckhoff, 2002); and *Les codes de la différence: Religion, origine, race en France, Allemagne et Etats-Unis* [Codes of otherness: Religion, ancestry, and race in France, Germany, and the United States] (2005). Her new research focuses on nationalisms without territory.

CECILIA MENJÍVAR is Cowden Distinguished Professor of Sociology in the School of Social and Family Dynamics at Arizona State University. Her publications include *Fragmented Ties: Salvadoran Immigrant Networks in America* (2000) and *Enduring Violence: Ladina Women's Lives in Guatemala* (2011). She is editor of *Through the Eyes of Women: Gender, Social Networks, Family and Structural Change in Latin America and the Caribbean*, and coeditor of *When States Kill: Latin America, the U.S., and Technologies of Terror* (2005) and *Latinos/as in the United States: Changing the Face of América* (2008). She has received several awards for her research, including the Julian Samora Distinguished Career Award from the American Sociological Association Latino Section.

ADIL NAJAM is the Vice Chancellor of the Lahore University of Management Sciences (LUMS), Pakistan, and Professor of International Relations at Boston University. He has served as the Frederick S. Pardee Professor of Global Public Policy at Boston University and the Director of the Pardee Center for the Study of the Longer-Range Future. He is the author of *Portrait of a Giving Community: Philanthropy by the Pakistani-American Diaspora* (2006) and his other books include *Civic Entrepreneurship* (with Tariq Banuri; 2002), *Environment, Development and Human Security: Perspectives from South Asia* (editor; 2003); *Envisioning a Sustainable Development Agenda for Trade and Environment* (co-editor; 2006).

RHACEL SALAZAR PARREÑAS is Department Chair and Professor of Sociology at the University of Southern California. She is a labor and migration scholar. Specializing primarily on the emigration of women from the Philippines, she is the author of *Servants of Globalization, Children of Global Migration* and, most recently, *Illicit Flirtations*.

ALEJANDRO PORTES is Howard Harrison and Gabrielle Snyder Beck Professor of Sociology and the founding director of the Center for Migration and Development at Princeton University. His most recent books are *Economic Sociology: A Systematic Inquiry* (2010) and, with Lori D. Smith, *Institutions Count: Their Role and Significance in Latin American Development* (2012).

MIN YE is the director of the East Asian Studies program and assistant professor of International Relations at Boston University. Her selected publications are *The Making of Northeast Asia* (coauthor, 2010), "Diffusion and Direct Foreign Investment in China" (2009), and "Critical Junctures and East Asian Regionalism" (2004). She was a postdoctoral fellow at the Fairbank Center for Chinese Studies at Harvard University (2008–9) and completed her manuscript "Embedded States: Foreign Direct Investment in China and India."

transnationalism, 19, 22, 34–35, 38, 107, 115–16, 138–40, 153, 213–14, 218, 226

Turks, 2, 4–5, 19, 25, 129, 138–55; government, 19, 143, 151

unauthorized immigrants, 10, 117, 128–29

unemployment, 30–31, 164, 223

United States, 3–6, 8, 10, 14–15, 22, 31, 39; and China, 59, 63, 69, 71–78; and Cuba, 92–113; and El Salvador, 22, 213–33; and India, 39, 75–91; and Mexico, 33–34, 114–37; and Latin America, 35, 37; and Western Europe, 31

violence, 34, 124, 223–26, 228

visas, 39, 77–79

wages, 32, 35, 131, 157–59, 163–66, 174, 180

Washington, 9–10, 14, 25, 98, 128, 226, 228

women, 7, 11, 23–24, 172, 192–93, 196–97, 200–202, 206–9, 234–35, 238–47; emigration of, 23–24

workers, 11, 13–14, 32, 35, 39, 41, 66, 103, 125, 130–31, 144, 156–57, 164–68, 172, 174–75; better, 124, 126; domestic, 191–92, 200–201, 204–7; emigrant, 167; nonmigrant, 175

World War II, 1, 5, 7, 9, 53

Xi Zhongxun, 62

youth, 22, 34, 122, 223–25, 228

youth gangs, 213–33

Yugoslavia, 60

Zhao Ziyang, 66–67